D0557723

STRUCTURE AND CHANGE:

An Economic History of Quebec
by Robert Armstrong

3 9345 00809398 5

SIMON FRASER UNIVERSITY

W.A.C. BENNETT LIBRARY

HC 117 Q4 A8 c.3

To my mother and to my father

ROBERT ARMSTRONG

STRUCTURE AND CHANGE

An Economic History of Quebec

Copyright © 1984 Gage Publishing Limited

All rights reserved. No part of this publication may be reproduced in any form without permission in writing from the publisher. Reproducing passages from this publication by mimeographing or by photographic, electrostatic, or mechanical means without the written permission of the publisher is an infringement of copyright law.

CANADIAN CATALOGUING IN PUBLICATION DATA

Armstrong, Robert, 1946-

  Structure and change : an economic history of Quebec
Includes index.
ISBN 0-7715-5588-1

1. Quebec (Province) - Economic conditions. I. Title.

HC117.Q4A75   330.9714   C83-098291-4

Co-ordinating Editor: Kathy Austin

Editor: Terry-Lee Wheelband

Designer: Susan Weiss

ISBN 0-7715-5588-1

1 2 3 4 5 AP 88 87 86 85 84

Written, Printed, and Bound in Canada

Cover Design: **Michael van Elsen Design Inc.**

Cover Illustration: Map of "Le Canada, ou Nouvelle France, & c." By Nicolas Sanson from the book *From Sea Unto Sea: Art and Discovery Maps of Canada* by Joe C.W. Armstrong.

More Gage Books in History

Quebec History

The Dream of Nation: A Social and Intellectual History of Quebec —Susan Mann Trofimenkoff

The French Canadians 1760-1967, Revised Edition in Two Volumes —Mason Wade
Volume I 1760-1911
Volume II 1911-1967

French-Canadian Nationalism —Ramsay Cook

Economic History

Canadian Economic History —W.T. Easterbrook and Hugh G.J. Aitken

Canada: An Economic History —William L. Marr and Donald G. Paterson

Other

Canada and the Burden of Unity —edited by David Jay Bercuson

Canada: A Story of Challenge —J.M.S. Careless (*LL30*)

Colonists and Canadiens 1760-1867 —edited by J.M.S. Careless

Part One of The Canadians 1867-1967 —edited by J.M.S. Careless and R. Craig Brown

The Maple Leaf Forever, Revised Edition —Ramsay Cook

Canada's First Century —Donald Creighton (*LL43*)

STRUCTURE AND CHANGE:

An Economic History of Quebec
by Robert Armstrong

Table of Contents

Preface

This book traces the history of the Quebec economy from the sixteenth century to World War II and offers a new view of institutional change and economic growth. The economic history of Quebec is an exciting area of study that has been extensively revised and expanded in the last twenty years. Until now, no comprehensive survey of Quebec's economic history has been available in either French or English. The present volume aims to redress this situation.

The academic literature on the history of the Quebec economy is extensive on many subjects and virtually untouched in others. To avoid producing a work that amounts to a collection of loosely related topics, I have attempted to fill in some of the gaps. The book therefore contains both an analytical exposition of recent research results and a chronological story with an economic bias. The book's contents are divided into four periods. Each period is sub-divided into four chapters. The subjects of the chapters vary from period to period in tune with the changing structure of the economy. The analysis focuses on the composition of economic activity and the chapter headings reflect a sectoral approach. Some chapters contain more narrative than others. The quantity of descriptive material in each chapter reflects my judgement as to how much historical background should be assumed for the average reader. So too with the volume of theoretical abstraction. The book contains some of the technical language used by the economics profession, but I hope that it will appeal to a wide audience. The Introduction is the most abstract part of the work and may be omitted by those unfamiliar with economic theorizing. A select bibliography accompanies each chapter. Although Quebec's history certainly stands on its own, the book can be used as a complement to existing Canadian economic history texts: until the middle of the nineteenth century, Quebec history encompasses a very large part of Canadian history.

Several issues are inadequately treated for want of source material. The resident fisheries and the service sector of the Quebec economy are two such topics. Other issues, such as the history of money and financial institutions after Confederation, are best discussed in the overall Canadian context. The history of the early Amerindian economy in the St. Lawrence basin is touched upon only briefly. Economic historians are more knowledgeable about some topics than others; general surveys inevitably reflect the author's areas of specialization.

I am endebted to a number of economists and historians who have taken the time to read and comment upon portions of this book at various stages in its preparation. A special thanks to Paul Davenport, George Grantham, Gilles Grenier, Marvin McInnis, Jacques Mathieu, Gilles Paquet, Jean-Claude Robert, Normand Séguin, and Irene Spry. None of them is responsible for the opinions expressed here. Portions of the manuscript have been used in the teaching of undergraduate courses in economics at McGill University, Duke University, and the University of Ottawa. I am grateful to have had the opportunity to improve the presentation of the material at these institutions. Ginette Rozon of the Secretariat de la Recherche at the University of Ottawa and Delise Alison of McGill University assisted in the typing of the manuscript. Terry-Lee Wheelband, Elana Kivity and Charlotte Hussey assisted with the editing.

Robert Armstrong
May 1983

Introduction

This book contains an analytical review of Quebec's economic history up to the beginning of World War II. Economic theory, particularly price theory, underlies the analysis though much of the theory is implicit rather than explicit. The repetition of basic economic principles has been restricted in the interest of narrative coherence and in the hope of reaching a wider audience. The study uses the results of empirical studies by economists but is not limited to these findings; the volume of empirical studies pertaining to Quebec's economic history is relatively small. Although the analysis proceeds by example and suggestion, economic theory is often employed in an *ad hoc* fashion to suggest why events occurred. The expression 'economic theory', of course, covers a wide range of doctrines; no single economic model can explain the growth process in Quebec since the sixteenth century. Various instruments from the economist's tool kit are used to shed light on economic behavior where they seem appropriate.

For many years, the staple approach was the perspective most often employed in historical analysis of the Quebec economy. Unlike classical trade theory, which explains trade and growth in terms of the optimal use of immobile resource endowments, the staple approach explains regional growth in terms of factor migration. Labor and capital move to the frontier in response to the high returns offered by natural resource commodity production and export to the metropolitan country. The take-off of staple production may result from a shift in metropolitan demand, technological change, or a new resource discovery. Through time, the growth of the staple industry creates linkage effects to manufacturing and the service industries. The size and composition of these effects differ from one staple commodity to another, but eventually the export sector becomes a minor employer in comparison to the dependent industries. The development process may be interrupted, however, if the region's comparative advantage in natural resource commodity production decreases before diversification has occurred. The regional prices of production factors in the staple industry will then decline causing capital and labor to migrate to other industries and regions. If a part of the labor force is relatively immobile, in other words, prepared to accept lower incomes rather than migrate, then the region may stabilize in self-sufficient resource exploitation. M.H. Watkins has called this no-growth situation, the 'staple trap'.

> In the absence of alternative opportunities, factors will tend to accumulate excessively in the export sector or in subsistence agriculture. In the former case, growth may become 'immiserized' as the terms of trade turn against the country. In the latter, the economy will face a problem common to most underdeveloped countries: development will depend on the interdependent growth of agriculture and industry.[1]

A simplified version of the staple approach can be formally represented by a one sector neo-classical growth model. (See Baldwin, Scott, Watkins) In this model, the staple product consists of a natural resource commodity whose price is established in metropolitan export markets. The staple is produced in an unsettled region by means of labor and *in situ* natural resources.[2] The growth of staple production in the region results from changes in metropolitan demand, technical progress, or new resource discoveries. Any one of these changes will cause the wage rate in the staple economy to rise. The size of the wage increase depends upon the structure of the labor market. The above changes will also affect the market value of *in situ* natural resources, except where common property and free access eliminate all natural resource rents. In the absence of common property resources, an increase in the wage rate in the staple economy relative to that in the metropolitan economy will stimulate some migration and settlement on the frontier, as long as the wage rate differential between the two regions more than compensates for the net social costs of moving. This adjustment process may be very slow owing to imperfections in the international flow of information during the early stages of frontier development. The presence of common property, free access resources will lead to higher wage rates, employment levels, and migration rates, though very rapid depletion, such as the excessive trapping of a beaver population, may reverse the growth rates of these variables if the maximum sustainable yield of the resource is surpassed. (See Southey)

The one sector model of staple growth can accommodate the addition of a non-tradeable domestic goods sector without changing the previous results. The price of 'home' goods is endogenous and dependent upon the domestic wage rate as determined in the staple goods sector. Home goods are priced independently of international prices because the regional economy is relatively unsettled and frontier markets, apart from the staple commodity market, are not yet integrated with the metropolitan economy. As the staple economy grows, the amount of labor in the home goods sector remains a fixed proportion of the total size of the labor market because of final demand linkages. Even a sustained decline in the size of the staple producing sector may not alter this relationship. A steady fall in the domestic wage rate may produce emigration to other regions or a shift into subsistence resource exploitation.

This simple model of the staple economy loosely accounts for the economic growth process in Quebec until about the middle of the nineteenth century. Fish, furs, wheat and timber provided the chief export opportunities for the St. Lawrence Valley region. Fluctuations in staple export prices explain the major changes in the level of colonial income per capita and in the composition of colonial output. The distribution of the economic rents flowing from staple production affected the size and composition of final demand linkages. However, a large proportion of new immigrants to the St. Lawrence Valley directly entered the agricultural sector upon their arrival. The shadow wage rate available from subsistence agriculture in the newly settled region approximated the expected wage rate available in the staple sector. By the end of the seventeenth century, staple production employed a relatively small proportion of the colonial labor force. Subsistence producers operated outside the confines of the market economy, but were ready to enter the labor market if the market-determined wage rate in the staple sector proved attractive. An explanation of the *level* of per capita income in Quebec before 1850, as opposed to *changes* in the level of income, requires an understanding of the seigneurial land tenure system, peasant agricultural production, and domestic economic exchange, which the staple approach does not provide. Watkins has described Innis's staple approach as "a unifying theme of diffuse application rather than an analytical tool fashioned for specific purposes," (Watkins, p. 50) and it is in this spirit that the staple approach will be considered in the first half of the book.

The 'Annales' school has exercised an influence upon Quebec historians because of its concern with the social, demographic, and economic aspects of the seigneurial system and peasant agriculture. Unfortunately, the Annales approach has never been formalized and its methodology is unclear. (See Forster) The Annales approach favors the quantification of demographic and economic phenomena, but avoids any precise analytical framework. At least one analytical tool used by those partial to the Annales approach— wheat prices as an index of colonial economic welfare—seems disingenuous in the light of modern price theory. (See Chapter 2) Studies associated with the Annales approach have nonetheless contributed to our understanding of the colonial economy. Typically, these studies have embodied an empirical approach to the past, and their attention to demographic, social and institutional issues has substantially improved our understanding of production in a seigneurial setting.

As a resource-based economy grows through time, the simplified version of the staple approach becomes less and less relevant. In addition to the staple producing sector, a non-staple tradeable goods sector often develops. The introduction of a sector producing either exportable or import-competing manufactured goods alters the results derived from the one sector model of staple production. In a two sector neo-classical model of advanced staple development, with a natural resource commodity export and a tradeable manufactured good, commodity prices are determined exogenously in international markets. Under assumptions of diminishing returns to labor inputs in the staple goods sector and constant returns in the non-staple tradeable goods sector, the wage rate is determined in the non-staple goods sector. (See Chambers and Gordon, Copithorne)

Several new results can be derived from the basic two sector model. If an internationally priced manufactured good is worth producing, the economy's wage rate will be determined in the manufacturing sector and fed to the staple sector. Should a non-tradeable home goods sector also exist, the price of home goods will also depend upon the domestic wage rate as determined in the tradeable manufactured goods sector. A rise in staple demand, new resource discoveries, or technical change in the staple sector will no longer influence the economy's wage rate. Any one of these changes will increase the size of the staple sector and reduce the size of the manufactured goods sector without altering the level of wages. The ensuing increase in gross national income accrues not to labor but to *in situ* natural resource owners in the form of rents. To the extent that these resources are foreign-owned, the increase in gross national product (GNP) is reduced. In the two sector model of growth, labor productivity must increase in the tradeable manufactured goods sector in order for the wage level to increase.

For this and other reasons, it has been argued that the two sector neo-classical model is an inadequate representation of the staple approach and an unrealistic simplification of how economies behave. The conditions necessary for the existence of a non-staple tradeable goods sector may not be encountered in the real world. (See Dales, McManus and Watkins) The validity of this criticism depends upon the pricing of manufactured goods in the domestic economy. Were domestic manufactured goods produced in isolation from international markets and trade so that their relative prices bore little or no relationship to international prices? Or did the prices of domestic manufactured goods reflect international opportunity costs so that they constituted 'tradeable' goods, whether or not they were actually exported? No definitive answer to the question is yet possible for nineteenth century Quebec, but in this writer's view, the relative prices for most of Quebec's manufactured goods were probably aligned with those in the northeastern United States by the close of the 1850s. The parallel movement of business cycles in Canada and the United States since at least 1873 lends indirect support to this contention. A more important problem with the neo-classical two sector model lies in the realm of consistent capital aggregation: in a multi-sector context, the neo classical parable and its implications are generally untenable. (Brown, p. 387)

Economic growth models usually abstract from the institutional environment. Until recently, many economists have ignored the changes in economic efficiency and equity that resulted from institutional change. Because institutions, such as the legal system, were considered a part of the constraint set, property rights received little formal attention. Times have changed and it is now widely recognized that legal institutions, laws and law-making can be considered as parameters subject to economic analysis. In this study the institutional environment is given a central place. For each historical period, institutional change is examined with reference to economic opportunities and behavior. The neo-institutional approach developed by Lance Davis and Douglass North has provided a source of inspiration. Using a blend of the theories of public choice, property rights, and technological change, Davis and North argue that profit-seeking economic agents seldom operate within a given institutional framework; they seek changes in the framework itself. In their work, Davis and North define the institutional environment as follows:

> The institutional environment is the set of fundamental political, social, and legal ground rules that establishes the basis for production, exchange, and distribution. Rules governing elections, property rights, and the right of contract are examples of the type of ground rules that make up the economic environment . . .

They explain institutional change in the following way:

> Economic institutions are innovated or property rights are revised because it appears desirable for individuals or groups to undertake the costs of such changes; they hope to capture some profit which is unattainable under the old arrangement.[3]

There are, of course, a wide variety of circumstances that can generate new sources of profits, and attempts to reform or revise institutions in one way or another.[4] Unfortunately, in Davis and North's work, the institutional framework is arbitrarily divided into an exogeneous 'institutional environment' and endogeneous 'institutional arrangements'. This study will abandon any such formal distinction as no universal breakdown is possible. Davis and North unnecessarily limit their analysis to four economic phenomena that influence changes in institutional arrangements: the realization of economies of scale, the elimination of externalities, the reduction of risk and uncertainty, and the lowering of transaction costs. Davis and North also assume consumers are almost invariably made worse off by government enterprise and regulation. In fact, while government enterprise and regulation can make consumers worse off, so too can the institutions of private enterprise and private contract. As Olmstead and Goldberg succinctly argued in their critique of Davis and North's book, the State has no monopoly on coercion and the redistributive aspects of institutional change.

NOTES

[1] Melville H. Watkins, "A Staple Theory of Economic Growth," *Approaches to Canadian Economic History*, pp. 63-64, eds. Easterbrook and Watkins, reprinted by permission of Carleton University Press.

[2] *In situ* natural resources should be distinguished from atmospheric conditions or climate. Although climate may be thought of as a part of the aggregate resource endowment, analytically, the effect of favorable climatic conditions on production is quite different. In a one sector growth model, *in situ* natural resources are a factor of production while climate is indistinguishable from neutral technical change. The effect of favorable atmospheric conditions may appear as an additional locational rent to land, or in the form of higher prices for all productive factors in the region. (Cf. Copithorne, p. 27)

[3] *Institutional Change & American Economic Growth*, pp. 6, 10, by Lance E. Davis and Douglass North © 1971, reprinted by permission of Cambridge University Press.

[4] Davis and North's analytical framework applies to rent seeking as well as profit seeking. (See Chapter 11)

SELECT BIBLIOGRAPHY

Baldwin, Robert E. "Patterns of Development in Newly Settled Regions." *The Manchester School of Economic and Social Studies.* May 1956.

Brown, Murray. "The Measurement of Capital Aggregates: A Postreswitching Problem," in Dan Usher, ed., *The Measurement of Capital.* Chicago: The University of Chicago Press, 1980.

Buchanan, James M., R.D. Tollison, and G. Tulloch, eds. *Toward a Theory of the Rent Seeking Society.* College Station: Texas A & M University Press, 1980.

Buckley, Kenneth H. "The Role of Staple Industries in Canada's Economic Development." *Journal of Economic History.* December 1958.

Chambers, Edward J. "Late Nineteenth Century Business Cycles in Canada." *Canadian Journal of Economics and Political Science.* August 1964.

Chambers, Edward J. and Donald F. Gordon. "Primary Products and Economic Growth: An Empirical Measurement." *Journal of Political Economy.* August 1966.

Copithorne, Lawrence. *Natural Resources and Regional Disparities.* Ottawa: Economic Council of Canada, 1979.

Dales, John H., John C. McManus and Melville H. Watkins. "Primary Products and Economic Growth: A Comment." *Journal of Political Economy.* December 1967.

Davis, Lance E. and Douglas C. North. *Institutional Change and American Economic Growth.* New York: Cambridge University Press, 1971.

Dubuc, Alfred. "L'influence de l'école des Annales au Québec." *Revue d'histoire de l'Amérique française.* December 1979.

Forster, Robert. "Achievements of the Annales School." *Journal of Economic History.* March 1978.

Lee, Susan Previant and Peter Passell. *A New Economic View of American History.* New York: W.W. Norton & Co., 1979.

McClelland, Peter. *Causal Explanation and Model Building in History, Economics, and the New Economic History.* Ithica: Cornell University Press, 1975.

McCloskey, Donald. "The Achievements of the Cliometric School." *Journal of Economic History.* March 1978.

Olmstead, Alan L. and Victor P. Goldberg. "Institutional Change and American Economic Growth: A Critique of Davis and North." *Explorations in Economic History.* July 1975.

Ouellet, Fernand, Jean Hamelin and Richard Chabot. "Les prix agricoles dans les villes et les campagnes du Québec d'avant 1850: aperçus quantitatifs." *Histoire Sociale-Social History.* May 1982.

Paquet, Gilles and Jean-Pierre Wallot. "Sur quelques discontinuités dans l'expérience socio-économique du Québec: une hypothèse." *Revue d'histoire de l'Amérique française.* March 1982.

Scott, Anthony D. "Policy for Declining Regions: A Theoretical Approach," in N.H. Lithwick, ed., *Regional Economic Policy: The Canadian Experience.* Toronto: McGraw-Hill Ryerson, 1978.

Southey, Clive. "The Staples Thesis, Common Property and Homesteading." *Canadian Journal of Economics.* August 1978.

Watkins, Melville H. "A Staple Theory of Economic Growth," in W.T. Easterbrook and M.H. Watkins, ed., *Approaches to Canadian Economic History.* Toronto: McClelland and Stewart, 1967.

Part I

QUEBEC BEFORE THE CONQUEST 1500-1763

1

Fish and Furs

At the beginning of the sixteenth century, very few Europeans were aware the North American continent existed. As adventurous ocean travellers in search of a route to the Far East gradually accumulated knowledge about the North Atlantic region, entrepreneurs and governments developed a growing interest in the New World. European labor and capital began moving across the Atlantic Ocean in response to the profitable opportunities arising from resource discoveries in North America. Fish, the initial pole of attraction, brought mobile factors of production as a magnet attracts iron filings. The flow of European fishermen, equipment and supplies was sponsored and enacted by private economic agents. The State played a secondary role largely confined to the gathering of information, the enforcement of contracts, and the provision of naval protection for the national fishing fleet.

The shallow waters over the continental shelf and the off-shore banks along the North American coast provided an abundance of fish that attracted fishermen from all over Europe. Within a few years of Jean Cabot's voyage to Newfoundland in 1497, French, Spanish, Portuguese and English fishing boats were sailing to Newfoundland's off-shore waters on a seasonal basis. Jacques Cartier's voyages of 1534, 1535-1536, and 1541-1542 extended fishing westward to the St. Lawrence Gulf. At the same time, European population growth was creating a rising demand for fish products, a protein substitute for meat. The French population, being Roman Catholic, absorbed more fish than the English on a per capita basis. The French supplied the English market in the first half of the sixteenth century but with the subsequent rise of competition from the English fishing industry, French fishermen turned to their sizeable domestic market.

Fish are a renewable resource which, unlike non-renewable resources such as mineral deposits, will reproduce if left to themselves. Bottom-dwelling fish, such as cod and haddock, are relatively non-migratory; a feeding ground divided by deep water channels usually defines the spatial limits of a given fish population. Each fish population therefore has a maximum sustainable yield—a maximum catch that leaves the fish population intact. Overfishing this limit reduces the catch attainable in the future. Moreover, ocean fish are a common property resource and do not become private property until a catch is made. The fish that one operator leaves in any given feeding ground today may be recovered by another operator tomorrow. In the long run, free entry to a feeding ground leads to depletion of the fish population unless the catch is regulated in some way.

The emergence of national States in the sixteenth century stimulated international competition in the fisheries, and the North Atlantic fishing zone became a theatre for the extension of European rivalries. Since fishermen could not stake formal claims over open bodies of water, individual fishing boats often required naval protection from the home government. International conflict stemmed from attempts to regulate access to feeding grounds and landing rights in one or other national interest. But in the absence of internationally recognized legal institutions, attempts at regulation (such as the system whereby the first captain in a port distributed fishing rights for the season) proved unsuccessful. The threat of armed conflict and the need for naval protection induced fishing boat operators to favor particular regions according to national origin. By the end of the sixteenth century, England controlled the western Newfoundland waters around the Avalon Peninsula while the small scale, competitive French fisheries had been pushed into less accessible areas around the St. Lawrence Gulf.

Two distinct methods of curing permitted fishermen to preserve the catch while making the slow journey to market. The English employed the 'dry' curing technique on shore in Newfoundland. French fishermen, on the other hand, preferred salting their catch on-board ship without necessarily setting foot on land. As a result, the French fisheries contributed to the exploration of the North American coastline, but not to the penetration of the St. Lawrence Valley. The fisheries generated some knowledge of the Gulf region, reducing the eventual costs of settlement, but contact with the land and Indian people was limited. For all of the European

Chart 1.1

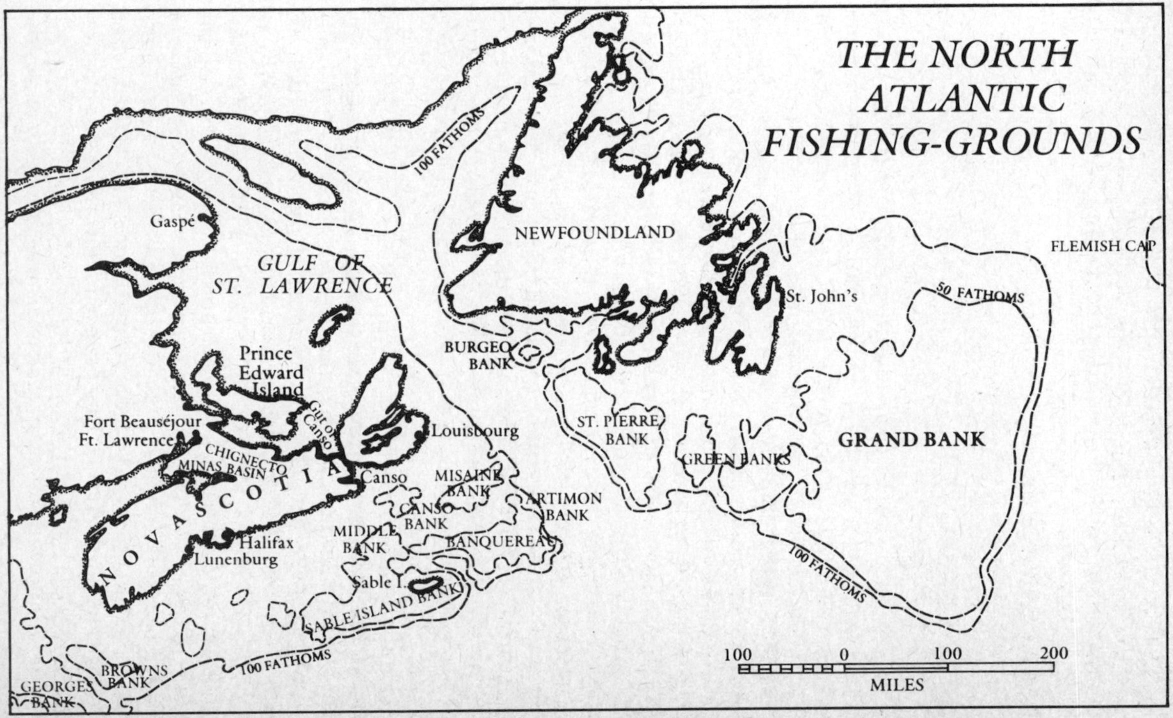

THE NORTH ATLANTIC FISHING-GROUNDS

FLEMISH CAP

50 FATHOMS

GRAND BANK

St. John's

100 FATHOMS

GREEN BANK

ST. PIERRE BANK

NEWFOUNDLAND

BURGEO BANK

Louisbourg

ARTIMON BANK

MISAINE BANK

BANQUEREAU

GULF OF ST. LAWRENCE

Canso

CANSO BANK

MIDDLE BANK

SABLE ISLAND BANK

Sable Island

Gaspé

Prince Edward Island

Gut of Canso

CHIGNECTO

Fort Beauséjour
Ft. Lawrence

MINAS BASIN

Halifax

Lunenburg

NOVA SCOTIA

100 FATHOMS

BROWNS BANK

GEORGES BANK

MILES

100   0   100   200

Canadian Economic History, p. 29, by W.T. Easterbrook and Hugh G.J. Aitken, reprinted by permission of the authors.

countries, the North Atlantic fisheries constituted an off-shore seasonal activity that failed to induce permanent settlement in the sixteenth century. Cod fishing produced few linkage effects with other forms of economic activity that could have given rise to colonization. Not until the first decade of the seventeenth century, after a hundred years of non-resident fishing, did Europeans establish permanent outposts in the Atlantic region of North America.

The Fur Trade

The physical layout of North America established the pattern of exploration, resource discovery and migration. Water transportation was the only means of travel to the new land; once on the continent, the spatial distribution of navigable waterways determined traffic and settlement patterns. For Europeans, the Appalachian Mountains running parallel to the Atlantic seaboard constituted the principal barrier of entry to the interior. Of the four means of access to the interior, the St. Lawrence Valley offered the most efficient route. To the south, the Hudson River and the Mohawk Valley provided an alternate passage to the Great Lakes. But aside from these two thoroughfares, penetration to the continental interior required either a northern voyage by way of Hudson Bay, or a southern circuit by way of the Gulf of Mexico and the Mississippi River. Early settlement took place mostly in the temperate regions closest to Europe—along the Atlantic coast, especially at New York, and at several points in the St. Lawrence River Basin. (See Chart 1.2)

During the 1580s, French merchants in Rouen and La Rochelle organized the first fur trading expeditions. Until this time fur trading with the indigenous people had been an incidental spillover from the fisheries. The rise in demand for beaver furs was dependent upon the demand for felt hats (a luxury good) in Europe. J.F. Crean attributes the growth in French demand for Canadian beaver to the rise of Sweden as a great power during the sixteenth century and an associated change in European tastes in favor of the Swedish-style beaver felt hat. By the time of Champlain's voyage inland in 1610, the primary motivation for French exploration in North America had shifted from the fishing industry to development of the beaver fur trade.

The task of hunting fur-bearing animals was generally left to the Indian people who possessed the skills and information necessary to accomplish the hunt efficiently. European traders acquired fur pelts in exchange for processed commodities through trade. Euro-

Chart 1.2

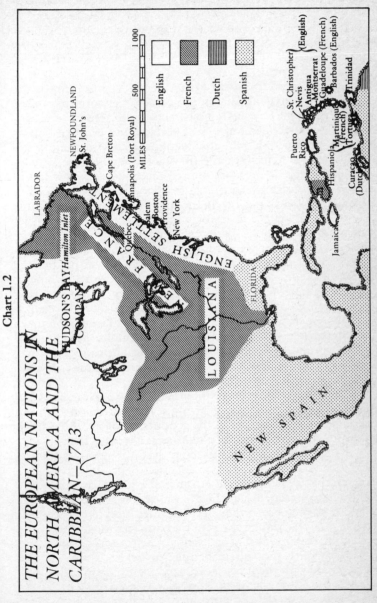

THE EUROPEAN NATIONS IN NORTH AMERICA AND THE CARIBBEAN—1713

LABRADOR

HUDSON'S BAY *Hamilton Inlet*
COMPANY

NEWFOUNDLAND
St. John's

Cape Breton

FRANCE

Quebec

Annapolis (Port Royal)

ENGLISH SETTLEMENT

Salem
Boston
Providence
New York

FLORIDA

LOUISIANA

NEW SPAIN

MILES
500   1 000

English

French

Dutch

Spanish

Puerto Rico

Hispaniola

Jamaica

Curaçao (Dutch)

Tortuga

Trinidad

St. Christopher
Nevis   } (English)
Antigua
Montserrat
Guadeloupe (French)
Martinique (French)
Barbados (English)

Canadian Economic History, p. 101, by W.T. Easterbrook and Hugh G.J. Aitken, reprinted by permission of the authors.

pean demand, by offering rewards to Indian tribes that engaged in the fur trade, upset the established social and economic equilibrium that had prevailed in the pre-European era. The acquisition of new weapons technology by some tribes led to new alliances and power struggles. At the end of the sixteenth century, the more northerly hunting tribes (Montagnais, Algonkians) displaced the agricultural Indians of the St. Lawrence Valley (Iroquois), who moved west and south.

The economic growth of New France depended primarily on the fur trade. The collecting of animal furs for export to Europe constituted the first colonially-based economic activity. An agricultural sector developed during the seventeenth century, and by 1700 many more people were involved in agriculture than in any other economic activity. But the fur trade remained the basis of colonial exports and the main source of economic growth and change. While subsistence farming provided the major proportion of the average level of per capita income, fluctuations in income per capita varied with fur exports and other market activities related to overseas trade.

The concept of comparative advantage is helpful to the understanding of interregional or international specialization and the expansion of the fur trade in the northerly part of the continent. Just as specialization and economic exchange within a given region may make the regional economy more efficient, specialization among regions, combined with interregional trade, can make the trading partners better off. Atmospheric conditions, abundant natural resources, or economies of large scale production may favor one region over another in the production of some commodities. Higher quality fur pelts, for instance, are found in colder climates, but agricultural production in these areas is often restricted because of the short growing season. A region is said to enjoy comparative advantage in the production of a commodity if it can produce the commodity relatively cheaply, that is, at a comparatively lower opportunity cost than the region's trading partners.

The concept of comparative advantage between regions does not apply in the presence of explicit or indirect coercion, nor where the trading parties are unequally informed about alternatives. There are many examples of plunder, international theft, and unequal exchange in colonial and modern history. With the exception of barter with the Indian people, however, it appears that European trade with the newly colonized regions of North America was carried out on the basis of comparative advantage.

Furs proved to be the only product in which New France was able to establish a clear comparative advantage in trade with

Europe. Their importance did not lie solely in their contribution to wages and profits: furs played an important role in the process of international factor migration by attracting European labor, skills and capital to the St. Lawrence region. Fur trading created a demand for export services such as shipping, and public goods such as the policing of contracts and military protection. By improving information about the regions adjacent to the St. Lawrence Valley, the trade affected the early pattern of settlement in North America. Fur trading did not, however, induce many subsidiary economic activities. Links with extant colonial industries (agriculture, fishing, lumbering) were relatively few. The fur trade made itself felt on these industries, not through commodity markets, but through the labor market. In providing risky though potentially rewarding employment opportunities to the adventurous, fur trading was akin to prospecting for gold. As such, the fur trade undermined government attempts to diversify the economy and attract labor into alternative economic activities.

The most influential analysis of the impact of furs on the economy and society of New France is contained in Harold Innis's *The Fur Trade in Canada*. This work, first published in 1930, is a classic example of the staple approach to Canadian economic history. Innis demonstrated how French labor and capital moved to the St. Lawrence Valley in response to the high returns offered by fur trading. The comparative advantage in furs arose as a result of changes in demand on the part of both Europeans and Amerindians, and gave rise to a resource-intensive or 'staple' export trade controlled by metropolitan merchants. The growth of the staple trade raised the level of per capita income and induced labor and capital migration to Canada.

Beaver furs, like fish, constituted a renewable resource. But since no provision was made for the animals' reproduction, the supply of beaver in the areas immediately adjacent to the St. Lawrence River was gradually depleted. The fur trade, which began in the St. Lawrence Gulf region in the sixteenth century, extended first to the Saguenay River, then via the St. Lawrence and Ottawa Rivers to the Great Lakes in the seventeenth century. By the middle of the eighteenth century, the trade reached across the headwaters of the Hudson Bay drainage basin to Lake Winnipeg and the Saskatchewan River, and as far south as the Ohio Valley and Mississippi River.

It appears unlikely that major changes occurred in fur trading productivity to offset the rising costs of inland transport. The westward expansion of the fur trade resulted in reduced transaction costs through learning-by-doing and institutional innovations such as the creation of inland fur trading posts. But it seems unreasonable to attribute substantial savings to these changes. Of greater significance was the reduction in the costs of ocean shipping stemming from the reduction of piracy, privateering, and related hazards. James Shepherd and Gary Walton have attributed the dramatic decline in the real costs of American colonial shipping over the period 1675-1775 to improvements in the security of overseas travel. Although it has not been demonstrated that pre-Conquest French colonial shipping benefited from similar changes, it is probably safe to assume this was so. The decline in ocean shipping costs would help to explain why the fur trade was able to support higher inland transport costs as trading moved westward.

Although Innis's staple approach provides a useful way of analysing the fur trade, a number of his specific conclusions have now been revised. In his discussion of market structure, Innis emphasized that fur trading in New France possessed the characteristics of a natural monopoly: fur trading operations involved high start-up costs and the scarcity of water routes to the continental interior invited monopoly control of the St. Lawrence River. These characteristics were reinforced by a series of 'artificial' monopolies created by the French State. Beginning in 1603, a succession of fur trading companies received charters granting the exclusive right to sell furs on the French market. Innis does not make clear, however, that as of 1665 these licenses applied only to beaver and moose hides. With the subsequent decrease in the supply of quality beaver pelts (castor gras), the European demand for felt hats declined. After 1700 beaver furs represented less than half the total value of furs exported to France (Eccles, 1979, p. 436). Innis does admit the 'artificial' monopoly aspects of the fur trade extended only to market sales in France and not to the development of the trade within North America. Dutch and English settlements in the Hudson River Valley, and beginning in 1670 the Hudson's Bay Company in the north, provided alternate and competing opportunities to Indian hunters and traders. As the Indians engaged in the fur trade secured better information about European goods and trading alternatives, they obliged French traders to pay more competitive prices. Even in the French domestic market, however, there is no evidence the French fur trading companies were able to restrict output over the long run in the way an effective monopolist would be expected to do. As Louise Dechêne points out, there is no reason to believe that the Company of the West Indies, which controlled fur exports in the century after 1674, earned anything more than the going rate of profit for large companies in France (some 10 to 15 percent).

Innis conducted his analysis in terms of a monopolistic market structure and maintained the fur trade monopoly induced or favored centralized control within all of New France's major institutions. In his view, government regulation, the Church, and the seigneurial system exhibited authoritarian behavior in contrast to the competitive, decentralized economic and political activities of New England. In fact, there is no evidence that centralized political administration and institutions (if this characterization is accurate) resulted from the fur trade. Other French colonies where the fur trade was of little or no importance, such as Louisiana and the French West Indies, possessed the same institutions, and attributing "centralized" institutions in New France to the "monopoly" character of the fur trade is therefore misleading.

Another widely held belief stemming from Innis' work concerns unbalanced colonial economic development. Innis maintained that the growth of the fur trade hampered the diversification of colonial economic activity. By drawing off labor and capital from all other sectors, the fur trade allegedly inhibited the kind of economic diversification occurring in New England. It is not clear, however, that specialization in fur trading reflected anything other than a comparative advantage in fur pelt production. (See Table 1.1) Profits and wages in fur trading stemmed from the productivity of capital and labor in trading activities; the size of the agricultural sector in the St. Lawrence Valley followed from the modest returns that farming in the St. Lawrence lowlands offered potential migrants. It is conceivable that the fur trading companies reduced the flow of labor into agriculture by restricting immigration to Canada in the early years; there were only 3 200 people in the Laurentian Valley by 1665. But the situation did not change significantly thereafter when the French government exercised direct responsibility for immigration. Only 10 000 immigrants settled in Canada over the entire 1608-1760 period. According to Harris and Warkentin, 5 percent of these immigrants came without being subsidized in some way. Colonial agriculture did not enjoy a comparative advantage with respect to the French domestic agricultural sector and, except for the period 1727-1741, the habitants did not produce for export to any considerable degree. The small size of urban markets (about 17 500 people in 1760), the relatively high costs of production stemming from land clearing requirements and unfavorable climatic conditions, and the costs of transport to markets in Europe and the West Indies, continued to limit agricultural growth even in the nineteenth century. The fur trade and agricultural settlement were not fundamentally incompatible, they simply offered different rates of return.

Table 1.1

VALUE OF EXPORTS FROM CANADA, BY COMMODITY AND DESTINATION, EXPRESSED AS A PERCENTAGE OF TOTAL VALUE, 1739

By commodity	Percentage
Beaver furs	24.1
Other furs	47.3
Agricultural products	17.9
Fish	8.9
Lumber	0.6
Iron and scrap iron	1.2
TOTAL	100.0

By destination	
France	79.9
West Indies	7.6
Acadia and Isle Royale*	12.5
TOTAL	100.0

*A part of these exports was destined for shipment to the West Indies in the following year.

Denys Delage, "Les structures économiques de la Nouvelle-France et de la Nouvelle-York," *L'Actualité Economique*, Vol. 46, No. 1, pp. 95-96, (avril-juin 1970), reprinted by permission.

Similarly, manufacturing production was appropriately scaled to the size of the domestic market. It is true that French mercantile policy, like English policy, discouraged colonial manufacturing in some sectors, (see Chapter 4) but French mercantile policy is not specifically attributable to the fur trade. The size of the fur trading sector reflected a comparative advantage with respect to Europe in spite of transport costs. Aside from the cod fish, this comparative advantage extended to few commodities. The size of the manufacturing and agricultural sectors in the St. Lawrence Valley corresponded to the size of the domestic market and the eighteenth century value of Canadian resources.

Innis also suggests the Indian people engaged in the fur trade were aware of the differential in prices offered by French and English traders. He argues that France was incapable of maintaining the fur trade as a viable economic activity in the face of English competition, and implies that the British Conquest was inevitable. His argument rests on two assumptions concerning the advantages that eighteenth century English fur traders enjoyed over their French counterparts. Innis maintained the English supplied cheaper and better commodities in trade with the Indians and, second, that they enjoyed lower transport costs to European markets because of their control of Hudson Bay and the Hudson River. However, both of these assertions have been contested. The relative price or quality advantage of English goods has never been demonstrated. Eccles suggests prices for comparable trade goods were about the same and the quality of French and English commodities no different prior to the Industrial Revolution (circa 1760). Eccles also disputes the claim that the Bay route was less costly than trading via Michilimachinac, the main Canadian post. Inland costs were higher via the Bay route, and food supplies had to be imported as they could not be produced locally. Larger canoes could be used on the Great Lakes than in the Hudson Bay drainage basin, permitting an economies of scale advantage on the Great Lakes route. For all of these reasons the French would appear to have had a less costly trade route than the English. Arthur J. Ray's data indicate the total money value of furs received by the Hudson's Bay Company at York Factory, Fort Albany and Fort Churchill declined unevenly from the early 1730s until the late 1750s, when the French were forced to withdraw. The average annual value of furs entering England was about 40 percent of that entering the French port of La Rochelle over the forty years leading up to the Conquest. In fact, the British share in North American trade was declining over this period. Innis's suggestion that the French fur trade was on the decline prior to 1759 and that the British Conquest was inevitable is not supported by available data.

The fur trade constituted the basis of colonial exports and the main source of economic growth and change. But despite its importance to the economy of New France, the trade was not of great significance to the economic well-being of the metropolitan merchant class or the French economy as a whole. The value of exports from New France to the French port of La Rochelle, the most important centre for Canadian goods, averaged about one million livres per year over the period 1718-1761. This constituted less than one percent of the value of all French imports from the colonies—the important items being sugar, coffee, indigo, chocolate and fish. France's true imperial success in the Western Hemisphere occurred in the West Indies (Guadeloupe, Martinique and Saint-Dominique). Eccles interprets French interest in Canada as being largely political or strategic, as opposed to economic: fur trading maintained military alliances with the Indians and assured effective control of the American mid-west. It seems unlikely, however, that this strategic interest can be divorced from long run economic objectives, that is, ownership of continental resources. In the seventeenth century the size of the French-speaking population corresponded to the resource base in the St. Lawrence and Mississippi drainage basins, as perceived at the time. By midpoint in the eighteenth century perceptions had changed. However, the French government did not have the financial means to organize the settlement of the continental mid-west, something the British American colonies were preparing to do.

SELECT BIBLIOGRAPHY

Crean, J.F. "Hats and the Fur Trade." *Canadian Journal of Economics and Political Science.* August 1962.

Dechêne, Louise. *Habitants et marchands de Montréal au XVIIe siècle.* Montreal: Plon, 1974.

Easterbrook, W.T. and Hugh G.J. Aitken. *Canadian Economic History.* Toronto: Macmillan, 1963.

Eccles, W.J. "A Belated Review of Harold Adams Innis, The Fur Trade in Canada." *Canadian Historical Review.* December 1979.

Eccles, W.J. "A Response to Hugh M. Grant on Innis." *Canadian Historical Review.* September 1981.

Grant, Hugh M. "One Step Forward, Two Steps Back: Innis, Eccles, and the Canadian Fur Trade." *Canadian Historical Review.* September 1981.

Hamelin, Jean. *Economie et société en Nouvelle-France.* Quebec: les Presses de l'Université Laval, 1970.

Harris R. Cole and John Warkentin. *Canada Before Confederation: A Study in Historical Geography.* Toronto: Oxford University Press, 1974.

Innis, Harold A. *The Cod Fisheries: A History of an International Economy.* Toronto: University of Toronto Press, 1940.

Innis, Harold A. *The Fur Trade in Canada.* Toronto: University of Toronto Press, 1956.

Innis, Harold A. *Select Documents in Canadian Economic History, 1497-1783 .* Toronto: University of Toronto Press, 1929.

Lawson, Murray G. *Fur: A Study in English Mercantilism 1700-1775.* Toronto: University of Toronto Press, 1943.

Mackintosh, W.A. "Economic Factors in Canadian History," in W.T. Easterbrook and M.H. Watkins, eds., *Approaches to Canadian Economic History.* Toronto: McClelland and Stewart, 1967.

McManus, John C. "An Economic Analysis of Indian Behavior in the North American Fur Trade." *Journal of Economic History.* March 1972.

North, Douglass C. and Robert P. Thomas. *The Rise of the Western World: A New Economic History.* Cambridge: Cambridge University Press, 1973.

Pritchard, James S. "The Pattern of French Colonial Shipping to Canada before 1760." *Revue française d'histoire d'Outre-Mer.* Vol. LXIII, no. 231 (1976).

Ray, Arthur J. *Indians in the Fur Trade: their role as hunters, trappers and middlemen in the lands southwest of Hudson Bay, 1660-1680.* Toronto: University of Toronto Press, 1974.

Shepherd, James F. and Gary M. Walton. *Shipping, Maritime Trade and the Economic Development of Colonial North America.* Cambridge University Press, 1972.

Trigger, Bruce G. *The Indians and the Heroic Age of New France.* Ottawa: The Canadian Historical Association Booklets, No. 30, 1979.

Trudel, Marcel. *Histoire de la Nouvelle-France*, Vol. I, *Les vaines tentatives 1524-1603.* Montreal: Fides, 1963.

Watkins, Melville H. "A Staple Theory of Economic Growth", in W.T. Easterbrook and M.H. Watkins, eds. *Approaches to Canadian Economic History.* Toronto: McClelland and Stewart, 1967.

2
Agriculture and Settlement

French settlement in North America covered a remarkably broad geographical area. The largest colony, Canada, rested on the banks of the St. Lawrence River, but small pockets of French-speaking people also located in two other regions: in the sheltered coves of the Gulf of St. Lawrence and the Bay of Fundy, and beyond the British American colonies south and west of the Great Lakes. In the Gulf region, settlements developed in association with the fisheries on the Iles de la Madeleine, Ile St-Jean (Prince Edward Island), and Ile Royale (Cape Breton). In the Bay of Fundy area, some 500 immigrants established a successful agricultural colony in the region known as Acadia, prior to the capture of Port Royal (Annapolis Royal) by the English in 1710. South and west of the Great Lakes, fur trading posts sprung up in the eighteenth century to serve both economic and military objectives in the French North American design. By the 1740s, however, the total population in the Mississippi Valley had attained some 4 000 and the only settlement west of the Appalachians was at the port of New Orleans.

Immigration to Canada

Complex and varied considerations influenced the decision to migrate to North America. Social and cultural factors, such as the desire of migrants to break away from existing organizational and religious constraints, played a significant role. But an underlying motive for international migration was the desire to increase personal income and wealth. The discovery of new resources and profitable opportunities in fishing, fur trading, and agricultural production raised the average expected level of income from migration. Potential migrants did not base their migration decision solely on the expected level of income in the Americas. Their migration decision depended on the net difference in income between the Old World and the New, as perceived at the time, subject to various incentives offered by the State. The income differential was a 'net' calculation in the sense that it amounted to the present value of the difference in expected income after the total costs of moving had been taken into account. Of course the average working person's perception of this differential was vague and subject to considerable error. But this did not prevent potential migrants from comparing expected opportunities in the New World with the income to be earned from selling their labor in Europe, and moving if the net difference was positive.

France furnished relatively few settlers to the New World in comparison to England, partly because of domestic economic conditions. (See Table 2.1) Despite the repeated onslaught of plagues, England's population is estimated to have grown by as much as 25 percent during the seventeenth century. This population increase placed downward pressure on agricultural wages in the English countryside, providing an economic incentive to emigrate to the New World. In France, famines, epidemics and the Huguenot emigration took a higher toll than in England, suspending French population growth altogether during the seventeenth century. French peasants and workers did not face the same economic incentives to migrate to North America as the English did. Moreover, French Protestants were forbidden to settle in New France. The decline of real incomes in England accelerated emigration and, together with the intensity of religious strife, contributed to the marked difference in the rates of immigration and settlement in the British American colonies as compared with Canada.

Immigration depended on pull as well as push factors. That is, the rate of migration to the various regions in North America also depended on the expected rate of return from settlement and resource exploitation in each region. France supplied relatively few migrants to the New World primarily because of the nature of the resources in the northeastern part of the continent. In contrast to the export-oriented fisheries of New England, the resident fisheries in Canada did not induce permanent settlement of any significance. The land in the Gulf region was ill-suited to agriculture and port facilities were open to attack by the English. The resident fisheries in the Gulf of St. Lawrence remained a minor economic activity compared to the metropolitan fisheries.[1] The fur trade

Table 2.1

TOTAL POPULATION IN CANADA AND THE BRITISH COLONIES OF NORTH AMERICA, SELECTED YEARS, 1630-1760

Canada		British American Colonies	
Year	Population	Year	Population
1641	240	1630	5 000
1665	3 215	1660	89 000
1692	12 431	1690	209 000
1720	24 434	1720	466 000
1760	70 000	1750	1 171 000

Census of Canada, 1871. Reprinted by permission of the Minister of Supply and Services Canada.
Historical Census of United States, Colonial Times to 1957. Reprinted by permission of the U.S. Bureau of the Census.

exercised a greater, though limited, impact on the demand for labor in New France. By the time of the Conquest, about 2 500 people were directly engaged in the fur trade. (cf. Ouellet, p. 358) Most of the immigrants who came to Canada engaged in agriculture.

Agricultural settlement in the St. Lawrence Valley offered only modest economic returns. With the St. Lawrence River frozen from mid-December to the end of March, commercial relations and communications with the metropole came to a standstill for six months every year. Although mean summer temperatures and total summer rainfall compared favorably with that in western France, the growing season was shorter causing lower quality yields and less crop variety. The January mean temperature in Quebec City and Montreal is at least 15°C lower than in northern Brittany and the discomfort must have discouraged potential migrants as well. Soil resources were no more than adequate. In R.C. Harris's words,

> All in all, the soil resources of early Canada were scanty. There were bands of potential farmland along either shore of the St. Lawrence and up some of the tributaries, and a triangle of fertile land from the Isle de Montreal to Lake Saint-Pierre and south toward Lake Champlain, but the best land was to the west in what is now Ontario, and was then the territory of the fur trade.[2]

The difference in average agricultural incomes between Canada and the English colonies affected the quantity and nature of immigrants coming to the two regions. By 1700 the population of the English colonies was twenty-five times as great as that in the French colonies. Ratner, Soltow and Sylla indicate that about half of all migrants to the English colonies had come voluntarily. These migrants appear to have been moderately wealthy because they were able to pay their own transport and settlement costs. As mentioned in Chapter 1, only 5 percent of the 10 000 immigrants who arrived in New France during the years 1608-1759 did so without being subsidized in some way. According to Harris, the other 95 percent consisted of 4 000 indentured workers, 3 500 ex-soldiers excused from military service, 1 000 prisoners (predominantly salt smugglers) and 1 000 women (mostly from Parisian orphanages). Not surprisingly, there were almost no wealthy migrants among French Canadian colonists. The vast majority of settlers were low income, unskilled or semi-skilled people.

Seigneurial Institutions and Settlement

Settlement and cultivation of the land in North America required a system of land granting and tenure. For this purpose the French State introduced the seigneurial system to the colonies. Almost all of the laws governing French seigneurial institutions were transferred to the colony with the Coutume de Paris in 1663. The Crown intended the seigneurial environment to serve not only an economic role, but a social and political function as well. Through the seigneurial system, the French government expected to recreate the seventeenth century French social structure in America. But over time the institutional environment adapted to the economic conditions prevailing in the St. Lawrence Valley. The set of property rights inherent in the French seigneurial system gradually adjusted to the abundant land and relatively low economic returns from farming in Canada. As a result the seigneurial system in Canada came to play an economic role similar to that later played by the English system of free and common socage in Ontario.[3]

Seigneurial institutions were initially introduced to Acadia in the first decade of the seventeenth century, and to the St. Lawrence Valley in 1627. In that year the Company of New France, also called the Company of One Hundred Associates, acquired legal title to most of eastern North America with the stipulation that seigneuries be granted and colonists invited to settle. But the Company was more concerned with the fur trade than with settlement; the fur trade was where Canada's comparative economic advantage lay. By 1663 the largest seigneuries to be granted in

Canada had been distributed to associates of the Company, their wealthy friends, and the Jesuits. The seigneuries of Beaupré, Lauzon, the Ile de Montréal, Bastiscan, Cap-de-la-Madeleine and Cap des Rosiers, for example, far exceeded one hundred square miles each. The seventeenth century value of these forested lands, however, was not very great. In 1663 no more than 10 of the 70 seigneuries granted by the Company, largely around the towns of Quebec, Trois-Rivières and Montreal, had any settlers at all. For this reason among others, the Company of New France lost its charter and Canada reverted to the administrative control under the French Crown.

Under the aegis of colonial government, agricultural settlement grew at an accelerated pace. Between 1665 and 1672, the European population in the St. Lawrence Valley expanded from some 3 200 to about 6 000. In his last year as Intendent, 1672, Jean Talon granted 46 seigneuries of modest size, more or less completing the concession of river frontage between Quebec and Montreal. Governor Frontenac conceded another 40 seigneuries between 1672 and 1698. But at the end of the seventeenth century the total population of the colony was little more than 11 000. Despite the considerable extent of seigneurial concessions, most of the land in cultivation lay on the north shore of the St. Lawrence within twenty-five miles of the urban markets in Quebec City, Trois-Rivières and Montreal. (See Chart 2.1) Settlement west of Montreal was forbidden by the Crown in an attempt to prevent settlers from engaging in the fur trade.

Between 1698 and 1740 the Crown granted another 78 seigneuries, but immigration did not proceed apace. In the last sixty years of French dominion, the returns to agriculture, together with government subsidies and incentives, attracted at most 4 000 immigrants to the colony. The total population expanded by nearly six times over this period, but this growth depended largely on natural population increase. At the time of the British Conquest, Canada consisted of two thin bands of settlement on the St. Lawrence: one along the north shore from la Malbaie to Vaudreuil, the other along the south shore from Beauharnois to Pointe-au-Père, and nearly all of the Lake Champlain area. The total population in the St. Lawrence Valley amounted to about 60 000 people.

From an economic point of view, the seigneurial system may be thought of as a land granting mechanism. Instead of making concessions directly to cultivators, the State (during the years 1627-1663, the fur trading companies) conceded property to seigneurs who in turn were expected to act as real estate agents by parcelling their concessions among settlers. Seigneurial income

Chart 2.1

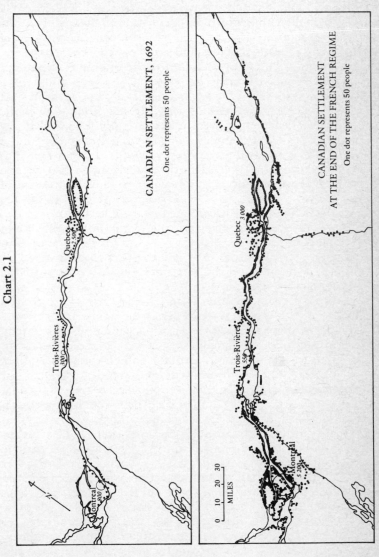

CANADIAN SETTLEMENT, 1692

One dot represents 50 people

CANADIAN SETTLEMENT
AT THE END OF THE FRENCH REGIME

One dot represents 50 people

Canada Before Confederation, p. 35, by R. Cole Harris and John Warkentin, Cartographer Miklos Pinther © Oxford University Press.

was derived from the seigneur's personal lands, the *reserve* or *domaine direct*, and from rents and charges, *cens* and *rentes*, collected from the residents of the seigneury, the *censitaires*. Each censitaire worked a concession called a *censive* or *roture*, usually a hundred to a hundred and twenty acres. The rental fees generally depended on the number of acres in cultivation, the quality of the soil, and the amount of river frontage, with other charges being collected for additional rights and services rendered by the seigneur—fishing rights, timber dues, the use of common pasture, grist mills, bake-ovens, and so on.

About a quarter of all the seigneurial land granted during the French regime was granted directly to the Roman Catholic Church. These seigneuries were more carefully tended than lay seigneuries. Of the 30 seigneuries held by religious orders, more than half were conceded by the Company of New France prior to 1663. R.C. Harris says, "The north shore within a fifteen mile radius of Quebec and both shores within a similar distance of Montreal were the most valuable and densely settled land in the colony, and almost all of it belonged to the Church" (Harris, p. 43). From the beginning, the clergy played an important role in providing education and social services, such as hospital care, to the population. Seigneurial land grants to religious orders may therefore be thought of, in part, as a subsidy or sub-contract for the provision of basic public services.[4]

The demand for agricultural land by settlers was a derived demand related to expected yields per acre. Seigneurial dues were variable from one seigneury to the next, depending largely on the economic value of the land in question. Overall, mediocre agricultural conditions and the small size of the domestic market resulted in low returns to agricultural activity, a modest demand for agricultural land, and in consequence, relatively low seigneurial dues.[5] Harris suggests that dues and charges were lowered from time to time in order to attract scarce agricultural labor. A period of prosperity, on the other hand, sometimes led to higher dues as seigneurs attempted to siphon off some of the transitory economic rents accruing to censitaires.

Under the seigneurial system, a small group of men acquired and retained property rights in Canadian lands. Until 1711 seigneurs could dispose of their land as they saw fit, either by sale or by lease to a censitaire. Because cleared land was a scarce resource, an initial payment or settlement fee was often required from a new censitaire in a cleared area. Once on the land, the censitaire could not easily be removed unless he failed to meet his contractual obligations. Censitaires were in turn entitled to buy and sell the rights to work seigneurial lands under certain conditions, including the payment of a sales tax or *lod* to the seigneur of one-twelfth of the selling price.

Beginning with the Edict of Marly in 1711, seigneurs were required to concede unoccupied land to whomever applied and forbidden to charge settlement fees. By law, though not in practice, censitaires who failed to work their concessions could have them withdrawn. The objective of the edict was to stimulate immigration and settlement at a time of high European cereal prices by eliminating speculation in unoccupied land on the part of both seigneurs and censitaires. The rate of immigration and settlement did not increase after 1711, however, and the Edict can therefore be judged as unsuccessful in attaining its objective.

Table 2.2

AGRICULTURAL PRODUCTION/STOCK
PER CAPITA IN CANADA, 1706, 1719, 1734

	1706	1719	1734
Cultivated land (arpents)	2.6	2.8	4.3
Land in pasture (arpents)	0.3	0.4	0.5
Wheat (minots)	12.9	10.5	19.6
Corn (minots)	n/a	0.3	0.1
Oats (minots)	n/a	2.2	4.3
Peas (minots)	2.6	2.1	1.7
Flax (pounds)	n/a	2.0	2.4
Hemp (pounds)	n/a	0.2	0.1
Tobacco (pounds)	n/a	n/a	4.4
Horses	0.1	0.2	0.1
Cattle	0.8	0.8	0.9
Sheep	0.1	0.4	0.5
Pigs	0.5	0.6	0.6

1 arpent = 0.845 acres, 1 minot = 1.107 bushels

Government of Canada, *Census of Canada*, 1871, Vol. IV. Ottawa, 1876.
"Economic Development in New France, 1713-1760," by A.J.E. Lunn. Unpublished Ph.D. Thesis, McGill University, 1942.

Agricultural Output

In the absence of reliable data on agricultural production, exports, and prices in Canada, it is difficult to do more than catalogue various impressions. This is not to disparage the careful quantitative work accomplished by some historians of the colonial economy. It is simply to reaffirm the lack of time series data on most key economic variables and the riskiness of general conclusions about the agricultural sector during this period.

The short growing season (150 days at Montreal and 130 days at Quebec City), and the middling quality of the soil in the St. Lawrence Valley, conditioned the nature, quantity, and quality of agricultural output. Wheat generally occupied about three-quarters of the land in cultivation so the colony was ordinarily self-sufficient in wheat and flour. Peas, oats, barley and maize accounted for most other crop lands in use. (See Table 2.2) Sheep, pigs and horses were raised by almost all of the habitants, but the market for these products remained limited.

The agricultural techniques employed in Canada reflected the quantity and nature of the resources available. Fewer than a quarter of all the immigrants to Canada appear to have had previous agricultural experience in France. Furthermore, the colony was settled prior to the agricultural revolution in the mother country. Agricultural knowledge was a scanty resource in Canada, but land was relatively abundant. Settlers in North America generally practised a somewhat antiquated, extensive form of agriculture that European visitors often described as "sloppy". In North America, skilled labor rather than land was the scarce resource commanding economic rents; agricultural technique and organization differed between Europe and America because of the differing resource base.

Louise Dechêne has stressed the fragility of any generalizations about agricultural productivity, but until more research is done in this area, Harris's conclusions remain the most authoritative. Harris says, "Yields per acre and seed-to-yield ratios in Canada during the French regime compare very unfavorably with contemporary standards, and probably were little better than those in medieval Europe when seed-to-yield ratios of 1:3 or 1:4 were characteristic." (Harris, p. 154) Compared to Western Europe, more land per capita in Canada compensated for less productive agricultural labor.

The absence of accessible markets for food products constituted a major constraint on agricultural growth in the colony. About a quarter of the total domestic population lived in towns which provided a potential market for farm products, but many town dwellers kept their own gardens and livestock. Rapid agricultural growth required an export market. Given the high costs of overseas transport, however, a substantial export market did not arise. Travel time from Quebec to La Rochelle, for instance, was double the travel time to the West Indies or the Ile St. Jean because of the difficult St. Lawrence River passage; the navigation season was only half as long.

Agricultural exports were virtually non-existent in the seventeenth century. The agricultural sector was small, the costs of shipping high, and the colony beseiged by the Five Nations Iroquois Confederacy during the last two decades of the century. At the same time, New England, because of geographical proximity, could provide all of the foodstuffs in demand in the French West Indies at lower shipping cost. By importing sugar, molasses and rum for the American colonial population, New England merchants further lowered their average transport costs per ton/mile.

In the eighteenth century, agricultural exports rose to a modest position in the balance of Canadian trade. A fall in shipping costs associated with the decline in Indian wars, a reduction in ocean piracy and the cessation of hostilities with the English after 1713 appear to account for this change. European crop failures in 1709 and 1710 induced Canadian exporters to establish trade relations with other Franco-American colonies—the French West Indies, the Ile Royale and the Ile St. Jean. The export of small amounts of flour, biscuit, and peas became customary. Poor harvests caused the colonial government to curtail exports from 1714 through 1718, but intercolonial trade was restored in the late 1720s, as is evident in A.J.E. Lunn's data culled from government censes (Lunn, p. 449). Owing partly to colonial government regulation, the years of agricultural export corresponded to years of surplus beyond the colony's domestic needs. The period 1727-1741 was relatively prosperous. (See Table 2.2) No agricultural exports occurred from the mid-1750s as a result of the economic turmoil caused by the military build-up leading to the Seven Years War.

The Annales Approach

Given the paucity of data on agricultural production and exports during the French colonial regime, Jean Hamelin has attempted to make inferences about colonial production and welfare on the basis of individual commodity prices. Using prices paid at the Séminaire de Québec, Hamelin compiled a wheat price index for the years 1674-1750. For the Montreal region, Louise Dechêne has constructed a comparable index from post-mortem inventories and notarial documents for the years 1655-1725. The similarity of price movements in the two regions during the years 1674-1725 reflects the extent of domestic trading. Both authors take pains to describe the limitations of their data, but contentious issues in the computation of these price indices remain.[6]

A major limitation on the use of Hamelin and Dechêne's price indices arises because they are presented in money rather than deflated terms. It would admittedly be difficult to construct a reliable general price index for the French colonial period. But without such an index, the interpretation of individual commodity price indices in terms of constant purchasing power is problematic. An individual commodity price index expressed in money terms may illustrate a qualitative description of events, but it is not very useful in isolation from other commodity price indices for the same years. It is the relative price of wheat, as of other products, that is of interest to economic historians, and not the money price of wheat alone.

Hamelin, in line with the work of the French Annales school, attempts to use the money price of wheat as an index of economic welfare in the colony. Reasoning that the decrease in supply caused by a bad harvest drives up the price of cereals, Hamelin argues that average farm revenue, and therefore aggregate colonial expenditures declined in proportion to the increase in wheat prices during the years 1708-1750. This conclusion is acceptable only on the basis of restrictive assumptions. As Landes has written:

> It is quite evident that a disastrous harvest, with all that it implied in the way of hunger and unrest, was quite capable of crippling every sector of the economic life of the nation. It is one thing, however, to show that famine or near famine could have this effect, and another to prove an inverse proportional relationship between farm prices and farm income.[7]

Agricultural prices, and the price of wheat in particular, depend on both supply and demand conditions. An inversely proportional relationship between wheat prices and farm income would hold under the following assumptions:

(1) that wheat revenues so outweighed all other sources of farm income as to constitute the dominant factor in agricultural economic welfare at all times (i.e. that little or no substitution occurred between wheat and all other farm products over time);

(2) that the colonial demand for wheat was relatively price elastic so that a rise in the price of wheat always led to a fall in the total revenue accruing to the farm sector.

While the first assumption may have held, the second implies that as a consumption good, wheat had close substitutes. But this possibility (there is no firm evidence one way or the other) is rejected by Hamelin himself. Hamelin says that wheat had no close substitutes and that grain imports were insignificant. This statement implies that the demand for wheat was price *in*elastic. If wheat in fact had no close substitutes as a consumption good, then a rise in the price of wheat should have led to a *rise* in average real farm income, except in times of famine or near famine. The implication of Hamelin's analysis, that a trend increase in the price of wheat was associated with a deterioration in the economic welfare of agricultural producers in the four decades after 1708, is not logically coherent.[8] The entire question of money, prices, and economic welfare in New France remains open.

Seigneurial Institutions and Agricultural Output

There has been disagreement among historians of New France over the impact of the seigneurial system on agricultural production. In Europe the seigneurial system was accompanied by a rigid social structure with a vertical system of political authority and conditional property rights. Once transplanted, did similar institutional arrangements impose constraints on agricultural production in the St. Lawrence Valley? From an economic point of view, the question concerns not only the seigneurial system as an allocative mechanism among farmers, but also its effects on the allocation of resources between agriculture and the other sectors of the economy. Did the seigneurial system permit the functioning of markets in agricultural labor and land so as to allow those resources to find their best use? In other words, was the pricing of productive factors in the colony determined primarily by markets or, was it determined, on balance, by judicial, military, and political power, custom and other types of relationships commonly associated with feudalism that constrained the growth of agricultural output?

Unquestionably, the seigneurial system imposed few constraints on labor mobility. The habitants could move freely from one seigneury to another if economic returns proved profitable. In contrast to the servile tenure of mediaeval feudalism in France, the land-man ratio in Canada offered censitaires a considerable degree of autonomy. The extra-economic coercion of labor, typical of the feudal mode of production, was by and large absent from the colonial labor market in Canada.

The situation with respect to the allocation of land is more difficult to characterize. Even though serfdom had died in Western Europe by 1650, the seventeenth and early eighteenth centuries are usually regarded as a transitional period between feudalism and market capitalism. The Canadian seigneurial system evolved into a system of shared property rights. But seigneuries were regulated by such diverse laws, conventions and customs that one must wonder whether a market for land truly existed. Disposition of the land was subject to numerous colonial regulations, as well as the Coutume de Paris. Both seigneurs and censitaires traded in land, either through buying and selling land itself or leasing the customary rights to work the land through a procedure called *sous-arrentement*. This trade gave rise to an informal land market that permitted experienced farmers and productive soils to find their most economic use through the price mechanism. The Edict of Marly (1711) placed some restrictions on this process, by obliging seigneurs to concede unworked land at zero price on a 'first-come, first-served' basis. But the regulation does not appear to have had a significant impact. *Cens* and *rentes* continued to vary according to the economic value of the land in question.

The right of inheritance associated with the Coutume de Paris did tend to constrain the land market. Revenues from the 'sale' of a *roture* had to be divided among the family's heirs. This common property provision reduced the incentive to transfer farm property and may have inhibited the accumulation of farm lands by the more prosperous. Large scale farming and the systematic hiring of agricultural labor, typical in some of the American colonies, never appeared during the French colonial regime. However, the modest size of initial concessions to censitaires and the comparatively low returns from agricultural activity in the St. Lawrence Valley contributed more to the development of small-holder family farming than the institutional constraints imposed by the seigneurial system. Although it functioned awkwardly, a market for land did develop under the guise of the seigneurial regime. The *de facto* system of property rights associated with the seigneurial system adapted to the modest agricultural conditions prevailing in St. Lawrence Valley. The high opportunity costs of working in agriculture, as opposed to the fur trade, further contributed to modifications in the seigneurial system as originally designed by the metropolitan government.

During the eighteenth century, the seigneurial system does not appear to have constrained agricultural resource allocation in a serious way. Farmers enjoyed relatively secure tenure, freedom of movement, and positive incentives to increase output on the supply side. The chief impediments to agricultural growth in pre-Conquest Canada appear to have been the costs of migration, settlement and land-clearing, soil quality, climatic conditions, and the costs of transport to the markets of Europe and the French West Indies.

NOTES

[1]By the time of the Conquest, the French metropolitan fisheries employed some three thousand ships and fifteen thousand fishermen around Newfoundland and the St. Lawrence Gulf, about twice the number of British seamen. (Eccles, p. 215)

[2]*Canada Before Confederation*, p. 17, by R. Cole Harris and John Warkentin, Cartographer Miklos Pinther © Oxford University Press.

[3]For a revisionist viewpoint that emphasizes the persistence of traditional rights and customs, see Dechêne, 1971. Dechêne argues that seigneurial institutions had relatively little impact on the economic and social development of the colony.

[4]In addition to revenues from their own lands, the clergy collected 3.8 percent (1/26) of the annual grain harvest on lay seigneuries in the form of a *dime* (tithe).

[5]On average, about 10 to 14 percent of gross revenues from *rotures* in lay seigneuries went to seigneurs. Except for very productive soils, this percentage probably equalled the censitaire's rate of gross saving. (Dechêne, 1971, p. 180).

[6]For example, does the redemption of card money (1714-1719) by the French government at one half of its nominal value justify Hamelin's doubling of wheat prices for those years? In other words, was the real (exchange) value of card money, as opposed to its nominal (face) value, cut in half at the time? This author does not believe so. (See Chapter 3)

[7]"The Statistical Study of French Crises," by David Landes, *Journal of Economic History*, p. 197, May 1950.

[8]Hamelin also identifies the variance of wheat prices as a factor contributing to the low level of average agricultural income during the first half of the eighteenth century. The alleged 'instability' of wheat prices is asserted rather than demonstrated by comparison to some reference standard.

SELECT BIBLIOGRAPHY

Courville, Serge. "La crise agricole du Bas-Canada, éléments d'une réflexion géographique (deuxième partie)." *Cahiers de Géographie du Québec.* December 1980.

Davis, Lance E. and Douglass C. North. *Institutional Change and American Economic Growth.* New York: Cambridge University Press, 1971.

Davis, Ralph. *The Rise of the Atlantic Economies.* Ithica: Cornell University Press, 1973.

Dechêne, Louise. "L'évolution du régime seigneurial au Canada. Le cas de Montréal aux XVIIe et XVIIIe siècles." *Recherches Sociographiques.* May-August 1971.

Dechêne, Louise. *Habitants et marchands de Montréal au XVIIe siècle.* Montréal: Plon, 1974.

DeVries, Jan. *Economy of Europe in an Age of Crisis.* New York: Cambridge University Press, 1976.

Eccles, William J. *France in America.* Toronto: Fitzhenry & Whiteside Ltd., 1972.

Forster, Robert. "Achievements of the Annales School." *Journal of Economic History.* March 1978.

Hamelin, Jean. *Economie et société en Nouvelle-France.* Québec: Les Presses de l'Université Laval, 1970.

Harris, R. Cole. "The Extension of France into Rural Canada," in James R. Gibson, ed., *European Settlement and Development in North America: Essays on Geographical Change in Honour and Memory of Andrew Hill Clark.* Toronto: University of Toronto Press, 1978.

Harris, R. Cole. *The Seigneurial System in Early Canada: A Geographical Study.* Madison: University of Wisconsin Press, 1966.

Harris, R. Cole and John Warkentin, *Canada Before Confederation: A Study in Historical Geography.* Toronto: Oxford University Press, 1974.

Landes, David. "The Statistical Study of French Crises." *Journal of Economic History.* May 1950.

Lunn, A.J.E. "Economic Development in New France, 1713-1760." Unpublished Ph.D. Thesis. McGill University, 1942.

Mathieu, Jacques. *Le commerce entre la Nouvelle-France et les Antilles au XVIIIe siècle.* Montreal: Edition Fides, 1981.

Ouellet, Fernand. "Libéré ou exploité! Le paysan québécois d'avant 1850." *Histoire Sociale-Social History.* November 1980.

Ratner, Sidney, James H. Soltow and Richard Sylla. *The Evolution of the American Economy: Growth, Welfare and Decision Making.* New York: Basic Books, Inc., 1979.

Trudel, Marcel. *Les débuts du régime seigneurial au Canada.* Montreal: Fides, 1974.

Trudel, Marcel. *The Seigneurial Regime.* Ottawa: The Canadian Historical Association Booklets, No. 6, 1971.

3

The Monetary System

The search for a common currency continued throughout the French regime and resulted in a variety of monetary experiments. Means of exchange ranged from commodity monies, such as beaver pelts and measured quantities of wheat, through near-monies, such as promissory notes and bills of exchange, to currencies including French, Spanish and Portuguese coins, and colonial government issues of playing cards and other paper monies. The modern definition of money (bank deposits plus currency) is not directly applicable to the French colonial regime. The economy of Canada did not possess formal banking or credit institutions, nor did a single medium of exchange displace all others before the Conquest. Metropolitan French currency served as a unit of account in the colony, but the means of exchange were many and varied. There was, however, a general trend toward reducing the number of commonly accepted monetary instruments and a tendency to replace barter with transactions based on domestically issued paper money.

Monetary instability resulted from the overissue of paper money rather than from colonial monetary innovations *per se*. Inflation became a recurring problem in the eighteenth century colonial economy. The inflation rate appears to have varied with the nominal supply of money, but this relationship was modified by growth in real money demand (i.e. the money stock/price ratio). The demand for real money depended upon real output growth and institutional change involving the monetization of the colonial economy. When the nominal money supply increased faster than the demand for real money balances, inflation ensued. The overissue of paper money became a serious problem during the colonial military build-up preceding the British Conquest.

A Barter Economy

At the time of Jean Talon's arrival at Quebec in 1665, economic exchange in Canada took place primarily by barter. Beaver pelts constituted the most commonly traded commodity, but other goods such as moose skins, wildcat pelts, and liquor served as alternative media of exchange. These goods were familiar to the colonists, lightweight, durable, and available in standardized units. Together they facilitated exchange and served as a store of wealth—important attributes of any monetary system.

Economic exchange based on a common currency has three economic advantages as compared with a barter system. These advantages stem from the services offered by money as a medium of exchange, as a store of value, and as a unit of account.

The use of a primary product as a medium of exchange raises a number of problems relating to divisibility, perishability, safekeeping, and transport costs. Recourse to beaver pelts gave rise to such difficulties since pelts had to be guarded and shipped at non-negligible expense to the trading parties. As the colonial government and service sectors grew in size, economic exchange between the monetized and non-monetized parts of the economy became more difficult. Transactions with the monetized metropolitan economy also proved more burdensome. A common currency overcame these difficulties by reducing the costs of storage and transport. This is the function of money as a medium of exchange.

The use of commodities as a store of value complicates economic exchanges that occur over time. With some colonial goods, such as wheat, physical deterioration or spoiling resulted in a net loss of wealth to owners of the stored commodity. With an asset such as beaver pelts, market price fluctuated unpredictably in response to demand and supply conditions in the felt hat market—an undesirable characteristic for a community's store of wealth. Confidence in the future value of a monetary instrument depends largely on its past stability. In principle, one of the major advantages of a standardized currency is that it can be managed to grow in step with the demand for money in an expanding economy, without reference to relative price fluctuations in individual markets. This is the function of money as a store of value.

Finally, a barter system requires a great deal of information about all of the *numéraire* commodities in use. With several numéraire in circulation, everyone wishing to make an economic exchange must know each of the independent exchange ratios to do the best one can. Prices must be quoted in terms of each of the numéraire goods (or currencies if more than one is in use). When a common currency prevails, all exchange ratios can be expressed with a single unit of account. As Brunner and Meltzer have pointed out, the gain from the use of a single monetary unit of account is analogous to the gain arising from introducing any common unit in the measurement of temperature, weight, or height.

As long as the fur trading companies administered the colony, commodity monies sufficed as a means of exchange. The lack of metropolitan notes and coins did not constitute an effective constraint on colonial growth until the middle of the seventeenth century. Even metropolitan taxes were paid directly in fur pelts; fur pelt taxes were stored and shipped to France in separate vessels. In the case of imported goods, selling prices in terms of French currency were usually marked up by 50 percent to pay for the costs of transport and by $33\frac{1}{3}$ percent to allow for handling costs, risks of piracy, and a return on capital investment. This mark-up amounted to a fee for services and did not constitute a colonial 'devaluation' of French currency in the economic sense of the word.

The absence of a domestic currency in Canada did not hinder economic growth as long as the colony was small and closely tied to the metropolitan economy. Commodity monies were used in domestic transactions and French currency in the export sector. With growth in the number of domestic market transactions, however, the inconvenience of widespread barter began to make itself felt. In the traditional literature on the subject (Shortt, Lester, Hamelin), the monetary problems of the colony are attributed to a shortage of currency stemming from a chronic deficit in the balance of trade. The annual value of imports that flowed into the country exceeded the annual value of exports that flowed out. Unfortunately there is no hard evidence that the recurring deficit in the overall balance of *trade* extended also to a regular deficit in the overall balance of *payments*. The net flow of currencies between countries and foreign exchange rates depend on the total balance of payments (including metropolitan government expenditures, spending by the religious orders, and smuggling) rather than on the official balance of trade in physical commodities alone. New England, New York and Pennsylvania, for instance, all had trade deficits with Britain in the eighteenth century. In the American context, Roger Weiss has argued there is no empirical evidence that colonial merchants' complaints about liquidity shortage amounted to more than self-pity. The same can be said of merchants in Canada. Temporary currency shortages undoubtedly occurred, but there is no evidence of a chronic deficiency in the aggregate money supply.

Early Monetary Experiments

In 1661 the French government raised the value of metropolitan gold and silver coins circulating in Canada by 25 percent relative to their nominal values in the metropole. (Shortt, Vol. 1, p. xii) A distinction arose between the value of currencies accepted as legal tender in France (*valeur monnaie de France*) and their nominal value in the colony (*valeur monnaie de pays*), a distinction that was officially retained until 1717. The ordinance of 1661 was designed to induce currency imports, favor the monetization of economic exchange in Canada, and integrate colonial economic activity with that of the metropole. But the revaluation of gold and silver coins in Canada led to an inflow of poor quality French coins containing a large proportion of copper, and crumbling Spanish coins, both of which metropolitan merchants tended to refuse. According to most accounts, the price level in Canada gradually increased to accommodate the revaluation so that the purchasing power of metropolitan currency was unchanged in the long run.

The transfer of New France from private to public administration in 1665 accelerated the transition from barter to monetary transactions. The fall in the relative price of furs caused by the dissolution of the internal monopoly of fur trading in North America, deregulation of wheat prices, and expansion of the colonial government sector stimulated this change. The parallel growth of towns and market exchange in the colony rendered commodity monies increasingly uneconomic. Fur pelts continued to be used as a means of exchange and a unit of account on the frontier, but merchants and administrators in Montreal and Quebec City increasingly favored metropolitan notes and coins.

In 1665 the French government authorized the Company of the West Indies to mint coins in lieu of French currency, for exclusive use in the colonies. Being of no value in commercial transactions with the metropolitan country, these coins were unacceptable to merchants in Canada and most of them ended up in the French West Indies. Louise Dechêne reports no trace of them in the available inventories of Montreal merchants' post-mortem assets, and it is reasonable to assume their acceptance in Canada was temporary.

There are constant references to liquidity shortages in the colonial correspondence of the 1660s and 1670s. In 1672 the French government raised the nominal value of French currency in most of the overseas colonies to one-third more than its face value at home. Whether this regulation was enforced in Canada is unclear.[1]

Playing Card Currency

One of the most interesting monetary experiments in the New World occurred in 1685 with the introduction to Canada of a domestic paper currency. The French government usually paid • colonial administrators and employees in French currency that arrived in the autumn, allowing for monetary transactions during the winter months when ports were closed. In the autumn of 1684 the annual appropriation failed to arrive and the Intendent of the colony, DeMeulles, borrowed funds and dipped into his personal savings to pay colonial officials and troops. Finally, in June 1685, the appropriation still to arrive, DeMeulles collected most of the playing cards in the colony and issued them, signed and sealed in various denominations, as paper money. Drawing on his knowledge of Quebec merchants' credit notes, the Intendent promised redemption of the playing cards once the annual appropriation from France arrived. Playing card money circulated as fully backed legal tender during the summer of 1685 and was completely redeemed in the following September.

The playing card issue did not receive prior sanction by metropolitan authorities. DeMeulles subsequently justified it as a temporary expedient. But the issue so successfully fulfilled its objectives that the experience was repeated the following year, with the cards again being fully redeemed in the summer of 1686. Because playing card money was fully backed by funds arriving from France, and fully redeemed when those funds arrived, it did not constitute a permanent addition to the colonial money supply. In the beginning, therefore, the issue of playing card money was noninflationary.

As of 1690 card money was issued annually, with the colonial administration no longer employing playing cards alone, but also white paper cards of comparable size and shape. Once again, the printing of card money initially served as a temporary expedient to reduce the loss at sea of French government funds. War between the French and English (1689-1697) had extended to the North American colonies and the issue of Canadian paper money largely obviated the need for costly shipments of metal currency back and forth across the Atlantic. Eventually, in 1705, card money became a legal tender authorized by the metropolitan government.

As the colonial government issued paper money on a regular

basis, and as confidence in the new monetary instrument grew, the population began to regard card money as a stable asset and to retain a proportion instead of redeeming their entire holdings every year. The content of the colony's aggregate portfolio of monetary assets shifted in favor of card money. This gradual change in behavior allowed colonial authorities to issue card money in excess of the French government's annual appropriation. As long as the colonial issue of card money exceeded the colonial budget by no more than the amount the colonists were prepared to hold in the form of cash balances, the issue did not pose a repayment problem for the French Crown. Card money simply took its place alongside the existing forms of currency: metal coins, bills of exchange (metropolitan government credit notes), merchants' notes and barter commodities. And as long as the total value of the colony's means of exchange expanded in step with the number of goods and services produced in the monetized sector of the economy, the issue of card money remained non-inflationary.

The supply of card money in Canada increased at a higher rate in the years after 1700. Once again European conflict, in this case the war of the Spanish Succession (1701-1714), extended to the French and English colonies in North America. Colonial military spending rose continuously, and at the same time growth in the supply of card money considerably outstripped growth in the annual colonial budget. Playing card money in circulation in Canada rose from some 120 000 livres (the unit of account) in 1702 to some 2 000 000 livres ten years later. On a per capita basis, this increase represented a rise from about 11 livres to about 108 livres by 1712.

As early as 1705 the French Crown refused to redeem all of the card money presented to it because its nominal value exceeded the metropolitan government's appropriation for that year. This action on the part of the Crown amounted to a devaluation of card money, to which the colonial authorities responded by printing more. By this time the metropolitan government was encountering severe financial problems at home. After 1708 the French government abandoned the silver standard causing an effective devaluation of all paper assets in the metropolitan country. To accommodate the ensuing demand for monetary assets in Canada, the colonial authorities issued more and more card money. A part of the increase in the card money supply, therefore, was accommodated by the substitution of card money for other assets, as metal currency disappeared from circulation and French bills of exchange rapidly diminished in value. Although its issue may have been excessive during these years, the emission of card money in

Canada provided a badly needed monetary instrument. Certainly the colonial population retained confidence in card money. When, in 1712, the French government attempted to redeem Canadian card money in exchange for City of Paris bonds bearing 4 percent interest, less than four percent of all card money in circulation was voluntarily turned in.

In order to reinforce imperial ties with the metropole, the French government decided to put an end to colonial card money after the war. Between 1714 and 1719, card money was retired from circulation at half its nominal value in silver coins.[2] By 1720, the possession of card money was forbidden, and Canada had returned to the pre-1685 situation with its money supply dependent on the balance of payments with France. Once again economic fluctuations in the metropolitan economy were transmitted directly to the colony, the inhabitants no longer enjoying the economic buffer provided by a separate currency and flexible exchange rates. In earlier years the value of card money had been fixed in terms of French currency, but in practice its value had fluctuated in response to the colonial balance of payments.

When the redemption program was announced, merchants and habitants in the colony sought to protect the value of their assets by doubling prices (Hamelin, pp. 42-43). The colonists holding card money may have perceived its conversion at one-half of nominal value as a loss of net wealth amounting to confiscation. They undoubtedly resented the conversion because the system of card money rendered a useful economic service to the population. In any case, a part of the population, including government employees and creditors, could not maintain their pre-conversion level of expenditures. In the long run the price hike of 1714 could not be sustained, and by the end of the redemption period in 1719, the aggregate price level had fallen to its level of 1712.

The monetary instability of the years 1712-1720 stemmed primarily from the regulatory policies of the French government and the vacillations of metropolitan monetary authorities rather than from conditions internal to the colony or to the card money system. Indeed it could be argued that the French government ended the card money experiment, not because of its failure from the colonist's point of view, but because of its success. The economy of Canada expanded during the years 1709-1713, and it appears the French government used monetary reform to tax away some of the economic gains accruing to the colonists. An important part of the Canadian currency 'problem' consisted of a basic conflict between the metropole and the colony over shares in the colonial income.

During the 1720s the deficiencies inherent in a partially monetized, dependent economy surfaced once again. The colony reverted to its pre-1685 status characterized by dependence on French currency, on the French government's monetary policy, on metropolitan prices, and on European economic conditions in general. French currency that managed to reach the colony without returning to pay for imports was withdrawn from circulation and held as a form of savings. The uncertainty surrounding credit notes issued by colonial merchants made them a poor currency substitute. Colonial merchants complained bitterly of the situation and in the late 1720s petitioned the colonial government for a return to the card money system.

The Return of Paper Currency

In 1729 card money returned to Canada in the form of a single issue authorized by the French Crown. The popularity of this issue allowed for modest expansion of the total card money supply in 1733, 1742 and 1749, roughly in proportion to the growth of monetized economic transactions. Parallel to the re-issue of card money, the colonial government authorized the issue of 'orders' (*ordonnances*) by the military, making them legal tender in 1733. This new monetary instrument was initially designed to serve as a promise-to-pay, redeemable for bills of exchange, in outlying regions where currency and even card money was in short supply. However, unlike the issue of card money, 'orders' could be issued by any number of military officers; control of their supply lay beyond both the Intendant and the metropolitan government.

As early as 1735 colonial expenditures on the frontier began to exceed the official colonial budget because local military officers issued 'orders' above and beyond their authorized budgets.[3] This practice amounted to inflationary financing—the debasing or taxing of all colonial paper money to finance unauthorized military spending. Although unauthorized military spending on the fur trading frontier was not officially condoned by the colonial government, it was unofficially sanctioned as long as 'orders' retained the status of a legal tender (i.e. the colonists were legally required to accept them). The supply of 'orders' expanded rapidly following the outbreak of war between France and Great Britain (1744-1748). Merchants and habitants attempted to discount 'orders' by demanding higher prices for payment in this form, while seeking to hold their own savings in card money and metal coins.

The inflationary financing of military expenditures that began about 1744 never really ceased before the Conquest. The Treaty of Aix-la-Chapelle (1748) settled none of the outstanding questions between France and Great Britain, and fighting began again in North America by 1754. In the interim, the French military continued spending heavily to reinforce its position on the frontier and encircle the British American colonies from the west. During the Seven Years War (1756-1763), the French army retained as many as 20 000 soldiers on the continent—about a third of the civilian population at the time. This military contingent was financed by army 'orders' issued in the colony. Jean Hamelin writes that the nominal value of 'orders' circulating in New France tripled between 1750 and 1755, and grew again by five-fold between 1755 and 1759. Not surprisingly, by the time of the Conquest, the price level (measured in 'orders') had risen from five to ten times its level in 1751. (Heaton, p. 661) This inflation had its origins in the war and the proliferation of paper money issued to pay for military expenditures. It is inaccurate, therefore, to attribute the welfare costs of colonial monetary management to the balance of payments deficit or the structural weaknesses of the colonial economy (cf. Hamelin). Responsibility for monetary instability and hyper-inflation in the 1740s and 1750s lay squarely with the metropolitan government's military commitments. The French State used inflationary financing (a tax on the colonists) to help pay for the war.[4]

A complete evaluation of monetary history in Canada cannot be undertaken without comprehensive monetary data and a general price index for the colony as a whole. This information has not yet been assembled. On the basis of the partial evidence available, however, and excepting the 1720s, paper money appears to have circulated with success until about 1744. From all appearances, the colonies did not experience the long run price decline that would have accompanied a chronic deficiency in the supply of money. Whenever a shortage of monetary instruments arose, new instruments were introduced. Though by no means optimal, the money supply in Canada proved quite adequate.[5] During the years preceding the Conquest an important component of the total colonial money supply expanded, not because of a change in the level of economic activity but in response to imperial conflict between France and England. When the French State abused the monetary system in Canada, naturally the system showed signs of strain.

NOTES

[1]A. Shortt suggests that the decree of 1672 was applied only in the West Indies. (Shortt, Vol. 1, p. 37)

[2]It should be noted that France left the silver standard in 1708 and that card money had circulated at less than its nominal value in silver since that time, and possibly since as early as 1705.

[3]When the colonial treasury judged the demand for redemption of 'orders' to be excessive, it issued temporary receipts which circulated as an additional form of paper money.

[4]"In the colonial era, few individuals held large paper balances or lived on fixed incomes. Bank deposits did not exist. Depreciation was thus less of a threat than today in terms of destroying accumulated wealth or eroding real incomes. Colonists seeking a monetary store of wealth invariably held specie. To the extent that wealth was eroded somewhat by depreciation, urban residents, who were more deeply involved in money transactions, probably felt the effects more than farmers." (*The Economy of Colonial America*, p. 117, by Edwin J. Perkins, © 1980. Reprinted by permission.)

[5]As Richard Sylla has said of colonial American experience: "The inflationary side effects of colonial monetary innovations have received disproportionate attention from historians. The beneficial effects—the removal of what otherwise would have been most serious constraints on colonial economic growth and development—are often downplayed or ignored. Colonial monetary innovation was a rational, purposive activity motivated by perceived economic opportunities." (*The Journal of Economic History*, p. 25, March 1982, by Richard Sylla. Reprinted by permission.)

SELECT BIBLIOGRAPHY

Bordo, Michael D. and Anna J. Schwartz. "Issues in Monetary Economics and their Impact on Research in Economic History." in Robert E. Gallman, ed., *Research in Economic History*. Supplement 1, 1977.

Brunner, Karl and Allan H. Meltzer. "The Uses of Money: Money in the Theory of an Exchange Economy." *American Economic Review*. December 1971.

Dechêne, Louise. *Habitants et marchands de Montreal au XVIIe siècle*. Montreal: Plon, 1974.

Hamelin, Jean. *Economie et société de Nouvelle-France*. Quebec: les Presses de l'Université Laval, 1970.

Heaton, Herbert. "The Playing Card Currency of French Canada." *The American Economic Review*. December 1928.

Lester, Richard A. "Playing-card Currency of French Canada." in E.P. Neufeld, ed., *Money and Banking in Canada*. Toronto: McClelland and Stewart Ltd., 1964.

McCusker, John J. *Money and Exchange in Europe and America, 1600-1775: A Handbook*. Chapel Hill: University of North Carolina Press, 1978.

Perkins, Edwin J. *The Economy of Colonial America*. New York: Columbia University Press, 1980.

Shortt, Adam. *Documents Relating to Canadian Currency, Exchange and Finance during the French Period.* 2 volumes. Ottawa: King's Printer, 1926.

Sylla, Richard. "Monetary Innovation in America." *The Journal of Economic History* . March 1982.

Weiss, Roger W. "The Issue of Paper Money in the American Colonies 1720-1774." *Journal of Economic History.* December 1970.

4
Merchants and the British Conquest

The British Conquest ended a century-and-a-half of French colonization in North America. Although war was not declared until 1756, France began a military build-up in the New World as early as 1748. Tensions heightened in 1752 when settlers from Virginia tried to occupy a part of the Ohio Valley previously reserved for the fur trade. With the help of Indian alliances the French patrolled the region west of the Alleghenies, but it was colonial Americans who were prepared to settle the area. By and large, however, the Seven Years War (1756-1763) was an extension of French-English conflict in Europe. The French army and navy proved unequal to the British armed forces with the result that Louisbourg (1758), Quebec City (1759), and Montreal (1760) fell successively to the enemy. In 1762 France, by secret agreement, sold all of the land west of the Mississippi to Spain. In the Treaty of Paris (1763), France abandoned to Britain virtually all remaining claims in North America in exchange for the captured French West Indies. The exceptions consisted of fishing rights on the north shore of Newfoundland and two non-fortified island ports, St. Pierre and Miquelon.

The impact of the British Conquest on Quebec society is the most controversial issue in the history of the region. From an economic perspective, the question concerns the extent to which the change in metropole represented a critical turning point in the growth of the colonial economy and a determining influence on the distribution of income between French and English speaking Quebecers in later years.

Historians such as Michel Brunet have argued that at least two thousand colonials left for France during the decade 1760-1770. The emigrants, it is said, constituted the merchant or entrepreneurial class during the French regime. By precipitating this emigration, the British Conquest 'decapitated' the colonial social structure and removed essential human capital. In this way the Conquest created a vacuum that English speaking entrepreneurs subsequently filled. For French speaking people, life in Quebec after the Conquest no longer offered the prospects of economic and social mobility that had existed before the Seven Years War.

The Conquest debate really consists of three issues. One issue concerns the relative size and wealth of the domestic merchant class in Canada before the Conquest. Because this question cannot be directly answered with available data, it has usually been considered indirectly through an analysis of the strengths and weaknesses in the structure of the colonial economy. Evidence of colonial economic growth and diversification is assumed to reflect domestic entrepreneurship; evidence of economic stagnation or staple dependency is taken as a sign of commercial domination by the metropole. The second issue concerns the emigration of merchants during the years 1760-1770. To what extent did the movement of population back to France represent an irreplaceable loss of French speaking entrepreneurship? The third issue concerns the role of merchants and economic welfare after 1760. Did the British colonial regime, in the application of monetary, fiscal and commercial policy, and in the distribution of property rights, impose constraints on economic activity in Quebec or on the welfare of Quebecers? This chapter will address one of these constraints, monetary policy in the 1760s, leaving the bulk of the discussion of the post-Conquest period to subsequent chapters.

Entrepreneurship Before the Conquest

"Entrepreneurship" is a difficult phenomenon to define. The absence of a consensus on what entrepreneurs do has contributed to the fuzziness of many discussions on the subject. Entrepreneurship has been referred to as a factor of production comparable to resources, capital, and labor. More entrepreneurship in a region is often thought to produce more economic activity as undeveloped markets are brought into existence. Entrepreneurship is believed to be especially important in newly settled regions where internal markets are weak or non-existent. According to Nathaniel Leff, entrepreneurship refers to a capacity for innovation, investment and active expansion in new markets or with new techniques. Entrepreneurs may possess superior information that reduces the risk of investing in new ventures, or they may have special attitudes toward taking risks and bearing uncertainty. Entrepreneurship is not, however, a variable independent of the economic environment in which it originates. In Habakkuk's words,

Entrepreneurs are, of course, not to be considered only as the causes of economic development, they are also a product, a consequence, of economic development. Shall we say that economic progress was rapid in a particular country because the entrepreneurs of that country were unusually adventurous, or that the entrepreneurs were successful because the country was developing rapidly for quite independent reasons?...It is always difficult to know how much importance we should attribute to the entrepreneur and how much to the economy in which he works, to the nature of the market he supplies, to the character of his labour supplies and the extent of the natural resources. The entrepreneur is not a deus ex machina: he is part of a complicated social process.[1]

Before the Conquest, France, like most European powers, discouraged colonial manufacturing beyond the stage of primary processing except in those industries producing strategic materials. The French government forbade linen cloth making in 1704 and fur hat manufacturing in 1736 because these activities competed with French industry. But small colonial manufacturing firms, such as brick and tile works, tanneries, and sawmills, did succeed in supplying the domestic market. Shipbuilding yards based on local timber appeared during the last third of the seventeenth century, and then again during the 1730s and 1740s with the help of government subsidies and contracts. Shipbuilding in turn created profitable opportunities in ancillary activities—tar, rope, sail making and iron hardware. Forges using local bog iron ore were established on the St. Maurice River near Trois-Rivières in 1733. But ten years later the forges had to be taken over by the colonial government because they could not be operated at a profit. The growth of manufactured exports was hampered by the high price of importing skilled labor, the costs of transport to European markets, and metropolitain government regulation. Essentially, it is the colony's comparative advantage in natural resource commodity production and colonial demand for a wide array of processed goods that explain why importing and exporting services played an important role in aggregate economic activity. The majority of entrepreneurs found that wholesaling, retailing, and fur trading offered the highest rates of return.

Well-known studies by Jean Hamelin and Cameron Nish present substantially different views on colonial welfare and the extent of entrepreneurship before 1760. By emphasizing the structural weaknesses of the colony, Hamelin infers that per capita colonial income was comparatively low and domestic entrepreneurship virtually absent during the French regime. Nish, on the other hand, finds that per capita economic activity in Canada compared favorably with that in colonial America during the years 1729-1748. Nish uses this and other indirect evidence to support his contention that a sizeable merchant class operated in the colony prior to 1760. The work of these two authors can be taken as representative of two opposing views concerning the size and nature of the merchant class in pre-Conquest Canada.

In his study *Economie et société en Nouvelle-France*, Jean Hamelin argues that low levels of income and domestic saving characterized the colonial economy under French rule. These magnitudes, while not directly measurable, are reflected in the structural weaknesses of the colonial economy. One by one Hamelin reviews the economic deficiencies of the fur trading sector, the agricultural sector, and the monetary system, concluding with a discussion of the slow growth of skilled labor immigration.

The fur trading sector does not appear to have bolstered the domestic savings rate or enriched colonial merchants. Except for the years 1645-1663 and 1700-1705, the fur trade was in the hands of metropolitan merchants. Hamelin estimates that only 14 percent of gross revenues (revenues before costs) from the legal trade in beaver remained in the hands of Canadian merchants during the period 1675-1760. Another 14 percent flowed to labor and service industries. On the strength of this calculation, Hamelin concludes that the fur trade as a whole could not have provided an important source of domestic savings. Although his computations are crude, the conclusion seems warranted. It is weakened, however, by the fact that the legal beaver trade (leaving aside illicit trade with the English colonies) represented less than half of total colonial fur export value after 1700. In addition, Hamelin is critical of one group that did represent a source of domestic entrepreneurship. The *coureurs-de-bois* or backwoods traders, he argues, squandered potential savings by indulging in lavish spending on imported goods. This criticism is partly an exercise in debunking aimed at traditional historiography. But the implication that traders displayed abnormally high propensities to consume and to import luxury goods is not empirically supported by the author.

In his discussion of agriculture, Hamelin similarly comes to a strong conclusion on the basis of weak empirical evidence. By all contemporary accounts, the volume of agricultural sales was insufficient to serve as an economic base for a sizeable merchant class. Louise Dechêne confirms this point of view when she writes of the habitants, "ils n'entrent jamais qu'accessoirement dans les plans mercantiles." (Dechêne, p. 490) Although the potential for profitable entrepreneurial activities in the rural sector appears to have been limited, a detailed study of net agricultural income in the colony has yet to be written.

Hamelin's discussion of the monetary system is similarly one-sided. As indicated in Chapter 3, there is no direct evidence that the quantity of money in circulation constrained economic growth and/or reduced the savings rate in peacetime. The monetary history of New France is no more uneven than that of colonial America. Entrepreneurial activity may have been minimal in Canada; but if so, this was probably attributable to the rate of return on domestic economic activities rather than to an exceptionally misguided monetary policy.

Hamelin estimates that some 11 percent of the 10 000 immigrants who came to Canada before 1760 possessed skilled labor qualifications or experience. The situation is blamed on the failure by the French State to organize the immigration of skilled people. As indicated in Chapter 2, labor migration is primarily a function of expected income differentials. If economic opportunities are unavailable, government incentives to encourage immigration will be unsuccessful. The absence of skilled labor immigration was as much a reflection as a cause of slow economic growth in the colony.

In his concluding chapter, Hamelin draws on varied information to support his contention that "the absence of a vigorous French-Canadian bourgeoisie in 1800 appears as an achievement of the French regime, not as a consequence of the Conquest". (Hamelin, p. 137) Reviewing official correspondence, taxes paid, the financial positions of the principal shareholders of the beaver trade monopoly for 1708, bills of exchange between France and the colony for the year 1746 (which indicate that only 27 percent of colonial trade was in the hands of Canadian merchants) and so on, Hamelin concludes that the emigration of merchants in 1760 may have been part of a phenomenon that had existed every autumn for some time. But all of the evidence used to illustrate his underdevelopment thesis is indirect, and therefore inconclusive.

Cameron Nish adopts a different methodological approach in his study of merchants and entrepreneurship during the French regime. In *Les bourgeois-gentilshommes de la Nouvelle-France 1729–1748*, Nish tries to demonstrate the existence of a sizeable colonial merchant class by concentrating on comparative levels of trade and commerce with reference to the British American colonies of the time. In other words, Nish uses British metropolitan-colonial relations as a benchmark against which to measure the extent of Canadian trade and development. He finds that per capita economic activity in the French and English colonies was similar. In

Canada, the volume of foreign trade per capita was at least as great as that in the colonies to the south. Moreover, during the 1730s and 1740s furs became proportionately less important as trade expanded, which suggests the colonial economy was in the process of diversifying. Although Canada had a significant balance of trade deficit with the mother country. But most of the American colonies also imported more than they exported, with Virginia and Maryland the only exceptions. In contrast to the American carrying trade, however, the lion's share of Canada's commercial transactions overseas was carried out by metropolitan residents.

On the question of comparative standards of living, Nish is more circumspect. The absence of reliable data and the difficulty of computing meaningful exchange rates make comparisons hazardous. With virtually no empirical support, Nish asserts that unskilled workers, artisans, and government administrators earned comparable wage and salary rates in New France and the British American colonies. When it comes to evaluating the contribution of the fur trade and the monetary system of economic growth, Nish adds little to our knowledge. Documenting the existence of fur traders and import-export merchants, Nish fails to improve our understanding of their net contribution to the growth of the colonial economy.

In the major portion of his study, Nish emphasizes the complementary and often identical roles played by merchants, military officers, administrators, and seigneurs. Out of this analysis arises the expression 'bourgeois-gentlemen', the term Nish employs to describe the commercial activities and aristocratic pretensions of what he identifies as a distinctive colonial social class. The interdependence of the fur trade and military posts around the Great Lakes and to the south implicated military officers in fur trading. The tendency for seigneurs to live in towns, and to lose interest in their seigneuries, made them more bourgeois than feudal or aristocratic. Nish also uncovers considerable intermarriage among families of merchants, fur trade seigneurs, and administrators.[2] Throughout his study he disparages Hamelin's analysis, but ultimately delivers an empirically weak counter-hypothesis. While underlying the fragility of Hamelin's conclusions, Nish offers a plausible, yet no more reliable interpretation of the importance of merchant activity in the pre-Conquest period.

The Conquest

There is no doubt that a group of colonial merchants existed in early Canada and lived comfortably. Some of them held seigneuries as well as important administrative and military positions. But just how wealthy were these merchants at the time of the Conquest? This is one of the questions that José Igartua examined in several publications drawn from his doctoral thesis. Igartua proceeded by identifying the merchants and traders of Montreal in 1750, estimating their wealth, and then analysing their situation again in 1775, fifteen years after the Conquest.

Montreal was the second largest town in the St. Lawrence Valley. Quebec City was the chief port of entry in trade with the exterior, but Montreal was the base camp for fur trading expeditions to the interior. Montreal merchants comprised a group of more than 200 people in a town population of some 5 000. To a greater degree than their counterparts at Quebec City, these merchants were integrated into the pattern of colonial life and domestic market activity. For this reason, says Igartua, few Montreal merchants took the opportunity to depart for France after the Conquest.

Igartua demonstrates that the Montreal merchants did not constitute a wealthy social class: it is doubtful the wealthiest earned as much as shopkeepers in the American colonies. The most commercially successful were import and wholesale merchants, followed by fur trade outfitters. But the modest extent of commercial activities is surprising. Of 55 merchants identified as fur trade outfitters, for example, 32 made an average of less than one engagement per year between 1750 and 1775. Only four merchants averaged more than four engagements per year over this period. Igartua concludes as follows:

> There was little wealth within the merchants community as a whole and social mobility was quite restricted. Such a situation would put the body of Montreal merchants at a disadvantage after 1760...The weight of tradition which hung over their business and their meagre financial resources held them back in the post-Conquest struggle for the control of the fur trade. The British merchants' advantage of familiarity with British business practices and the British military's suspicions about the Canadian fur traders' activities among the Indians only compounded the difficulties and obstacles which were all at once thrown in the path of these merchants.[3]

Igartua's research focuses on the merchant community in Montreal. What of the larger picture? Did the Conquest induce the emigration of merchants from Quebec and the rest of the colony? One inventory of emigrants taken by Governor Carleton in 1767 covered 228 wealthy Canadians, of whom 102 had departed. Fernand Ouellet refers to these emigrants as members of the nobility rather than the merchant class. Their military, administra-

ive and seigneurial functions took precedence over their contribu-
ion to economic activity. There is no doubt, says Ouellet, that
members of this *noblesse militaire* foresaw an end to the government subsidies, privileges and patronage that had sustained them
up to the Conquest. Many returned to France after 1759.

Recent research points to a middling position between proponents and opponents of the 'decapitation' metaphor. Igartua's
snapshot of the Montreal merchant community in 1750 suggests
that merchants' incomes and the average level of colonial economic activity attained only modest levels. Although no massive
evacuation of people occurred as a result of the Conquest, some
merchants did leave because the application of British laws, such as
the Navigation Acts, interrupted commercial lines of communication with continental Europe. The management of the Canadian
money supply in the 1760s imposed further costs on those who
stayed.

Imperial Monetary Policy After the Conquest

The impact of the British Conquest was experienced directly
through the monetary system. In October 1759, after the capture
of Quebec City, the French Crown suspended payment on all
outstanding colonial bills of exchange. These credit notes had
been a linchpin in the colonial monetary system, especially after
the introduction of 'orders' that were payable in terms of bills of
exchange. The renunciation of debt by the French government did
not put an immediate end to the paper money system in Canada.
As long as paper currency retained the confidence of the colonial
population as a monetary instrument, it did not require backing. A
month later, however, Brigadier Murray, commander of the British forces in Canada, completely outlawed the use of all paper
money in colonial commercial transactions. Murray's aim was to
impose the Pound Sterling as a unit of account and force the
substitution of metal currency as a means of exchange. In September 1760 the ban on paper money was extended to Montreal.
Together, these two events, renunciation of the French government's outstanding debt and the British occupant's prohibition of
paper money, resulted in a considerable net welfare loss to all
Canadians holding paper money as an asset.

French speaking Canadians were not the only losers from the
abolition of paper money without compensation. As early as 1762
English merchants doing business in Canada petitioned Lord
Egremont, the British Secretary of State, to consider compensation. Otherwise, argued the petitioners, the reduction in colonial

wealth and the ensuing loss of confidence in the monetary system would affect aggregate colonial demand to the detriment of English traders. In fact, the prohibition of paper money was not uniformly enforceable and, consequently, not entirely respected. Certain contracts, signed before publication of the policy, specified payment in paper currency denominations for which the British equivalent was unclear. Many colonists could not make payment in anything other than paper currency thereby obliging importers to accept paper money or return their merchandise. In these situations paper currency often changed hands at considerable discount. Creditors were effectively speculating on the likelihood of some form of compensation for colonial paper money—a risky undertaking.

In November 1762 the French government indicated that it would be willing to consider partial compensation. This news and the accompanying expectations resulted in considerable trading of colonial paper money. To add to these hopes, the Treaty of Paris, signed in February 1763, guaranteed that bills and letters of exchange issued during the French regime would be fully redeemed at an unspecified date in the future. However, the wording of the Treaty suggests that only the holdings of British subjects would be entitled to such treatment. British merchants began criss-crossing the province offering to buy French colonial paper money at 15 to 25 percent of its nominal value. At the time of the census of paper money in the colony undertaken in 1764, 16.8 million livres was declared, a substantial decline from the estimated 30 million livres in circulation in 1759, and 49 million in circulation in 1763.

The French government announced a plan for the redemption of paper money in June 1764. As outlined by Ouellet, the plan included complete reimbursement for letters of exchange acquired by their owners prior to 1759, and of letters of exchange drawn in 1760 to pay for the upkeep of the French army. All other letters of exchange would be redeemed at one-half of their nominal value, and all other paper assets at one-quarter of their nominal value. The extent of losses to the colonists in terms of real purchasing power implied by this unexpectedly generous proposal, requires detailed information that is not available to historical researchers.

In fact, the French government never honored the redemption plan. In March 1766 France began redeeming the colonial money in question, not with hard currency, but with promissory notes paying $4\frac{1}{2}$ percent. Two months later, the market price of these notes in London had fallen to some seventy-four percent of their nominal value. Finally, in 1771, a bankrupt French State renounced repayment of this special issue leaving note holders in the lurch. Much as the British government was attempting to do with the American colonies, the French State passed the financial burden of the Seven Years War onto the colonists.

Ultimately, both habitants and merchants suffered from the monetary disruption of the 1760s. The switch to a new and unfamiliar unit of account, the Pound Sterling, entailed short term losses caused by economic uncertainty and a drop in economic activity. In addition, the abolition of paper money, much of it issued to pay for the Seven Years War, produced an important permanent loss of net wealth for the colonists. This loss would have been reduced if the French government had honored its commitments or if, as Murray proposed in 1763, the British government had authorized the issue of a substitute in exchange for French colonial paper money.

As it happens, the French government played a role in determining the distribution of the costs of monetary change in the 1760s. If paper money from the French regime had been prohibited without further ado by the British occupant, the burden of the Conquest would have fallen entirely on the Canadian population. The French government, by promising compensation for colonial paper money, sustained false hopes for almost a decade and effectively redistributed a part of the burden to British merchants and speculators. In this way the costs of monetary disruption to Canadians were reduced to some extent. Nonetheless, this experience with paper money frightened many colonists and impeded the growth of monetization and market exchange in the years that followed. (See Chapter 7)

The question of the extent to which the Conquest affected the economic growth of Quebec and the welfare of the francophone Quebecers is still in need of considerable research and analysis. The fate of French speaking entrepreneurs and the financial burden of the change in metropole are only two aspects of this question. In order to come closer to definite answers, an examination of the Quebec economy and its people in the post-Conquest era is required. This is the subject of Part II.

NOTES

[1]J. Habakkuk, "The Entrepreneur and Economic Development," in *Economic Policy for Development*, pp. 40-41, ed. I. Livingstone, Penguin Books Ltd., 1971.

[2]José Igartua has found this inter-marriage involved much horizontal social mobility, but very little vertical mobility.

[3]*Histoire Sociale*, p. 291, by Jose Igartua, Nov.-Dec., 1975, reprinted by permission.

SELECT BIBLIOGRAPHY

Bosher, John F. "A Quebec Merchant's Trading Circles in France and Canada: Jean-André Lamaletie before 1763." *Histoire Sociale-Social History.* May 1977.

Breckenbridge, Roeliff M. "The Paper Currencies of New France." *Journal of Political Economy.* Vol. 1 (1892-3).

Brunet, Michel. *French Canada and the Early Decades of British Rule, 1760-1791.* Ottawa: The Canadian Historical Association Booklets, No. 13, 1966.

Dechêne, Louise. *Habitants et marchands de Montréal au XVIIe siècle.* Montreal: Plon, 1974.

Eccles, William J. *France in America.* Toronto: Fitzhenry & Whiteside Ltd., 1972.

Habakkuk, J. "The Entrepreneur and Economic Development," in I. Livingstone, ed., *Economic Policy for Development.* Harmondsworth, England: Penguin Books Ltd., 1971.

Hamelin, Jean. *Economie et société en Nouvelle-France.* Quebec: les Presses de l'Université Laval, 1970.

Igartua, José. "The Conquest and the Marchands of Montreal." *CHA Historical Papers,* Canadian Historical Association, 1974.

Igartua, José. "The Merchants of Montreal at the Conquest: Socio-economic Profile." *Histoire Sociale-Social History.* Nov.-Dec. 1975.

Leff, Nathaniel H. "Entrepreneurship and Development: The Problem Revisited." *Journal of Economic Literature.* March 1979.

Mathieu, Jacques. *La construction navale royale à Québec 1739-1759.* Quebec: la Société historique de Québec, 1971.

Mathieu, Jacques. *Le commerce entre la Nouvelle-France et les Antilles au XVIIIe siècle.* Montreal: Editions Fides, 1981.

Miquelon, Dale. *Society and Conquest: The Debate on the Bourgeoisie and Social Change in French Canada, 1700-1850.* Toronto: Copp Clark, 1977.

Nish, Cameron. *Les bourgeois-gentilshommes de la Nouvelle-France, 1729-1748.* Montréal: Fides, 1968.

Ouellet, Fernand. *Histoire économique et sociale du Québec, 1760-1850.* Montreal: Editions Fides, 1966.

Ouellet, Fernand. "Propriété seigneuriale et groupes sociaux dans la vallée du St-Laurent (1663-1840)," in P. Savard, ed., *Mélanges d'histoire du Canada français offerts au professeur Marcel Trudel.* Ottawa: Editions de l'Université d'Ottawa, 1978.

Shortt, Adam. *Documents Relating to Canadian Currency, Exchange and Finance during the French Period.* 2 volumes. Ottawa: King's Printer, 1926.

Part II

QUEBEC AFTER THE CONQUEST
1763-1850

5
Institutional Change, Migration and Settlement

The province of Quebec experienced considerable population movement during the ninety years following the Conquest. Much of this migration coincided with the worldwide displacement of Europeans after 1815. English speaking immigrants flowed into the province and, after 1840, growing numbers of French speaking Quebecers began to leave their homeland. The expectation of higher economic returns explains the greater part of this migration but British colonial policy certainly affected its timing and intensity. Through the definition and enforcement of property rights, the British government influenced the rates of migration and land settlement.

Migration, settlement and land clearing in a given region depend upon the perception of economic opportunities. Expectations of agricultural opportunities in the future are formed on the basis of past and present experience: the demand for agricultural products, the supply of land, climate, and so on. The demand for land in an unsettled region is dependent upon the demand for agricultural products. Land supply depends upon the resource endowment and the institutional environment, that is, the set of rules governing the ownership and control of resources. The net income to be earned from farming in a newly occupied region varies according to the property rights enforced in the region. In the eighteenth century the seigneurial and freehold systems of property rights embodied different forms of land tenure. Each system contained a unique set of obstacles and opportunities for potential migrants desiring to settle in the St. Lawrence Valley.

Economic exchange is facilitated by knowledge of the prevailing property rights and rules of contract. Knowledge of the prevailing rights and rules may be passed along orally from person to person, from generation to generation. In a period of major institutional change, literacy can play a key role in the diffusion of new rules concerning property rights. The introduction of new rights and rules concerning property and contracts may hamper economic exchange unless these rights and rules are widely publicized and understood by all trading parties. The higher the cost of new information, the higher the costs of economic transactions, and the less freely markets will operate. During the years 1760-1850, the literacy rate of adult Lower Canadians was very low. When fundamental changes in the institutional environment occurred, it is not surprising that the mass of the French speaking population turned to the educated elite of its own language group for political and spiritual leadership.

Between 1760 and 1850, the province of Quebec was subjected to four major revisions of the institutional environment. The Royal Proclamation (1763), the Quebec Act (1774), the Constitutional Act (1791) and the Act of Union (1840) embodied distinct combinations of political and property rights. Each piece of colonial legislation contained different implications for potential migrants, potential profits and incomes, and the settlement of land in Quebec. This chapter will focus on the evolution of political and property rights as they affected the supply of land and labor. The demand for agricultural products and resources will be examined in the chapter that follows.

The Royal Proclamation

When the Treaty of Paris was signed in February 1763, the British government began organizing political and legal institutions to govern its acquisitions. The planned institutional environment for Canada was outlined in the Royal Proclamation announced in October 1763. The Proclamation, effective in August 1764, offered little hope for the long term continuation of a French presence in North America. The new institutions were modelled on those existing in the British American colonies. The free-holder land tenure system, free and common socage, and a qualified form of representative government were promised so as to provide a congenial setting to attract Anglophone immigrants. However, the introduction of new legal institutions, a new land tenure system, and ill-defined language and religious rights[1] created an atmosphere of confusion that hampered English speaking immi-

ration, as well as domestic economic growth. The costs of making
economic transactions increased as political, cultural, and economic uncertainty clouded the future of the province.

In the wake of changes caused by the Conquest and the Royal
Proclamation, the settlement of new lands in Quebec occurred
slowly. Brigadier Murray conceded new seigneuries to two British
army officers in 1762, but this practice was outlawed two years
later. The Royal Proclamation and subsequent instructions to the
colonial governor specified that Crown land should be granted in
free-hold tenure. In fact, no new property rights in land were
conceded during the following decade.

British colonial policy for the St. Lawrence Valley was part of a
larger imperial design. The British government created an institutional environment for Quebec in the context of political unrest in
the Thirteen Colonies to the south. Until 1763 imperial relations
between Britain and the American colonies contributed to a certain unity of vision. But after the Conquest of New France, the
British government delayed the sale of potential farm lands west of
the Appalachian Mountains because Britain feared American
expansion into this area. The question of ownership of the mid-
continent's vast resources and control of the rate of mid-continental land settlement developed into a serious bone of contention
between the British metropole and the Thirteen Colonies. As
suspicion and hostility between Britain and the American colonies
intensified, colonial policy for the St. Lawrence Valley became an
element in this larger conflict.

The Royal Proclamation limited the boundaries of Quebec to
the settled areas in the St. Lawrence Valley, east of the Ottawa
River. (See Chart 5.1) The vast region south and west of the
Ottawa River became part of an Indian land reserve where fur
trading was regulated by licence and agricultural settlement forbidden. The British government's refusal to allow settlement west
of the Appalachian Mountains annoyed many American colonists.
The Thirteen Colonies had participated enthusiastically in the war
with France on the assumption the continental mid-west would be
opened to British American settlement once victory was achieved.
Instead, the British government closed the western frontier and
imposed a series of direct and indirect taxes on the American
colonies (the Sugar Act, the Currency Act, the Stamp Act, the
Townsend duties, the Tea Act, and so on) to help pay for the war.
The final insult to American colonists came in 1774 when the old
French fur trading area west of Pennsylvania was annexed to
Quebec.

Chart 5.1

POLITICAL BOUNDARIES OF QUEBEC, 1763–1841

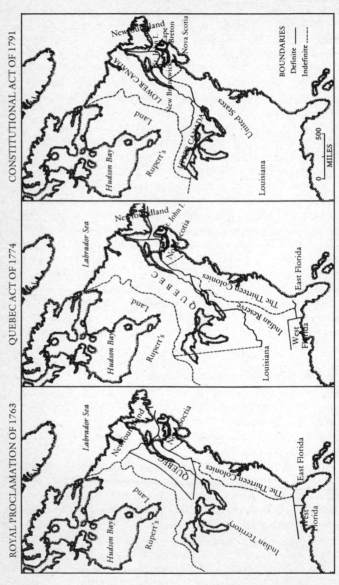

ROYAL PROCLAMATION OF 1763   QUEBEC ACT OF 1774   CONSTITUTIONAL ACT OF 1791

Canada Before Confederation, p. 64, by R. Cole Harris and John Warkentin, Cartographer Miklos Pinther © Oxford University Press.

The Quebec Act

The Quebec Act of 1774 accorded two new regions to the colonial administration at Quebec. Labrador, Anticosti Island, and the Iles de la Madelaine, which had previously been attached to Newfoundland, came under Quebec's jurisdiction.[2] More importantly, the British placed a substantial area of unsettled land surrounding the Great Lakes under the colonial administration in Quebec City. (See Chart 5.1) This action alienated colonial American land speculators and fur traders, particularly in Virginia, and cast Britain in the role previously played by France, that of the chief obstacle to American expansion.

The British government designed the Quebec Act to attain two political objectives: to contain the rebellious American colonies at a time of mounting tensions, and to secure the allegiance of a recently conquered French Canada should Anglo-American hostilities erupt. To meet this second objective, the Quebec Act legitimized the institutional environment existing *de facto* in the St. Lawrence Valley. By reintroducing French civil law into Quebec, the Act effectively guaranteed the continuity of the seigneurial system of land tenure.[3] At the same time, the Act legalized the collection of tithes by the Roman Catholic Church and affirmed the right of Quebecers to worship as Catholics. Finally, the Quebec Act revoked the right of Quebecers to a popular assembly, a right acknowledged by the Proclamation of 1763 but never fulfilled. The British government enacted laws for the colony and administered them through an appointed governor and council. This redistribution of political and property rights reinforced what remained of the French regime's colonial elite, seigneurs and the clergy. In effect the British Crown sought to purchase the loyalty of its French speaking subjects by reinstating the pre-Conquest social structure, while denying an institutional channel for the expression of popular will.

The strongest opposition to the decision to abandon the idea of an elected assembly was voiced by newly-arrived Anglo-American merchants. These merchants came to the province in the wake of the Conquest hoping to seize profitable commercial opportunities created by the economic disruption of the war years. They constituted a small proportion of the two to three thousand Anglophones in the colony by the mid-1770s, and formed a political action group distinct from British military administrators. Because the colonial government feared the 'capture' of any representative assembly by this articulate group, fired as they were by American Revolutionary ideas, the assembly promised in the Royal Proclamation of 1763 did not materialize. The Quebec Act made this *de facto* policy official. The institutional arrangements provided by the Quebec Act contained a complementary set of imperial policies: cultural, economic and legal concessions to French Quebecers; consolidation of mid-continental resources under the administration of a loyal colonial government at Quebec; and minimization of interference by the local population in the administration of the colony.

Although new immigrants did not stream into Quebec during the two decades after 1763, the indigenous French speaking population continued to grow as rapidly as it had in the first half of the century. The rate of natural population increase was high, but similar to the rate of increase in the British American colonies. Between 1765 and 1784, total population grew by some 62 percent to 113 000. This growth was accommodated by the clearing of new lands on established seigneuries and a rise in agricultural output. The area of cultivated land in Quebec expanded by some 66 percent during the years 1765-1784 in response to new export possibilities.

The province of Quebec offered economic opportunities to new immigrants in a rather limited number of activities—wholesaling, retailing, and the fur trade. British Army officers and wealthy merchants could take advantage of opportunities to buy seigneuries from French speaking seigneurs; by 1781 wealthy Anglophones controlled 32 percent of all seigneurial lands in Quebec. But a lack of information concerning the nature of the resources in the St. Lawrence lowlands and the functioning of the seigneurial system presented a barrier to the entry of Anglophone farmers. Profitable opportunities existed in Quebec agriculture, but a practical knowledge of the seigneurial system was necessary to reap the attendant rewards.

The American Revolutionary War (1776-1783) stimulated the creation of English speaking communities in the province: the break-away of the Thirteen Colonies provoked an influx of British Empire Loyalists into the remaining British American provinces. A 1784 census of loyalist emigrants in Quebec placed their number at 4 764 people, almost certainly an underestimate. (Ouellet, 1976, p. 24) In any case, the English speaking population in the province more than doubled between 1780 and 1784, rising from 4 to at least 9 percent of the total population. The motivation behind this migration was political rather than economic. While it is true that per capita income in the United States probably declined during the Revolutionary War years, few of the loyalist emigrants expected income gains from moving north. Many gave up all they owned in order to migrate.

Most of the loyalists who came to Quebec eventually settled in the region that was to become Upper Canada (Ontario). Royal instructions permitted interim concessions in free and common socage as early as 1783. The loyalists were a new political force on the scene—royalist, individualist, and desirous of English civil law, freehold tenure, and parliamentary institutions. By 1790, English speaking people constituted nearly 20 percent of the 172 000 people in the province. Anglophones increasingly exercised political pressure on the British government to change the existing institutional environment in their favor.

By providing loyalist immigrants to the region, the American Revolutionary War produced a significant change in the definition of Quebec's borders. In the Treaty of Paris of 1783 between Britain and the United States, the region west of the Appalachians and south of the Great Lakes was conceded to the newly independent republic. Up to this time European economic activity had been limited to fur trading with the Indian inhabitants. After 1783 both Indians and fur traders were gradually pushed out by an expanding frontier of American settlers.

The Constitutional Act

The Constitutional Act of 1791 introduced a new institutional environment to the province of Quebec. On the one hand, the Act and its accompanying regulations reaffirmed the concessions accorded by the British Crown in the Quebec Act, that is, retention of the seigneurial regime, French civil law and French customs in the St. Lawrence Valley. On the other hand, the accompanying instructions secretly amended the Quebec Act by recommending that all future land concessions be made in free and common socage. In this way the British government hoped to create an institutional environment favorable to settlement by English speaking immigrants. The occupation of Canadian soil by settlers loyal to the British Crown appeared all the more urgent in light of American independence and westward expansion.

The Constitutional Act also divided the former province of Quebec into two political units, Upper and Lower Canada, and introduced parliamentary institutions, though not ministerial responsibility, to both regions. By partitioning the province, the British Crown aimed to prevent Upper Canadian dependency upon the Lower Canadian assembly in matters affecting the economy and society. But Upper Canada's economic reliance on the St. Lawrence River (See Chart 5.1), and the financial dependence of both colonial governments on tariff revenues from imports, soon led to a long and acrimonious conflict over relative shares in the duties collected at the port of Quebec.

The institutional environment introduced by the Constitutional Act of 1791 corresponded to the demands of the newly arrived loyalists in the Great Lakes area. The English speaking merchant community in Montreal, however, greeted the Constitutional Act with mixed emotions. While favoring the creation of a representative assembly and the restoration of English civil law and freehold tenure, the merchant community objected to the political partitioning of the old province of Quebec. The Act committed the English speaking community to a minority status in the Lower Canadian Assembly. Furthermore, the Act relieved the Lower Canadian administration of political control over land policy (an important means of political patronage) and the rate of settlement in Upper Canada.

French speaking Quebecers reacted to the Constitutional Act according to their self-interest. Seigneurs, and to a lesser extent the clergy, feared parliamentary institutions and the partial return of English civil law because these innovations undermined their social prestige and political influence. French speaking merchants and professionals, on the other hand, generally supported the advent of parliamentary institutions and the new voice in colonial administrative decisions they promised. The Act created some resentment, however, offering separate political institutions for a population of only 12 000 in Upper Canada. The rural farm population's reaction to the Constitutional Act is difficult to gauge, but farmers appear to have remained relatively indifferent to the institutional changes of 1791. The property qualifications introduced for voting were lenient by the standards of the time. Later, however, as economic growth and change created a propertyless class of working people, these voting qualifications would exclude an increasingly large proportion of the population from participating in the electoral process. (Ouellet, 1976, pp. 41-42)

Up to this time, the privately owned portion of the St. Lawrence Valley had changed little since the French regime. Except for some settlement along the Richelieu River south of Montreal and the Chaudière River south of Quebec City, most seigneuries lay along the banks of the St. Lawrence. South of the seigneuries adjacent to the river, the land had not been conceded by either the French or British administrations. Generally speaking, these lands contained soils of mediocre quality and lacked communications facilities to link them to the St. Lawrence. Colonial policy under both the French and British regimes had reserved the region as a spatial buffer with the United States.

The Constitutional Act explicitly provided for the alienation of Crown lands in the form of two hundred acre concessions according to the English system of free and common socage. Secret instructions accompanying the Act stipulated that future land grants in Lower Canada should be made in freehold only. For the unceded lands south of the St. Lawrence River, the Governor in Lower Canada adopted a modified form of the New England "leader and associates" system to expedite concessions. In practice, this scheme permitted the acquisition of lands by government officials and their political allies. Although the scheme was formally abolished in 1809, it impeded the development of a freely functioning market for land in the Eastern Townships until the 1830s.

Under the leader and associates system, 'leaders'—members of the executive or legislative council, wealthy merchants, army or militia officers—were given large tracts of land, entire townships in some cases. Leaders in turn acted as real estate agents, distributing 1 200 acre blocks to 'associates' who had nominally agreed to work the land. Most of each block (legally 1 000 acres as of 1794) was returned to the leader as compensation for administrative expenses. In contrast to the situation in New England, the leaders and many associates in the Eastern Townships became absentee owners of unworked land. About two million acres was alienated in this way, over one-half of the total to wealthy Montreal merchants. The entire operation took place in the context of considerable uncertainty regarding survey dimensions, rents and royalties, the location of clergy and Crown reserves, and the system of common law in force.

Those immigrants who did settle in the Eastern Townships were northern New Englanders already familiar with an economic environment comprising the leader and associates system. Some had been British Empire Loyalists, but most came after 1791 in response to higher expected economic returns from farming.[4] Americans continued to settle in the Eastern Townships until the Anglo-American War of 1812 put an end to immigration. About 20 000 people lived in the Eastern Townships by this time, the majority English speaking.

Settlement in the regions north of the seigneuries along the St. Lawrence accompanied an increase in the relative price of Canadian timber in the first decade of the nineteenth century. (See Chapter 8) Forests previously regarded as an obstacle to agricultural settlement became an economic resource in their own right. River valleys such as the Ottawa, St. Maurice and Saguenay attracted migrants because of their forest resources and the available transport channel to the St. Lawrence.

According to Harris and Warkentin,

> Settlement of the townships north and west of the St. Lawrence lowland began in the Ottawa Valley in the early 1800s. New Eng-

landers arrived first, followed by a few Scottish and English settlers, then by Ulstermen and Irish Catholics, and a little later by French Canadians. Many of the New Englanders, the Scots, and the English brought capital, but almost all of the Irish and the French Canadians were destitute.[5]

As a result of the short growing season and the poverty of the soils in this fringe area, many farms failed to produce a surplus beyond that required for family subsistence. The primary value of most new land concessions lay in their forest reserves.

The population of Lower Canada continued to increase very rapidly in the twenty-five years following the War of 1812-1814. (See Table 5.1) The French speaking population grew by some 250 000 people between 1815 and 1840. This population growth was not unique to Lower Canada, however. During the years between 1790 and 1850 the population of the United States increased by almost six times, from 4 to 23 million. And more than two-thirds of this expansion was also attributable to natural population increase.

In Lower Canada, French speaking Canadians grew in numbers sufficient to double their population every 26 to 28 years. The birth rate of Francophones fluctuated around 51 per thousand population, a rate marginally lower than that of the eighteenth

Table 5.1

TOTAL POPULATION OF LOWER AND UPPER CANADA 1765-1851, SELECTED YEARS

	Lower Canada	Upper Canada
1765	70 000	—
1784	113 000	10 000*
1790	161 000	12 000*
1806	250 000*	71 000*
1814	335 000*	95 000*
1822	427 000*	—
1831	553 000	237 000
1844	697 000	—
1851	890 000	952 000

*Estimates

Government of Canada, *Census of Canada*, 1871, 1931.

century, and comparable to the birth rate in the United States. The death rate of Francophones, however, some 25 per thousand population, was higher than in the United States. More than 1 200 people in Montreal alone died of cholera in June 1832, and the total number of casualties in the province was thought to exceed 3 000. The advent of epidemics, armed conflict, and fluctuations in income affected mortality, marriage and birth rates on a year-to-year basis.

Immigration played a secondary role in Lower Canadian population growth after 1815. From 1792 to 1815 there had been virtually uninterrupted war in Europe: immigration to the Canadas was almost entirely American in origin during this time. After the War of 1812-1814, British imperial policy changed to discourage American immigrants and replace them with working class Britons. Between 1815 and 1840 nearly 400 000 British immigrants arrived in Lower Canadian ports, principally Quebec City. Quebec City surpassed even New York as the favored port of entry to the continent until 1832. The vast majority of immigrants moved on, however, to the southern portion of Upper Canada and to the United States. Between 1815 and 1840 British immigrants settling in Lower Canada numbered about 50 000 people.

The Lower Canadian economy accommodated nineteenth century demographic growth with increasing difficulty. The Constitutional Act of 1791 effectively ended the granting of lands in seigneurial tenure; thereafter new concessions were made in free and common socage. Growing population on a fixed quantity of seigneurial land meant that population per acre of seigneurial land increased steadily. During the first three decades of the nineteenth century, considerable demographic movement occurred in the seigneurial regions. This movement involved searching for cultivable property within the seigneurial environment. But, according to Harris and Warkentin, the economically cultivable seigneurial lands were largely occupied by 1800 and almost entirely so by the 1830s.[6]

As unoccupied cultivable land within the seigneurial environment disappeared, the question of land availability in the townships became more important. Demographic growth, the relative immobility of the Francophone population, and an increase in the relative price of colonial timber raised the demand for seigneurial land. The resulting rise in seigneurial dues, combined with poor harvests and price competition from newly settled western lands, reduced average net income per agricultural worker. In addition to charging higher dues, some seigneurs began charging a "start-up" fee to new occupants, a practice outlawed during the French regime by the Edict of Marly. Gradually, as the difference in rates of return from lands held in seigneurial tenure and those held in free and common socage became pronounced, Francophone farmers began moving into the townships north and south of the seigneuries bordering the St. Lawrence.

South of the seigneuries in the St. Lawrence Valley, the rolling highlands of the Appalachian range in the Eastern Townships were better suited for agriculture than the lands north of the river on the fringe of the Canadian Shield. The demand for agricultural produce in the United States, the communication links occasioned by a common New England heritage, and the high cost of overland transport to the St. Lawrence River tied the economy of the Eastern Townships to the United States. Once this trading pattern was established, the Lower Canadian assembly resisted proposals to finance roads to the river and Francophones hesitated to accept the social costs of settlement in the area. But after 1815 French speaking Canadians slowly began to move into the more prosperous townships. By 1831 Francophones formed more than 20 percent of the region's population.

Why Francophones hesitated to settle in the regions of Lower Canada administered in free and common socage is a question that has never been studied in detail. Several explanations are possible. Political patronage determined the co-ordinates of land concessions under the leader and associates system of land granting. Anglophone 'leaders' faced lower transaction costs if 'associates' were English speaking. For francophones, free and common socage, together with English civil law, created an unknown institutional environment in contrast to the conditional, but more familiar system of property rights embodied in seigneurial tenure. The purchase of land in freehold tenure also required an initial downpayment that may have been a barrier for low income farmers accustomed to the rental system in force on seigneuries. The Constitutional Act effectively enshrined two separate networks of institutional information: one in French based on the seigneurial system and French civil law, and the other in English based on free and common socage and English civil law. Only educated, bilingual people had access to both networks. For the majority of the population, illiteracy and the language barrier considerably reduced the gamut of economic opportunities available.[7]

The rate of settlement in the Eastern Townships by Francophones was consequently slow. The uncertainty surrounding property rights that had begun with the introduction of the leader and associates system, continued after 1815. Despite demographic pressure stemming from seigneurial over-population and immigrant arrivals, the total population of the townships increased to only 38 000 by 1825. To accelerate the rate of alienation and settlement of Crown lands, the Governor of Lower Canada introduced a new system of land sales by public auction, known as the New South Wales system, in 1825. The total population of the region climbed to 54 500 in 1831, but population density remained comparatively low.

In 1834 some 848 000 acres of Crown land was sold to the privately owned British American Land Company for the purpose of colonization. Half of the purchase price consisted of a commitment by the company to invest in public works, such as roads, that neither the government nor private entrepreneurs wished to undertake. The cash portion of the purchase price, was used by the colonial administration to finance the civil list, in other words, the salaries of the executive branch of colonial government. In this way the deal rendered the executive branch independent of the reform-minded assembly, and the British American Land Company became another source of political discord. The company ultimately completed some roads, but failed to meet its payment schedule or increase the overall rate of settlement in the townships.

Between 1760 and 1830 Lower Canada effectively 'de-urbanized' in the sense that the proportion of the total population living in towns fell from 25 percent to about 10 percent. Those English speaking immigrants who elected to remain in the province often chose to locate in Quebec City or Montreal. The proportion of English speaking people in Quebec City expanded from 28 percent in 1795 to 45 percent in 1831. The constant westward stream of immigrants through the two ports placed downward pressure on urban wage rates and made these towns unattractive for those without special skills until the intensity of the agricultural depression in the 1830s began to drive increasing numbers of Quebecers into urban areas in search of employment. Urbanization subsequently became a permanent feature of the provincial demographic scene.

The Insurrections of 1837-1838

The decline in net agricultural income per worker in the seigneurial regions during the 1830s intensified the demand for institutional change. This demand was channeled through the nationalist movement. The nationalist movement did not represent an isolated political phenomenon divorced from economic conditions. Nationalism and anti-colonialism attracted adherents for both political and economic reasons. Falling incomes in the agricultural sector accelerated the rate of diffusion of nationalist ideas among farm workers. Ultimately, in 1837, anti-colonial rebellions broke out in both Lower and Upper Canada. The two rebellions, though they differed in character and intensity, sought similar changes in the institutional environment.

The rise of nationalism in Lower Canada is attributable to a variety of factors: inequities in the institutional environment dating back to the eighteenth century, European nationalist ideas, elite political conflict, and a decline in average net agricultural income. Elite political conflict centred on control of government, political patronage, and reform of the seigneurial system. In an atmosphere of agricultural recession and growing economic uncertainty, many Lower Canadian agricultural workers looked to the educated Francophone elite for political leadership. Nationalist leaders used the climate of economic uncertainty to diffuse nationalist explanations for economic stagnation.

In the realm of economic policy, the nationalist movement favored taxes, tariffs and subsidies that redistributed income towards the French speaking majority: abolition of the civil list; reform of the land sale system, particularly in the Eastern Townships; subsidies for canal building on the Richelieu River rather than on the upper St. Lawrence; higher import duties on British goods, lower export duties, especially to the United States; restrictions on unskilled labor immigration from Britain; retention of the seigneurial system of property rights; and so on. These economic policies could not be enacted, however, without a radical change in the prevailing institutional environment.

The Patriotes political manifesto was contained in a document known as the '92 Resolutions'. The resolutions constituted a list of grievances against the colonial government and served as a manifesto for the *parti patriote* in the elections of November 1834. The 92 Resolutions did not contain a detailed economic program, but they did embody proposals for new institutions to regulate economic exchange. Eventually, in the British House of Commons, Lord Russel presented a series of resolutions that became the official response to the Patriotes' demands. The Russel Resolutions, enacted in 1837, rejected the constitutional proposals made by the Patriotes and authorized the colonial Governor to pay civil servants without the assent of the Lower Canadian assembly. In a calculated political risk, the British Parliament sided with the merchant elite, refused to liberalize the Canadian institutional environment, and threatened to unify the two Canadas under a centralized administration if reformers in the two provinces continued to press forward.

The insurrection of 1837 occurred almost exclusively in two localities, Saint-Denis and Saint-Charles in the Richelieu Valley, and the Saint-Eustache region north of Montreal. In 1838 the principal clash took place on the south shore of the St. Lawrence near Montreal. The Patriote leadership consisted of educated professionals, but the mass of followers, some five thousand in 1837, came from rural areas profoundly affected by the agricultural difficulties of the 1830s.

The Act of Union

The simmering conflict that erupted into armed rebellion during the years 1837-1838 resulted in administrative reorganization of the Canadas by the imperial government in London. Effective in February 1841, the British House of Parliament introduced a new institutional environment to both Lower and Upper Canada. The Act of Union resulted from the recommendations of John George Lambton, Lord Durham, in 1839. Lord Durham's Report on the political situation in the colony recommended two fundamental institutional changes:

(1) a limited form of colonial self-government, that included the cabinet system whereby the executive branch of government was "responsible" to the legislative assembly, but which left foreign relations, foreign trade, and the power of constitutional amendment in the hands of the British government;

(2) the unification of Lower and Upper Canada under one central government and the demotion of French from its status as an official language.

In the Act of Union, the British government adopted the second of these recommendations, but not the responsible government provision. The two provinces were united under one government in Montreal. Responsible government was dropped from the Act of Union, but introduced to the colony seven years later when Lord Elgin formed a cabinet in consultation with the legislative assembly.

The Act of Union did not alter the definition of property rights in Lower Canada. But it did transfer the responsibility for the administration and sale of property rights in natural resources, such as land, to the Union government. The Act of Union also reorganized the distribution of voting rights in a way so as to alter the nature and impact of government regulation of the economy. By 1841 the English speaking population in the two provinces exceeded the French speaking population; less than ten years later the population of Upper Canada (henceforth "Canada West") would exceed that of Lower Canada ("Canada East"). The Act of Union combined the votes of Upper Canadians and Lower Canadians into one constituency. Majority votes in the unified legislature could be obtained on tax, tariff and subsidy programs previously opposed in the Lower Canadian assembly. A government canal building program on the St. Lawrence between Lake Ontario and Montreal, for instance, was blocked in the 1830s. The Lower Canadian assembly had refused to participate in the subsidization of canals in the belief the majority of benefits would have flowed to farmers in Upper Canada and merchants in Montreal. In the new parliament, Canada East's rural votes constituted a minority and the canal building program was enacted. Under the Act of Union, the burden of taxation for development projects benefiting Canada West and the merchant community in Montreal could be extended to the entire population of Canada East.[8]

Rapid demographic growth continued in the 1840s. The natural rate of incease of population in Canada East actually increased: the crude birth rate maintained a level comparable to that of the first three decades of the nineteenth century while the crude death rate declined. Marr and Paterson suggest this decline in the death rate may be attributable to technical improvements in innoculation procedures. (Marr and Paterson, p. 158)

Demographic growth in the 1840s was also affected by immigration. Unfortunately the available data does not allow historians to identify the number of immigrant arrivals actually settling in Canada East at this time. But it does appear that the unified province of Canada became less and less attractive to British immigrants. Ouellet writes,

> Au cours des trois périodes quinquennales qui vont de 1838 a 1852, la position du Canada comme deversoir de l'immigration britannique recule. La proportion des éffectifs optant pour le Canada par rapport aux éléments allant en premier lieu aux Etats-Unis ne cesse de baisser: 1833-37: 68%; 1838-42: 53%; 1843-47: 53%; 1848-52: 15%. Les Maritimes se trouvent exactement dans la même situation par rapport aux Canadas: 25%, 26%, 19%, 2%. (Ouellet, 1966, p. 471)[9]

The population growth of the 1840s was not accompanied by an increase in average net agricultural income per worker. The differential between agricultural income per worker in Canada East and in the newly settled Great Lakes region probably increased. This growing income differential would explain the migration behavior of Quebecers after 1840. (See Chapters 6, 10) Some rural families left the seigneurial areas to settle in the surrounding townships. By 1844 French speaking Quebecers accounted for nearly 30 percent of the total population in the Eastern Townships. Other families moved to urban areas, reversing the de-urbanization trend that had characterized Lower Canada prior to 1830. In the pre-industrial era, however, the number of urban jobs was relatively few; by

1851, towns of over one thousand people contained only 15 percent of the total population.

Many migrant families chose to leave Canada East altogether. The sporadic emigration of French Quebecers to the United States had been a publicly debated phenomenon since at least the 1820s. In the 1840s emigration from Canada East became an issue of public policy. A committee of the Union legislative assembly estimated in 1849 that emigration had reached an annual average of four thousand over the previous five years. (McCallum, p. 44) In fact, the emigration phenomenon was not unique to Canada East. Northeastern states such as Vermont, New Hampshire and Maine lost native-born people for similar reasons.

Migration in the eastern regions of North America in the nineteenth century was the result of simple economic choice. In the presence of growing income differentials between rural and urban areas, many people began moving into towns. Others moved to the newly settled mid-western part of the continent where the productivity of land was relatively high. The decision to migrate depended on the present and future costs and benefits involved. Francophone Quebecers were less mobile than other North Americans because emigration from the St. Lawrence Valley often required a significant adjustment in language and culture. Only high expected net income gains could compensate for the social costs of leaving the region.

Some historians have suggested the constitutional reform of 1841 provoked the increase in the rate of emigration from Canada East in the 1840s. It is conceivable that changes in the institutional environment resulting from the Act of Union dampened expectations about the future. Greater pessimism about the future of average incomes in the seigneurial sector as well as the expectation of higher import taxes and fewer subsidies may have accelerated the rate of emigration after 1840. Given the present state of knowledge, however, this line of reasoning must be left to the realm of speculation. There is little doubt the underlying cause of emigration, which was bound to occur eventually, lay in the nineteenth century value of Quebec's resource endowment and the comparatively low level of net agricultural income per worker accruing to those operating in the seigneurial environment.

NOTES

[1]In a break with domestic policy in Britain, Roman Catholics were permitted to hold office in the colonial administration. But whether Catholics, the overwhelming majority of the Canadian population, would be eligible to sit in the promised representative assembly was a moot point.

[2]Labrador was returned to Newfoundland in 1809.

[3]The British government had issued instructions authorizing the concession of lands in seigneurial tenure three years earlier.

[4]By 1811 about 35 percent of Quebec's English speaking population earned its livelihood from agriculture. (Ouellet, 1966, p. 15)

[5]*Canada Before Confederation*, p. 88, by R. Cole Harris and John Warkentin, Cartographer Miklos Pinther © Oxford University Press.

[6]The quantity of cultivable land at any given point in time is dependent upon current and expected prices and costs. The quantity of cultivable land in a region may therefore change over time, as a result of higher product prices and technical change in agricultural practice and/or transport. Because all of the cultivable seigneurial lands appeared to be occupied in the 1830s did not preclude the profitable clearing of additional seigneurial lands later in the nineteenth century.

[7]"The literacy of Protestant, English-speaking settlers who arrived in the first half of the nineteenth century and that of their children was quite high, in striking contrast to their Francophone neighbours." (Greer, p. 331)

[8]In the case of the St. Lawrence canals, the project was largely financed through an increase in import duties. Consumers in both Canadas, particularly in the high import region of Canada West, eventually paid the bill.

[9]*Histoire Economique et Sociale du Québec*, *1760-1850*, p. 471, reprinted by permission of Les Editions Fides. During the three five-year periods between 1838 and 1852, Canada's position as a destination for British immigrants declined. The proportion of migrants choosing Canada as a port of entry diminshed steadily relative to those choosing the United States: 1833-37, 68 percent; 1838-42, 53 percent; 1843-47, 53 percent; 1848-52, 15 percent. The Maritime provinces found themselves in exactly the same situation relative to the Canadas: 25 percent, 26 percent, 19 percent, 2 percent. (Author Translation).

SELECT BIBLIOGRAPHY

Bernier, Gerald and Daniel Salée. "Appropriation foncière et bourgeoisie marchands: éléments pour une analyse de l'économie marchande du Bas-Canada avant 1846." *Revue d'histoire de l'Amérique française*. September 1982.

Breton, Albert. "The Economics of Nationalism." *Journal of Political Economy*. Vol. LXXVII, 1964.

Courville, Serge. "La crise agricole du Bas-Canada, Eléments d'une réflexion géographique (deuxième partie)." *Cahiers de Géographie du Québec*. December 1980.

Craig, Gerald M., ed., *Lord Durham's Report*. Toronto: McClelland and Stewart Ltd., 1963.

Davis, Lance E. and Douglass C. North. *Institutional Change and American Economic Growth*. New York: Cambridge University Press, 1971.

Graham, Gerald S. *British Policy and Canada, 1774-1791, A Study in 18th Century Trade Policy*. Toronto: Longmans, Green & Co., 1930.

Greer, Allan. "The Pattern of Literacy in Quebec, 1745-1899." *Histoire Sociale-Social History*. November 1978.

Harris, R. Cole and John Warkentin. *Canada before Confederation: A Study in Historical Geography*. Toronto: Oxford University Press, 1974.

Henripin, Jacques and Yves Péron. "The Demographic Transition of the Province of Quebec," in D.V. Glass and Roger Revelle, ed., *Population and Social Change*. London: Edward Arnold Ltd., 1972.

McCallum, John. *Unequal Beginnings: Agriculture and Economic Development in Quebec and Ontario until 1870*. Toronto: University of Toronto Press, 1980.

McGuigan, Gerald. "Administration of Land Policy and the Growth of Corporate Economic Organization in Lower Canada, 1791-1809," in W.T. Easterbrook and M.H. Watkins, *Approaches to Canadian Economic History*. Toronto: McClelland and Stewart Ltd., 1967.

McGuigan, Gerald. "La concession des terres dans les Cantons de l'Est au Bas-Canada, 1763-1809." *Recherches Sociographiques*. January-April, 1963.

Marr, William L. and Donald G. Paterson. *Canada: An Economic History*. Toronto: Macmillan of Canada Ltd., 1980.

Ouellet, Fernand. *Histoire économique et sociale du Québec, 1760-1850*. Montréal: Editions Fides, 1966.

Ouellet, Fernand. *Le Bas-Canada 1791-1840: Changements structuraux et crise*. Ottawa: Editions de l'Université d'Ottawa, 1976.

Paquet, Gilles and Jean-Pierre Wallot. *Patronage et pouvoir dans le Bas-Canada (1794-1812)*. Montréal: les Presses de l'Université du Québec, 1973.

Stigler, George. "Information in the Labour Market." *The Journal of Political Economy*. October 1962.

Wallot, Jean-Pierre. *Un Québec qui bougeait: trame socio-politique au tournant du XIX siècle*. Montreal: les Editions de Boréal Express, 1973.

6
Agriculture

During the years 1760-1850 the overwhelming majority of Quebec's population continued to earn its living in the agricultural sector. Subsistence agriculture provided the basis for rural living standards even though many farmers earned cash supplements from market transactions. The number of Quebec farmers producing a marketable surplus appears to have increased during the eighteenth century. But in the first half of the nineteenth century, this trend seems to have been reversed; many farmers returned to complete self-sufficiency. As pointed out in Chapter 5, the Quebec population was 'de-urbanizing' in the years prior to 1830. Rural people, who comprised 81 percent of the total population in 1790, accounted for 90 percent by 1825.

The gradual restructuring of relative prices in nineteenth century British North America profoundly influenced the evolution of Quebec agriculture. With the expansion of the North American frontier and the rise of wheat farming in the continental mid-west, wheat production in the St. Lawrence Valley became less profitable. Market-oriented agricultural producers responded by diversifying their output. As population per acre of seigneurial land continued to increase, Franco-Quebecers from the rural areas began migrating to local towns, to the Eastern Townships, and to the neighboring New England States. A similar phenomenon was occurring in all of the eastern regions of North America. Migration served as an equilibrating mechanism between low income and high income areas.

The effects of institutional change on the supply of agricultural land in Quebec after the Conquest was examined in the previous chapter. Because land and labor are complementary factors of production, the conditions surrounding the sale of land affected rates of migration and settlement. Within a given institutional environment, migration and settlement rates depended on the expected returns to land as an input into agricultural and timber production. Potential settlers made a crude estimate of the income, in cash or in kind, to be earned from land in the region before deciding on settlement and landclearing. This estimate depended on the productivity of the soil, the settlers' agricultural experience and, in the case of cash farming, on the costs of transport to market and the expected prices of commodities to be produced using the land as an input. The demand for land in commercial farming, like the demand for other factors of production, was dependent upon the relative prices of agricultural goods. Higher prices for agricultural commodities such as grains, meats and vegetables resulted in higher prices for land capable of producing these commodities for delivery to market.

This chapter will examine agricultural growth in Quebec focusing on product prices, output, and the evolution of net income per worker. The measurement of agricultural output and income is, of course, fundamental to a complete understanding of the Quebec economy in the eighteenth and nineteenth centuries. Unfortunately, the data problems that hamper close study of the evolution of the agricultural sector during the French regime recur for the period after the Conquest. Time series data on agricultural production for the years 1760-1850 do not exist. There are no census reports on agricultural production between 1739 and 1827. Assumptions about growth in farm output are usually made on the basis of discontinuous observations from a small number of regions, or from data on imports and exports. As far as prices are concerned, Jean Hamelin and Fernand Ouellet have constructed crude indices of individual commodity prices for Quebec City and Montreal on the basis of newspaper reports and accounts from religious institutions. These are complemented by Richard Chabot's rural prices series. Imperfect as they are, the parallel movement of these indices with similar indices for England, France and the United States testifies to the degree of international economic integration present in the second half of the eighteenth century. But all attempts to construct a general price index for Lower Canada that would allow for the translation of individual commodity prices from money values into real (deflated) prices have relied on exceedingly arbitrary assumptions. A satisfactory consumer price index for the period has not yet been developed. This chapter relies on scattered information that allows for a tentative appraisal of agricultural output and income to 1850.

After the Conquest

The Seven Years War disrupted all forms of market exchange in the St. Lawrence Valley. Part of the agricultural sector's labor force was requisitioned to battle, resulting in reductions in agricultural output. Established transport routes and marketing channels were interrupted creating shortages in some areas and undesired inventories in others. A high rate of inflation, caused by the massive increase in the money supply, contributed to the balkanization of markets by introducing an inflation tax on the cash balances held by individuals and firms. (See Chapter 4) Wartime disruption, however, was mostly limited to market-oriented economic activities. Subsistence farmers living at a distance from the battlefront were probably not affected.

There is no evidence that agricultural productivity improved during the decades following the Conquest, but there is evidence of an increase in aggregate agricultural activity. According to census data, the total population expanded by 62 percent between

Table 6.1

TOTAL EXPORTS OF WHEAT AND FLOUR FROM QUEBEC, 1763-1790 (000's minots)*

Year	Amount	Year	Amount
1763	57.2	1777	56.6
1764	29.2	1778	83.1
1765	—	1779	—
1766	—	1780	—
1767	16.5	1781	—
1768	24.1	1782	—
1769	—	1783	22.9
1770	59.2	1784	19.7
1771	197.9	1785	5.2
1772	240.5	1786	156.2
1773	276.8	1787	285.5
1774	467.4	1788	249.9
1775	187.5	1789	—
1776	61.3	1790	150.0

*1 minot = 1.107 bushels. The volume of flour exports has been converted to minots at the rate of 5 minots to the barrel.

"Colonial Economy and International Economy: The Trade of the St. Lawrence River Valley with Spain, Portugal and their Atlantic Possessions, 1760-1850," Table VII, by Fernand Ouellet, in J. Barber and A.J. Kuethe, eds., *The North American Role in the Spanish Imperial Economy, 1760-1819*. Manchester: Manchester University Press, 1983.

1765 and 1784, while the quantity of cleared land rose by 66 percent. Exports of wheat and flour grew particularly rapidly during the years preceding American Independence, 1770-1774. (See Table 6.1) The breakdown in commercial relations between Britain and the Thirteen Colonies created markets for Quebec produce in the metropole and in the British West Indies. With protection from American competition, wheat and flour exports to the West Indies increased to 82 percent of Quebec's total wheat and flour exports in 1774. The export demand for wheat and flour raised the relative price of wheat and increased the profitability of farming in the St. Lawrence Valley. The value of agricultural land increased and British merchants in the colony began acquiring seigneuries as productive assets.

Exports of wheat and flour declined during the years 1775-1778. According to Ouellet, the decline is attributable to a compensating increase in domestic demand stemming from the food requirements of British troops fighting the colonial American war. Reports from the time suggest that agricultural production remained at least constant and possibly increased during this period. Any rise in output was probably attributable to the increase in the quantity of land under cultivation rather than to an increase in total factor productivity (output per unit of input).

Table 6.2

TOTAL EXPORTS OF WHEAT AND FLOUR
FROM LOWER CANADA, 1791-1812 (000's minots)

1791	224.7	1802	1 151.0
1792	350.0	1803	447.5
1793	541.5	1804	273.1
1794	482.5	1805	115.0
1795	485.0	1806	151.9
1796	24.6	1807	333.8
1797	101.0	1808	399.0
1798	139.5	1809	301.8
1799	151.0	1810	233.5
1800	317.0	1811	97.6
1801	663.0	1812	451.4

"Colonial Economy and International Economy: The Trade of the St. Lawrence River Valley with Spain, Portugal and their Atlantic Possessions, 1760-1850," Table VII, by Fernand Ouellet, in J. Barber and A.J. Kuethe, eds., *The North American Role in the Spanish Imperial Economy, 1760-1819*. Manchester: Manchester University Press, 1983.

Agricultural production suffered from repeatedly poor harvests in the years 1779 to 1785. Exports of wheat and flour were virtually nil at this time.[1] Ouellet interprets the susceptibility of agricultural production to adverse atmospheric conditions as a sign of poor farming technique. From 1786 to the end of the century, however, with the exception of the years 1789 and 1796, Quebec agriculture seems to have been moderately productive. Exports of wheat and flour to Great Britain responded to high prices on the metropolitan market. Wheat exports appear to have had a stimulating effect on the entire agricultural sector; Ouellet refers to wheat as a 'staple' product for the years 1793-1802.[2] (See Table 6.2)

The comparatively high level of wheat and flour exports in the last decade of the eighteenth century reflects the income-maximizing outlook of Quebec farmers at this time. Subsistence farmers' resistance to change is sometimes attributed to incompetence or irrationality. But as with other economic agents, subsistence farmers usually behave in an economically rational manner when confronted with a choice of alternative opportunities. In this case, a rise in British wheat prices, caused by the interruption of Baltic and Mediterranean trade resulting from war between Britain and France (1793-1801), induced higher levels of wheat exports from the St. Lawrence Valley. Modest protective tariffs, together with special exemptions for colonial wheat imports, further stimulated Quebec exports. High wheat prices, combined with co-operative atmospheric conditions, probably contributed to greater production in Lower Canada. No doubt the increased demand for agricultural land and the accompanying rise in land values hastened the creation of an administrative device for alienating public lands in the Eastern Townships—the leader and associates system. But no change in agricultural technique is apparent. Although farm labor inputs and the quantity of land in cultivation increased, no increase in total factor productivity is discernable.

Despite active sales on the British market during the years 1793-1801, Quebec wheat and flour ceased to rival American produce on the West Indies market. American merchants, acting as 'neutral' intermediaries, handled nearly all of the carrying and re-export trade between wartorn Europe and the European colonies in the Caribbean. The scale of American trading activity reduced average transport costs to American grain exporters. As British subjects, Canadian merchant carriers could not participate in the wartime trade, other than with the British colonies. Without the advantages of the Navigation Laws, unenforced at this time, British North American wheat failed to compete in the Caribbean trade.

Agricultural Stagnation?

According to Fernand Ouellet, the decade 1803-1812 is one of the most important decades in the history of Quebec. These years bring an end to the modest economic growth based on fur trading and wheat production that had characterized the seventeenth and eighteenth centuries. In the social and political sphere, the liberal professions in Lower Canada begin to define a role for themselves as the purveyors of French Canadian nationalism. The rise of French Canadian nationalism weakened the collaboration between French and English speaking elites that had characterized colonial politics during the first forty years of British rule.

Ouellet's interpretation of this decade is controversial because he attributes the rise of French Canadian nationalism to an economic 'crisis' (*crise agricole*) in the agricultural sector. By Ouellet's interpretation, nationalism, as symbolized by the controversy surrounding the Gaols Bill in 1805[3] and the founding of the newspaper *Le Canadien* in 1806, is directly related to a trend decline in agricultural income per capita that begins in 1803. Most economic historians agree that average income in Lower Canadian agriculture probably decreased during the 1830s and 1840s. The controversy concerns the existence of a long term trend. If no trend is discernable before 1815, as Ouellet's critics suggest, then the rise of French Canadian nationalism in the first decade of the nineteenth century cannot be attributed to the agricultural 'crisis'. In other words, if Ouellet's economic analysis does not hold, then the origins of French Canadian nationalism can more easily be related to other forces, such as the institutional changes embodied in the Constitutional Act of 1791.

The debate on the precise dating of the agricultural 'crisis' stems partly from data deficiencies and partly from conceptual ambiguity. Essential information on output and relative prices is unavailable so that conclusions must be drawn on the basis of indirect indices such as quantities exported and money prices. The available production data, covering intermittent years and a small sample of seigneuries, is sufficiently incomplete that plausible explanations can be developed along different lines. Conceptually, it is not clear what constitutes an economic or agricultural 'crisis', nor consequently what characterizes the first symptoms of a crisis. Finally, there is no explicitly developed causal link between economic conditions and changes in political opinion. Even if average net agricultural income diminished steadily after 1802, this does not prove that manifestations of nationalism three years later are attributable to this decline.

Casual inspection of Figure 6.1 suggests that exports for wheat and flour from the port of Quebec declined between 1802 and 1812. However, the years 1801 and 1802 were years of exceptionally high exports, while 1804 was a year of crop failure that reduced exports in 1805. Considering this period in light of trade deficits for the years after 1815, Ouellet argues that a long run decline in wheat production began in 1803. Prices in England and the West Indies remained high, but a trend decrease in yields from Lower Canadian agriculture began to reduce the domestic wheat supply. According to Ouellet, the trend began in the oldest parishes as a result of exhausted soils and spread unevenly throughout the seigneurial regions in the years that followed.

How does Ouellet illustrate his thesis concerning a decline in agricultural income per capita during the first decade of the nineteenth century? He does so first and foremost by analysing the trend in wheat and flour exports. Total exports declined by 32 percent from the years 1797-1802 to the years 1803-1808. (See

Figure 6.1

NET EXPORTS OF WHEAT AND FLOUR FROM QUEBEC,
1792-1871 (thousands of bushels)

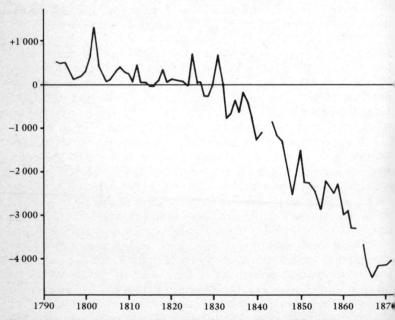

Unequal Beginnings: Agriculture and Economic Development in Quebec and Ontario Until 1870, p. 28, by John McCallum, reprinted by permission of University of Toronto Press.

Table 6.2) On a per capita basis, the decline is even more dramatic. (Ouellet, 1976, pp. 178-179) Unfortunately, this procedure for establishing trends is open to question because of the arbitrary way in which the trends have been dated. For example, if the exceptional years of 1801 and 1802 are excluded, the total export data indicates an increase of 41 percent from the period 1795-1800 to the period 1803-1808! As far as wheat exports are concerned, it is clear that Ouellet's results are sensitive to the way in which the data is grouped. Although Ouellet insists that any increase in wheat exports should be attributed to shipments that originated in Upper Canada and the United States, no time series data on wheat and flour imports are available to substantiate this claim.[4] Ouellet has therefore turned to tithe records and amassed a large array of information on field crop production that is consistent with his interpretation. But these records, dependent in time and location on pastoral visits, do not provide the year-to-year observations necessary to build a continuous time series data base covering both field crops and animal products.

Gilles Paquet and Jean-Pierre Wallot have offered an alternative explanation of the period 1802-1812. After underlining the fragility of Ouellet's conclusions, Paquet and Wallot offer another model that loosely accounts for the same data. Borrowing from price theory and the economics of development, Paquet and Wallot argue that the year-to-year variance in agricultural prices induced agricultural producers to diversify during the decade. Any fall in wheat and flour export receipts, according to Paquet and Wallot, was more than compensated by an increase in oats, barley and peas production. As rational economic producers, Lower Canadian farmers responded to wide variations in the relative price of wheat by substituting other products for home consumption. The wide variance in year-to-year prices on the imperial market for wheat and flour induced a 'restructuring' of the agricultural sector that included a return from cash cropping to agricultural self-sufficiency during the years 1792-1812. According to Paquet and Wallot's admittedly crude indices, average agricultural income, including imputed income for home farm consumption, increased during the period. (Paquet and Wallot, 1972, pp. 221-231)

There are weaknesses in Paquet and Wallot's analysis which, though not invalidating the argument, make it less than convincing. Their attempt to identify wheat supply and demand curves using money prices, for instance, is unsatisfactory. (Paquet and Wallot, 1972, pp. 197-201) The response of producers to price changes should be analysed in terms of deflated prices.[5] Paquet and Wallot's agricultural price data do indicate that wheat prices were more unstable than oats, barley or peas prices during the years

1805-1812, but no statistical trend in relative prices is evident. (See Table 6.3) The authors provide price data for an eight year period only, so that more general conclusions cannot be reached. Whether Lower Canadian producers really waited until the 1800s before responding to perennially unstable international prices, and if so, for what reasons, is not examined.

T.J.A. LeGoff has reviewed the debate on the beginnings of the agricultural 'crisis': on the basis of very crude estimates derived from tithe records, LeGoff suggests that Lower Canadian wheat and flour production probably leveled off after 1802. In the presence of rapid demographic growth, this leveling of total production would have resulted in a decline in wheat production per capita. The hypothesized increase in the production of substitute crops such as barley and oats, says LeGoff, should have produced a narrowing of the wheat price differential between Quebec and the United States. LeGoff's argument would not hold, however, if Lower Canadian wheat prices were set on the British market at this

Table 6.3

AGRICULTURAL PRODUCT PRICES AT QUEBEC, 1805-1812
(Monthly Average in Current Shillings)

| | Current Prices | | | | Relative Prices | | |
	wheat	oats	barley	peas	oats wheat	barley wheat	peas wheat
1805	6.9	2.0	2.8	5.0	0.29	0.41	0.72
1806	6.5	2.3	2.9	4.7	0.35	0.45	0.72
1807	6.6	2.1	3.0	5.1	0.32	0.45	0.77
1808	7.2	2.4	2.9	6.0	0.33	0.40	0.83
1809	7.7	3.1	3.3	7.7	0.40	0.43	1.00
1810	9.3	3.5	3.3	7.3	0.38	0.35	0.78
1811	10.4	2.9	5.0	7.3	0.28	0.48	0.70
1812	9.2	3.0	3.8	7.1	0.33	0.41	0.77
STANDARD DEVIATION (1805-1812)	1.47	0.54	0.73	1.22			

Gilles Paquet and Jean-Pierre Wallot, "Aperçu sur le commerce international et les prix domestiques dans le Bas-Canada (1793-1812)," *Revue d'histoire de l'Amérique française*, pp. 461-468, December 1967.

time. In any case, his entire discussion of Lower Canadian wheat prices (based on data generated by inspection from one of Ouellet's graphs) relies upon nominal values that ignore international differences in the cost of living. LeGoff's broad description of the rise in domestic food requirements seems reasonable, but his contention that net agricultural income per capita declined in the first decade of the nineteenth century remains unproven. LeGoff's rationale for choosing 1803 as a pivotal turning point is no more convincing than Ouellet's. There is no sharp discontinuity in the data available. Nor is any theory advanced to explain why 1803 should have constituted a turning point peculiar to Lower Canadian agriculture.[6] Wheat production fluctuated from year-to-year during the first decade of the nineteenth century, but there is as yet no reason to conclude that these fluctuations differed substantially from those of the eighteenth century.

There is no conclusive evidence that a secular fall in net agricultural income per worker occurred during the first decade of the nineteenth century. A product of diverse political and economic pressures, the birth of nationalism among French speaking professionals can more easily be attributed to the growing divergence of incomes between French and English speaking elites. Changes in the institutional environment resulting from the Constitutional Act of 1791, and the ensuing redistribution of political power and patronage, exemplified by land policy in the Eastern Townships, accentuated this divergence. The amendment of Ouellet's thesis on the origins of nationalism, however, does not in itself invalidate the rest of his analysis. The diffusion of nationalist ideas among the rural population may have resulted from the decline in net agricultural income per worker that occurred in the 1830s.

Agricultural Crisis

Net exports of domestically produced wheat and flour continued to fluctuate after 1815. Data on imports from the United States and Upper Canada indicate that Lower Canada became a continuous net importer of wheat and flour as of 1833. (See Figure 6.1) A series of wheat crop failures in the 1830s and 1840s resulted in the substitution of potatoes and barley for wheat on many Quebec farms. By 1851, wheat production had partially recovered. (See Table 6.4) Animal products accounted for about two-thirds of the value of agricultural output, once animal feed crops are netted out from total crop production. (See Chapter 10) In examining Table 6.4, however, it should be noted, that census years 1827, 1831 and 1851 were years of unusually abundant harvests, while census year

1844 was a year of unusual hardship.

There are several explanations for the trend decline in Lower Canadian wheat production over the first half of the nineteenth century. The most important is the increasingly competitive position of newly settled farms in Upper Canada and the mid-western United States. Wheat price competition from the west had its origins in falling transport costs, the high productivity of newly cleared land, relatively better climatic conditions[7] and technical improvements in soil preparation, seeding and cultivating. The resulting increase in total productivity reduced costs per unit of

Table 6.4

AGRICULTURAL PRODUCTION/STOCK PER CAPITA IN QUEBEC, CENSUS YEARS, 1827-1851

CROPS (bushels)	1827*	1831	1844	1851**
Wheat	6.2	6.2	1.4	3.7
Barley	0.8	—	1.7	0.6
Peas	1.7	1.8	1.7	1.7
Oats	5.2	5.8	10.4	10.7
Potatoes	14.4	13.3	14.2	5.2
LIVESTOCK (head)				
Horses	0.3	0.2	0.2	0.2
Cattle	0.9	0.7	0.7	0.7
Sheep	1.8	1.0	0.9	0.7
Swine	0.5	0.5	0.3	0.3

*The data for 1827 presented in 1871 census consists of a three-year average estimated by Joseph Bouchette.

**Following R.M. McInnis's re-examination of the 1851-52 Census of Agriculture in Lower Canada, Normand Séguin has produced revised estimates of cereal output for 1851. Séguin's estimates cover wheat, barley, oats, potatoes, and buckwheat production. They suggest that the published census data underestimated "true" output by an average of 5.08 percent. Séguin's estimates for 1851 have been employed here, together with a 5.08 percent correction for the published census figure for peas output.

"L'agriculture de la Mauricie et du Québec, 1850-1950," by Normand Séguin. *Revue d'histoire de l'Amérique française*, March 1982, pp. 557.

Government of Canada, *Census of Canada*, 1871, Volume V.

output and allowed western producers to underprice eastern farmers on eastern markets, despite the net transport cost differential. McCallum has succinctly placed the decline of Lower Canadian wheat production in its North American context:

> The decline of wheat [in the east] was a continental phenomenon. In the United States the centre of wheat production had shifted from eastern to northern and western New England in the early eighteenth century, to Pennsylvannia and the Mohawk Valley by 1800, to the Genesee Valley and Ohio after 1825, and to the mid-west after 1840. Over the years the same pattern repeated itself with dreary monotony: once transportation facilities became available the easterners were unable to compete with western producers, and they abandoned their farms or shifted from wheat to other commodities. The same was true of the efficient British farmers in the Montreal region during the 1830's and of the farmers in the older counties of Ontario in later years.[8]

Lower Canadian farmers were not alone in the problem they faced. By 1840 New England imported 80 percent of its wheat consumption, and the proportion was yet growing.

At the same time a significant change in the relative prices of agricultural and forest products accentuated Lower Canadian farmers' difficulties. The rise in the relative price of forest products gradually revalued timber stands; many lay adjacent to potential farm lands. Until the end of the eighteenth century, timber cutting was a costly obstacle to agricultural settlement. But in the nineteenth century timber cutting provided a source of potential revenue. (See Chapter 8) Because landowners could not be certain of enforcing their property rights in timber stands adjacent to cultivable lands, they gradually raised the price of agricultural land to reflect potential timber value. This rise in price affected land held in seigneurial as well as freehold tenure wherever forests occurred.

On seigneurial lands, new settlers were unaccustomed to paying a flat settlement fee to landowners. *Cens* and *rentes* were usually collected in proportion to output in a way comparable to royalty payments on natural resource exploitation in modern times. With an increase in the relative price of timber, seigneurs began to impose concession fees or insist on a downpayment prior to cultivation and harvest—practices outlawed during the French regime by the Edict of Marly. This raised the price of acquiring new lands and further accentuated the plight of agricultural workers seeking employment in the seigneurial environment. Other seigneurs refused to concede unsettled seigneurial lands for a period of time in anticipation of higher prices in the future. Subjected to an increase in the demand for agricultural land, the institutional arrangements embodied in the seigneurial system adapted to accommodate the market price system. The result was a significant increase in the unit costs of production on seigneurial land, associated with higher rental payments.

Did average yields on seigneurial lands fall during the first half of the nineteenth century? Wheat production, which represented 60 to 70 percent of the total harvest in the eighteenth century, declined dramatically to 22 percent of the total harvest by census year 1827 and to 4 percent by 1844. Agricultural producers switched from wheat to potato production (49 percent of the total harvest in 1831) and oats production (35 percent of the total in 1844). Diversification represented a rational response to western competition on the part of producers. The fact that none of the substitutes for wheat was exportable to neighboring regions suggests that these substitutes were comparatively high cost commodities on all but very local markets. It is possible, of course, that average yields on seigneurial lands remained more or less constant while the cost of mid-continental wheat delivered to eastern markets declined. The growing cost differential may have induced Quebec's commercial producers to diversify their output. On the other hand, the rapid decline of wheat production on self-sufficient farms that were relatively unresponsive to market prices lends credence to the view that structural problems existed on the agricultural supply side, and that average yields were declining.

Three explanations have been offered to explain falling crop yields on seigneurial lands. One approach emphasizes 'bad luck' by reference to the unusual frequency of poor atmospheric conditions, insects such as the wheat midge, and plant diseases such as wheat rust that also plagued the eastern United States in the late 1820s and 1830s. As a result of these misfortunes, Lower Canadians experienced a continuous deficit in the net balance of their wheat and flour trade as of 1833. A second explanation of low yields emphasizes soil exhaustion as the underlying causal factor. By the 1830s the most accessible seigneurial land had been cultivated for more than a century. In the absence of adequate crop rotation, seed renewal, field manuring, and the selective breeding of cattle, yield may have declined.[9] A change in techniques would then have been necessary to maintain the modest yields obtained in the eighteenth century. That technological change did not occur in Quebec wheat farming leads to a third explanation of low yields—the non-maximizing 'habitant' mentality that the seigneurial system allegedly preserved. (Ouellet, 1976) As has already been suggested, such an explanation is inadequate. Seigneurial practices were in a state of evolution under pressure from rapid population growth, the rise of the Lower Canadian timber trade, and the ensuing demand for seigneurial land. Illiteracy and the language barrier slowed the flow of market information and the diffusion of new agricultural technology among French speaking farmers in the St. Lawrence Valley. Within this context, Francophone farmers behaved in an economically rational way.

The issue of falling yields in the first half of the nineteenth century remains perplexing. Lower Canadians undoubtedly faced a severe economic recession from the mid-1830s to the mid-1840s, but there is no firm quantitative evidence that average agricultural income entered into a trend decline. Field crop output per capita appears to have fluctuated considerably from year to year. There were successive crop failures in the 1830s and 1840s and producers adjusted the structure of field crop output by diversifying away from wheat. But it has not been unambiguously demonstrated that net agricultural output per capita decreased continuously over several decades.

An interesting interpretation of the Lower Canadian agricultural 'crisis' has been presented by Serge Courville. Courville suggests that average yields remained more or less constant over the first half of the nineteenth century, but that average net agricultural income to producers in the seigneurial environment diminished all the same. Institutional changes involving the imposition of new rental charges, the revival of dues that had fallen into disuse, and the systematic collection of these payments by recourse to farm managers resulted in a redistribution of seigneurial farm income after 1820. The decline in net income to producers provided a disincentive on the supply side of production. Agricultural producers worked less in agriculture and turned to alternative sources of income such as lumbering and fishing, or else migrated out of the farm sector altogether. The poor harvests occasioned by insects, plant disease, and aridity in the 1830s and 1840s resulted in low yields during those years. But in the long run, the trend decrease in net agricultural output per capita occurred without any trend decline in total factor productivity. Courville's analysis could be taken to imply that a redistribution of income from censitaires to seigneurs reduced the savings rate of farm producers and slowed the rate of capital accumulation in Quebec agriculture.

Once an agricultural producer's output diminished to the subsistence level, the adoption of new techniques and crop patterns became a very risky venture. The rational subsistence producer may have been reluctant to shift from the traditional technology and a diversified crop pattern to new techniques and specialized production because of the potentially high costs of failure. Risk-averting farmers may prefer a production structure involving low 'mean' incomes with low variance to alternative structures promising higher 'mean' incomes with greater variance. Risk and uncertainty play an important role in the economics of subsistence agriculture.

The decline in average net agricultural income during the 1830s had a multiplier effect on incomes in the non-agricultural sector. Those employed in the rural service industries (lawyers, doctors, merchants and the clergy) felt the impact most directly. The return to subsistence production reduced rural demand for marketed goods and services, except in fringe areas where the growth of timber cutting provided cash incomes. The overall decline in the volume of rural market transactions slowed the development of economic specialization and the growth of markets, affecting urban as well as rural economic growth.

In 1836, poor harvests occurred not only in Lower Canada, but in the United States as well. The high price of imports affected the standard of living in both urban and rural Quebec. High domestic prices resulted from the reduction in the money supply that accompanied the suspension of specie payments in Lower Canada in May 1837. Instability in the banking system intensified feelings of economic and social malaise that culminated in the unsuccessful insurrections of 1837 and 1838.

From all appearances, the agricultural recession of the 1830s continued through the early 1840s. (See Table 6.4) The institutional changes contained in the Act of Union did not have any immediate effects on the structure or growth of the Quebec economy. Nor do the tariff changes of the 1840s appear to have had a significant impact on the agricultural sector. (Tucker, pp. 63-82) In 1846 the imperial government repealed the Corn Laws thereby abolishing tariff restrictions on wheat and flour imports to Britain from any source. The disadvantages of these adjustments in Britain's tariff structure were offset by innovations in transport infrastructure and accompanying changes in transport and transaction costs throughout North America.

During the 1840s net exports of Ontario wheat increased by a multiple of five, elevating wheat to the status of a staple product in that province. (McCallum, pp. 15-16) In the wake of the westward movement of wheat production, Quebec farmers confronted four basic options: they could shift to other types of farm output; they could leave the seigneurial regions for the townships; they could move to nearby urban areas and change occupation; or they could leave Quebec altogether. Each of these alternatives attracted some adherents.

Perhaps the least costly option was product diversification. Quebec farmers experimented with different mixes of crops and livestock seeking an improvement in output per farm worker. In the Eastern Townships, farmers exploited the opportunity to market dairy products in neighboring New England. Elsewhere, production shifted from wheat to barley, oats and potatoes for farm consumption. By 1851 Quebec imported nearly one half of all wheat consumed in the province. Only a few areas in the Montreal, lower St. Lawrence, and Saguenay regions continued to sow more than 25 percent of their cultivated lands in wheat. According to corrected 1851 census data, province-wide yields amounted to 9.2 bushels per acre sown. (McInnis, 1981, p. 227 and Séguin, 1982, p. 557) This figure compares favorably with the yields of 8 to 9 bushels being obtained in eastern New York State by 1845. (McCallum, p. 35)

Although Quebec farmers may have been slower to adopt new techniques than many of their counterparts elsewhere in North America, they were not antipathetic to new technology when informed of alternatives. Threshing mills, for example, were sparsely distributed over the province with the exception of one region. The adjacent districts of Islet and Kamouraska between Levis and Rivière-du-Loup accounted for 44 percent of all mills recorded. (Blouin, p. 97) According to the census of 1851, one of Quebec's three threshing mill manufacturing establishments was located in this region. When information on such innovations was readily available, and their adoption proved to be economic, Quebec farmers appear to have adopted new technology with alacrity.

Not only did Quebec farmers shift to other types of farm output, but some left the seigneurial regions to settle in the townships. This demographic movement, which had begun after 1815, accelerated in the 1840s. By 1844 French speaking Quebecers represented nearly 30 percent of the 82 000 people in the Eastern Townships. (Ouellet, 1976, p. 239) At the same time, Francophone Quebecers began moving to urban areas, principally Montreal and Quebec City, reversing the 'de-urbanization' trend characteristic of the years prior to 1830. Rural-urban migration depended upon expectations about vacancies in the urban job market and the growth rate of manufacturing industry. Migration into the province appears to have slowed considerably as information about Lower Canada's economic difficulties was diffused abroad.

The growing agricultural income differential between Quebec and the rest of North America also resulted in migration out of the region. A similar phenomenon was already underway in the United States as easterners headed west. Migration served as an equilibrating mechanism between low income and high income areas. The adjustment process was slower in Quebec for two reasons. First, information about the United States and Ontario relating to job vacancies and wage differentials was more imperfect because of the language barrier and the slower pace of growth in transport and communications infrastructure. And second, even when new labor market information became available, French speaking Quebecers displayed strong ties to their homeland. Emigration required a substantial linguistic and cultural adjustment that many Quebecers were unwilling to accept.

NOTES

[1] Wheat production accounted for sixty to seventy percent of total crop output in 1784. (Ouellet, Appendix, 1980)

[2] The contention that wheat production increased during the years 1793-1802 in response to high export prices has been contested by Gilles Paquet and Jean-Pierre Wallot. Paquet and Wallot assert that the higher level of exports resulted from a compensating reduction in domestic consumption.

[3] The controversy over the Gaols Bill amounted to a dispute over tax incidence. English speaking merchants wanted new jails to be financed through taxes on land, while French speaking professionals and farmers insisted on higher duties for imported goods from Britain.

[4] Imports of wheat and flour from Upper Canada amounted to an average of 7 percent of total exports from Quebec in 1801-1802 and 23 percent in 1806-1807, the only years for which data is available during this period. (Ouellet, 1976, p. 179)

[5] The price variable in the wheat supply function, based as it is on current rather than lagged price, is probably mis-specified in any case. (LeGoff, 1974, pp. 6-7)

[6] When England and France made temporary peace in 1803, the value of American exports plummeted much as Lower Canada's did.

[7] "Although the clay soils of the province [Quebec] were ideal for wheat-growing, springs were too late and summers too rainy to make good wheat country, and it is doubtful whether the crop can ever have been strong or yields high. But... wheat can be grown in a cool rainy climate if the farmer is satisfied with low yields and a poor quality grain." (Parker, p. 190)

[8] *Unequal Beginnings: Agriculture and Economic Development in Quebec and Ontario Until 1870*, p. 35, by John McCallum, reprinted by permission of University of Toronto Press.

[9] Modern soil science studies of wheat on the Canadian prairies and monoculture systems in Quebec and Ontario indicate that long run yields will decline in the absence of appropriate farming techniques (fertilizers and so on). Contrary to what R.M. McInnis appears to suggest (McInnis, 1982), the depletion of organic matter, phosphorous, and nitrogen will produce a trend decline in land fertility over long periods of time. Inclement weather, disease, and erosion by wind and water are separate matters of concern.

SELECT BIBLIOGRAPHY

Blouin, Claude. "La mechanisation de l'agriculture entre 1830 et 1890," in Normand Séguin, ed., *Agriculture et colonisation au Québec.* Montreal: les Editions du Boréal Express. 1980.

Bouchette, Joseph. *The British Dominions in North America.* London: Longman et al, 1832.

Courville, Serge. "La crise agricole du Bas-Canada, éléments d'une réflexion géographique." *Cahiers de Géographie du Québec.* Part I, September 1980. Part II, December 1980.

Danhoff, Clarence H. "The Tools and Implements of Agriculture." *Agricultural History.* January 1972.

Gallman, Robert E. "The Agricultural Sector and the Pace of Economic Growth: U.S. Experience in the Nineteenth Century," in David C. Klingaman and Richard K. Vedder, *Essays in Nineteenth Century Economic History.* Athens: Ohio University Press, 1978.

Greer, Allan. "Fur-Trade Labour and Lower Canadian Agrarian Structures." *CHA Historical Papers.* Canadian Historical Association, 1981.

Harris, R. Cole and John Warkentin. *Canada before Confederation: A Study in Historical Geography.* Toronto: Oxford University Press. 1974.

LeGoff, T.J.A. "The Agricultural Crisis in Lower Canada, 1802-12: A Review of a Controversy." *The Canadian Historical Review.* March 1974.

McCallum, John. *Unequal Beginnings: Agriculture and Economic Development in Quebec and Ontario until 1870.* Toronto: University of Toronto Press, 1980.

McInnis, Marvin. "Reconsideration of the State of Agriculture in Lower Canada in the First Half of the Nineteenth Century." *Canadian Papers in Rural History.* Vol. III, 1982.

McInnis, Marvin. "Some Pitfalls in the 1851-52 Census of Agriculture of Lower Canada." *Histoire Sociale-Social History.* May 1981.

North, Douglass C. *The Economic Growth of the United States 1790-1860.* New York: W.W. Norton & Co., 1966.

Ouellet, Fernand. *Le Bas-Canada 1791-1840: changements structuraux et crise.* Ottawa: Editions de l'Université d'Ottawa, 1976.

Ouellet, Fernand. *Eléments d'histoire sociale du Bas-Canada.* Montreal: Hurtubise HMH, Ltée, 1972.

Ouellet, Fernand. *Histoire économique et sociale du Québec, 1760-1850.* Montreal: Editions Fides, 1966.

Ouellet, Fernand. "Libéré ou exploité! le paysan québécois d'avant 1850." *Histoire Sociale-Social History.* November 1980.

Ouellet, Fernand. "Le mythe de l'habitant sensible au marché. Commentaires sur la controverse LeGoff-Wallot et Paquet." *Recherches Sociographiques.* January-April 1976.

Ouellet, Fernand, Jean Hamelin, and Richard Chabot. "Les prix agricoles dans les villes et les campagnes du Québec d'avant 1850: aperçus quantitatifs." *Histoire Sociale-Social History.* May 1982.

Paquet, Gilles, and Jean-Pierre Wallot. "Aperçu sur le commerce international et les prix domestiques dans le Bas-Canada (1793-1812)." *Revue d'histoire de l'Amérique française.* December 1967.

Paquet, Gilles and Jean-Pierre Wallot. "Crise agricole et tensions socio-ethniques dans le Bas-Canada, 1802-1812: éléments pour une re-interpretation." *Revue d'histoire de l'Amérique française.* September 1972.

Paquet, Gilles and Jean-Pierre Wallot. "The Agricultural Crisis in Lower Canada, 1802-12: mise au point. A Response to T.J.A. LeGoff." *The Canadian Historical Review.* June 1975.

Parker, W.H. "A Revolution in the Agricultural Geography of Lower Canada, 1833-1838." *Revue canadienne de géographie.* December 1957.

Ratner, Sidney, James H. Soltow and Richard Sylla. *The Evolution of the American Economy: Growth, Welfare and Decision Making.* New York: Basic Books, 1979.

Séguin, Maurice. *La "Nation Canadienne" et l'agriculture (1760-1850). Essai d'histoire économique.* Trois-Rivières: Le Boréal Express Ltée, 1970.

Séguin, Normand. "L'agriculture de la Mauricie et du Québec, 1850-1950." *Revue d'histoire de l'Amérique française.* March 1982.

Tucker, Gilbert N. *The Canadian Commercial Revolution 1845-1851.* Toronto: McClelland and Stewart Ltd., 1964.

7

Money and Banking

The growth of production and exchange in Lower Canada created a demand for reliable exchange media. The issue of debt instruments that served as money became one of the primary functions of early banking institutions. The banks originated as an appendage of the international and interregional trade sector and the practice of retaining savings in the form of bank deposits was generally restricted to densely populated commercial centres. Banking developed as an enclave-type activity with bankers manifesting little interest in the small lenders and borrowers that predominated the rural economy. Funds that entered the banking system were channeled to borrowers whose collateral and financial reputations proved acceptable to the bankers. As profit maximizers, bankers sought the highest rate of return possible for their shareholders. Given the institutional environment created by the State, this profit-maximizing behavior may have led to a net flow of funds out of the province during the slow growth periods of the nineteenth century.

This chapter examines money and the growth of financial intermediation after the Conquest and suggests how the State affected the monetary system, financial intermediaries, and the development of a domestic capital market. Unfortunately, the entire subject of inflation must be left aside because no general price index is available for the years prior to 1900. The discussion of financial intermediaries focuses on banking institutions owing to the small role played by non-bank financial intermediaries before 1850.

The slow growth of financial intermediaries appears to have

impeded savings, investment, and real income growth in the colonial economy. However, the growth rate of banking and other forms of financial intermediation was a result of, as well as a contributing factor to, the fragmented nature of colonial markets: the two were mutually interdependent phenomena. The relative price of any given commodity or service varied from one region to another owing to imperfections in the flow of information and high interregional transport costs. Considerable dispersion in both private and social rates of return ensued. Improvement in the efficiency of markets, the capital market in particular, was an important aspect of colonial economic development. Growth in the real stock of money was a necessary complement to domestic capital formation. Unfortunately, the British government never developed an overall plan for a colonial monetary system. The monetary and banking system that emerged by the middle of the nineteenth century resulted from piecemeal legislative innovations introduced by trial and error.

Money in the Post-Conquest Era

The usefulness of money as a financial instrument depends on the public's willingness to retain it. During the French regime, metropolitan currency was employed as the unit of account in the colony but diverse monetary instruments were accepted as media of exchange. Various metal currencies, card money, bills of exchange (metropolitan government credit notes), and merchants' promissory notes all contributed to the aggregate money stock. In October 1759, after the capture of Quebec City, the French Crown suspended repayment of the bills of exchange outstanding in the colony. Since most of the colony's paper money was payable in bills of exchange (that were, in principle, redeemable in metal currency), this action removed the colony's paper currency from the gold standard. But it did not undermine the utility of existing paper monies as media of exchange as long as Quebecers continued to accept them. A month later, however, Brigadier Murray outlawed the use of all paper money in the British occupied regions of the colony and in September 1760 the ban was extended to Montreal.

The British government's hostility towards paper money was not exclusive to that of the newly conquered colony in the St. Lawrence Valley. The parliament in London prohibited the use of paper currency in private transactions throughout its New England colonies in 1751.[1] In Quebec, the ban was not entirely enforceable. Paper money issued during the French regime continued to circulate in private transactions until about 1771 when the French government finally renounced its scheme for partial redemption. As indicated in Chapter 4, the entire episode involving the issue and abolition of paper money resulted in a net welfare loss to the colonists. Many Quebecers remained suspicious of paper money for decades to come.[2]

The progressive disappearance of paper money gradually removed a substantial component of the colony's aggregate money supply. Following the suspension of paper money as legal tender in 1759-1760, the colony experienced a currency shortage comparable to that of the 1720s. As before, colonists resorted to paper money substitutes: British Sterling, Spanish currency from the West Indies, and commodity money. French metal currency that had previously served chiefly as a savings instrument also appeared in economic transactions. The net reduction in the nominal money supply apparently exercised a downward pressure on the general price level. No comprehensive price index is available, but prices of the colony's principal agricultural products decreased by some 50 to 80 percent between 1760 and 1766. (Ouellet, p. 54)

To reduce the transaction costs associated with a monetary system consisting of several currencies, Brigadier Murray published tables of equivalence (official exchange rates) for the colony in November 1759. Henceforth, Quebec City operated on a bimetallic monetary standard, that is, fixed exchange rates with gold and silver coins available, in principle, at the published rates. In the hope of solving the problem of metal currency shortage, Murray rated all currencies in British pounds, shilling and pence using exchange rates current in Nova Scotia and Massachusetts (known as 'Halifax currency'). But Amherst, the commander-in-chief of British forces in America, established somewhat different exchange rates for Montreal in September 1760 based on rates current in New York (known as 'York currency'). Merchants and administrators soon began arbitraging between Montreal and Quebec City. French currency, which was relatively undervalued in New York and Montreal, disappeared from circulation in the Montreal area. The difference in exchange rates between Quebec City and Montreal induced a currency flow toward Quebec City that intensified Montreal's shortage of small change until the official rate for French currency in Montreal was increased in July 1762.

Governor Murray's administration published a single list of official exchange rates for the province of Quebec in September 1764 to take effect at the beginning of the following year.[3] The Murray administration designated British, French, Spanish, Portuguese, Mexican and German currencies as legal tender and rated them in terms of British Sterling. The new rates more closely approximated those in New York with the exception of French coins. French coinage was rated more highly than in New York as a sign of conciliation toward the defeated colonists and as an inducement to encourage the use of French coins as a medium of exchange. Overvaluation was the traditional remedy for a currency shortage, designed to attract the overvalued coins into circulation. But those Montreal merchants actively involved in trading with the American colonies, where French currency was less valued, resisted the imposition of the official rate for French coins. According to Ouellet, many Quebecers ignored official exchange rates in favor of black market rates more in keeping with real opportunity costs.

The American invasion of Quebec in 1775 ruptured commercial relations between Montreal and New York. Two years later, the colonial government realigned exchange rates so they corresponded with 'Halifax currency' values. An exception was made for French coins which were overvalued in relation to the Halifax rates. French and Spanish silver coins accounted for most of the metal currency in the province. Silver ceased to be legal tender in Britain for settlements of more than twenty-five pounds in 1774 and the resulting premium accorded to gold coins encouraged its use in transactions with the metropole. Consequently, gold coin became a scarce medium in the colony. In fact, the hazards of wartime discouraged the export of any British currency from the British Isles. Quebec became a repository for a variety of foreign coins, often in a state of decomposition, that were refused elsewhere.

Throughout the American War of Independence (1776-1783), British military spending exercised an important influence on the demand for marketed goods and services, the demand for money, and foreign exchange rates. The colonial agents of the British government's contractors in London supplied banking services to local merchants and military officers. These agents provided the liquidity necessary to accommodate the increase in domestic economic activity by accepting bills of exchange (promissory notes) issued by colonial merchants.

Although bills of exchange did not acquire the status of legal tender, they circulated as metal currency substitutes. Promissory notes issued by colonial merchants, also called *bons* as in "bon pour...", continued in use after the war. An anonymous writer made the following observation in 1792:

> During the War with America, the Expenses of Government at these [frontier military] posts, made more money necessary, and the princi-

pal trading house at each Post, having just given ample Security for the Payment of their Bills in Montreal, furnished the necessary supply. Other Houses afterwards took a share in this, till within these two years, it was understood that security of responsible houses in Montreal was necessary to render any paper Money Current. Since that time everybody has become a Banker. From the King's Receiver General to the Sergeant Major of the Rangers, from the first Commercial houses to the person who retails drams. Everybody makes Money. As to security that is not now thought of. In a payment the other day of twenty-five pounds I received the Bills of twelve different persons; To realize this by a draft on Montreal would require an application to as many different people, some at Detroit, some of York, some of the Lord Knows where.[4]

The growing array of coins and debt instruments in circulation constituted a burden on economic exchange in the colony. The filing and 'sweating' (chemical reduction) of gold and silver coins diminished their intrinsic worth. Because paper currency was not sanctioned as legal tender, the real value of merchants' notes was often uncertain. The variety of discount rates for paper added to the costs of making economic transactions. In rural areas there appears to have been frequent recourse to barter exchange.

Merchants in Lower Canada complained about the lack of currency throughout the two decades preceding the War of 1812. However, according to Ouellet, most agricultural prices nearly doubled between 1792-1793 and 1802, and again between 1802 and 1812. (Ouellet, p. 170) If these price increases are reflective of changes in the general price level of the colony, then it would appear that the nominal money supply was growing at a much faster rate than the marketed supply of goods and services. The monetary problem at the time was therefore one of quality (ie. confidence and security) as well as quantity. Debased metal coins and paper notes of uncertain value undermined the population's confidence in the monetary system. Institutional innovations to increase the efficiency of money and financial intermediation offered potential returns to all those involved in colonial economic exchange.

Early Banking Experiments

The large importing and exporting merchants often extended informal banking services to their customers. In 1792 three fur trading companies published notice of their intent to establish formal banking operations in Montreal.[5] To be named the 'Canada Banking Company', the principals would receive deposits, issue bank notes in exchange for such deposits, and discount merchants' notes. One of the desired results of the bank project was to reduce the transaction costs of economic exchange by setting standards for the vast array of paper monies in circulation. But the proposed company failed to obtain a bank charter from the Lower Canadian legislature, and the project ended in failure.

In 1793-1794 the legislature attempted to reduce some of the uncertainty surrounding colonial transactions by enacting legislation to regulate the negotiation of merchants' promissory notes. In legislating provisions relating to liability at maturity, endorsement and transfer of endorsement, the legislature improved the definition of contractual rights and obligations pertaining to paper money. The circulation of debased gold and silver coins continued, however, to impede economic exchange in the colony. As well as complicating economic transactions at home, decomposed coins were often unacceptable in transactions abroad. To improve the efficiency of metal currency, the legislature introduced several innovations in 1796. Official exchange rates were adjusted and the American dollar became legal tender in Lower Canada. To discourage the filing and sweating of coins, currencies denoted as legal tender were rated in terms of their weight. As of June 1797, all gold coins were valued exclusively in terms of their weight and karat rating. In any system involving fixed exchange rates, currency ratings must be adjusted periodically to accommodate structural changes in the balance of international payments and in 1808 the prevailing exchange rates were again revised to reflect changes in the composition of the colony's foreign trade. (See Chapter 8)

The project to obtain a legislative charter for the 'Canada Bank' in 1808 is another example of an innovation aimed at refinement of the monetary system. The wording of the legislation introduced to create this bank closely resembled the charter granted to the Bank of the United States in 1792. The Bank of the United States (1792-1811) was a hybrid institution that operated like any privately owned bank: receiving deposits and issuing bank notes. However, the United States government owned a part of the bank and served as its most important client. The Bank of the United States held government tax receipts, paid government bills, and made loans to the government at interest. Unlike the state-chartered banks, the Bank of the United States was authorized to operate branches throughout the nation. Indeed, it became a net creditor to most of the other banks, in other words, a sort of bankers' bank. When legislation was presented to introduce a similar kind of institution to Lower Canada, however, it was opposed and rejected as premature. Even so, the discussion surrounding the proposal served to inform the public about the principles of financial intermediation and helped to pave the way for the creation of banking institutions a decade later.

The economic advantages of granting the status of legal tender to paper money became apparent during the War of 1812. Although the British government employed the Pound Sterling as a unit of account in colonial affairs, Spanish dollars had been used to pay the troops stationed in Canada for some time. The outbreak of war with the United States rendered the trans-Atlantic shipment of specie precarious. To permit the financing of military expenditures in the colony, the legislature enacted the Army Bill Act in August 1812. The Army Bill Act outlawed the import and export of gold and silver coins for a five year period and authorized the Governor of Lower Canada, as Commander of the Army, to issue 'Army Bills' in the form of paper dollars. The bills were redeemable in coinage or bills of exchange on London at the Army Bill Office in Quebec City. Bills in small denominations prevailed; bills valued at \$25.00 or more carried interest at 6.1 percent per annum. By the end of the war, the value of Army Bills amounted to £1 249 000 (1£ = \$4). The legislature repealed the provisions relating to the export and import of specie in January 1817, and arranged for the redemption of all bills over the next four years. The Army Bill Office finally closed in December 1820.

The successful control and widespread acceptance of Army Bills demonstrated the advantages of legally sanctioned paper currency. The bills provided a close substitute for coins as a medium of exchange and a store of value. Legislative control over the bill issue prevented the total volume of money in circulation from rapidly outgrowing the demand for real cash balances. The public's confidence in paper money induced efforts by Lower Canadian merchants to imitate the Army Bill experience through the creation of financial intermediaries with note-issuing privileges. In this way, the monetary innovations that occurred during the War of 1812 contributed to the development of Lower Canadian banking institutions.

The Creation of a Banking System

Financial intermediation concerns the transfer of funds from surplus to deficit units in the economy. The issue of exchange media, such as bank notes, can be taken as a defining characteristic of 'banks' as opposed to other financial intermediaries. As an early form of financial intermediary, banks served the nascent capital market by accepting deposits for safekeeping and lending a proportion of bank funds to credit-worthy borrowers. In this process banks accepted 'primary securities', such as merchants' *bons*, that were the liabilities of ultimate borrowers, and created 'indirect securities', such as bank stocks, deposits, and bank notes, that became their own liabilities. Bank notes gradually multiplied to become an important component of the colonial money supply. The growth of financial intermediation may be attributed to the expansion of colonial economic activity, the growth of export income per capita, changes in the capital/output ratio, institutional innovations involving external financing by firms, and a rise in the demand for real money balances throughout the economy. Financial intermediation by the banks and other institutions improved the efficiency of the colonial capital market by reducing the cost of funds transfer from lenders to borrowers.

When Lower Canada's first bank opened in November 1817, it did so as a limited-liability company without a corporate banking charter. The articles of association that created the 'Montreal Bank' (later renamed the 'Bank of Montreal') derived directly from the unsuccessful legislation of 1808 and the 1791 charter of the Bank of the United States. Half of the Montreal Bank's stock had to be sold in the United States for want of subscribers in Lower Canada. The bank's notes were denominated in dollars. The Quebec Bank and Bank of Canada, both formed in 1818, modelled their articles of association upon those of the Montreal Bank. For this reason, Lower Canadian banking may be said to have had its origins in the post-revolutionary plans for a branch banking system in the United States.

All three Lower Canadian banks operated without banking charters until their incorporation by the legislature in 1822. The Bank of Montreal's charter authorized the bank to carry out the usual intermediary functions: to receive deposits, to issue promissory notes, and to deal in bills of exchange and other debt instruments at a discount. Although the charter did not specifically authorize bank branches, the new bank practiced multiple branch banking. The bank's charter forbid the bank from dealing in real estate, from mortgage lending or lending to foreign governments, and from exceeding the going interest rate ceiling on loans of 6 percent. To promote confidence in the banking system, the charter provided for stiff penalties to anyone convicted of theft, forgery, or counterfeiting.

The Bank of Montreal's charter limited the issue of bank notes by specifying that the bank's total debts (excluding deposits) could not exceed an amount equal to three times the value of its paid up capital stock. Although no minimum cash reserve requirements were imposed, the charter did oblige the bank to redeem its notes in specie on demand. The fear of a run initiated by depositors or

Table 7.1

**CASH RESERVE RATIO OF THE BANK OF MONTREAL,
1824-1841**
(Pounds Sterling)

Date	(1) Cash Deposits	(2) Bank Notes in Circulation	(3) Cash Reserves	(4) Reserve Ratio (3)÷[(1)+(2)]
1824 (Jan. 8)	96 809	92 727	102 300	0.54
1825 (Feb. 6)	105 518	137 580	65 109	0.27
1826 (Jan. 31)	142 555	133 005	99 511	0.36
1828 (Dec. 1)	94 785	148 039	72 808	0.30
1830 (Feb. 18)	111 643	178 552	80 164	0.28
1831 (Feb. 14)	139 285	223 558	98 513	0.27
1834 (Jan. 18)	184 882	227 439	73 870	0.18
1837 (June 1)	234 776	180 692	68 811	0.17
1841 (July 1)	234 686	227 048	125 175	0.27

The Canadian Banking System, 1817-1890, pp. 39, 52, 121, by Roeliff M. Breck-enridge. New York: Macmillan & Co., 1895.

another bank helps to explain why cash reserves stood at a high level in the early years. (See Table 7.1)

The reserve ratio declined as Lower Canadian bankers and the public gained more experience in banking operations. This decline in the reserve ratio corresponded to an increase in the total paper money supply. By the mid-1830s the cash reserve ratio in Lower Canada approximated that prevailing in the United States. (cf. Lee and Passell, p. 119)

The usury provision that appeared in all of the early bank charters reinforced a 6 percent interest rate ceiling introduced by the metropolitan government that had regulated commercial transactions in the colony since 1777. The usury regulations remained law until the 1850s, but it seems they were rarely enforced. By discounting a promissory note at the outset, for example, the effective rate of return to the lender could be raised. According to Neufeld, the usury regulations encouraged the banks to deal in foreign bills. With a foreign bill, the banks were able to make a return on the foreign exchange transaction as well as the discount. By the late 1820s, the Bank of Montreal was active in the loosely regulated financial markets in the United States through the bank's office in New York.

Government regulation of the early chartered banks in Lower Canada seldom extended beyond the provisions in each bank's charter. Since most charters were modelled on principles determined by the founders of the Bank of Montreal, rather than the legislature, the charters failed to provide adequate protection to the public.[6] Financial statements were not required unless specifically requested by the legislature. Restrictions written into the charters did not specify penalties for non-compliance except in the case of serious crimes involving theft or forgery. Nothing prevented the directors of a bank from receiving bank loans. By the winter of 1830-1831, the directors of the Quebec and Montreal Banks were liable, directly or indirectly, for more than a third of the banks' debts. (Breckenridge, 1895, p. 41) As the legislature and the banking public gained more knowledge and experience in banking transactions, however, some of the loopholes arising from uncertainty and misinformation were tightened. When the charter of a bank expired, as did the Bank of Montreal's in 1831, various provisions were revised before renewal so as to render the banking system more efficient.

The advent of commercial banking widened the array of currencies in use. Despite the British government's attempts to establish the Pound Sterling as the unit of account in all British colonies, the dollar functioned as the nominal standard in Lower Canada. Spanish, Mexican, British and American coins, often in poor physical condition, continued to circulate as media of exchange. French coins were frequently used in economic transactions, but they had no status as legal tender outside of Lower Canada.[7] By an act of the colonial legislature in 1830, the chartered banks were given a monopoly on the issue of paper money in denominations of less than $5 (£1.5s). When, in the same year, the legislature renewed the Bank of Montreal's charter, the total value of notes in circulation of denominations less than $5 was limited to one-fifth of the bank's paid up capital. This kind of limitation on paper money ensured a continuing demand for metal currency.

The Bank of Montreal and the Quebec Bank operated as commercial banks. Shareholders provided their single most important source of funds. (See Table 7.2) The commercial banks supplied bank notes and demand deposit services to firms involved in international and interregional trade, primarily to finance inventories. Because the commercial banks did not pay interest on deposits, several savings banks appeared in the shadow of the larger commercial banks to provide interest-bearing deposit services to small savers. The Savings Bank of Montreal began operations in Montreal in 1819 and was followed two years later by the Quebec Savings Bank in Quebec City. The savings banks relied

Table 7.2

CAPITAL STOCK, DEPOSIT AND BANK NOTE LIABILITIES OF THE BANK OF MONTREAL AS A PROPORTION OF TOTAL SELECTED LIABILITIES, 1824-1841
(Percentages)

Date	Capital Stock Paid Up	Deposits	Bank Notes in Circulation
1824 (Jan. 8)	49.7	25.7	24.6
1825 (Feb. 6)	43.5	24.5	32.0
1826 (Jan. 31)	40.5	30.8	28.7
1828 (Dec. 1)	46.4	20.9	32.7
1830 (Feb. 18)	44.9	21.2	33.9
1831 (Feb. 14)	40.8	22.7	36.5
1834 (Jan. 18)	37.7	27.9	34.3
1837 (June 1)	37.6	35.3	27.2
1841 (July 1)	52.0	24.4	23.6

The Canadian Banking System, 1817-1890, pp. 39, 52, 121, by Roeliff M. Breckenridge. New York: Macmillan & Co., 1895.

entirely upon savings deposits for their funds; they did not issue capital stock or bank notes. Savings banks were often considered 'charitable' institutions because of their reliance on voluntary management and their preoccupation with the welfare of small asset holders. In 1832, the Lower Canadian legislature enacted a law to regulate the nature of financial reporting by savings banks. The law prevented the payment of fees to bank trustees and established a ceiling of £50 on the total value of individual deposits. The trustee savings banks generally invested their funds in securities, including bank stocks, issued in the province.

During the mid-1830s, three new chartered banking institutions appeared in Montreal to challenge the regional monopoly on commercial banking services exercised by the Bank of Montreal. The City Bank of Montreal obtained a legislative charter in 1833 and two years later, the banking firm of Viger, DeWitt et Cie, known as the *Banque du Peuple*, began operations as a co-partnership without a bank charter. As an unincorporated company, the *Banque du Peuple* was not permitted to sue, to be sued, or to engage in certain banking activities reserved to the chartered banks. The Bank of British North America, founded by British investors, also opened a branch in Montreal in 1838. It operated as a private banking firm with a royal charter granted in Britain until its incorporation by colonial legislation in 1840.

A number of non-bank financial intermediaries appeared in Lower Canada during the mid-1830s. Fire insurance had been advertised in the colony since at least the 1790s; in 1804 the Phoenix Company of London opened an office in Montreal. The Quebec Fire Assurance Company, which began operations as a general insurance company in 1818, constituted the first indigeneous intermediary of this type. But fire and casualty companies provided a very modest source of savings before Confederation. Because their policies provided protection against specific types of risk, the total annual value of premiums was not large. Insurance companies invested funds in a small quantity of financial assets and their net contribution to the capital market was therefore limited.

Small open economies operating on a fixed exchange rate system are sensitive to economic conditions that affect their major trading partners. The financial crisis of 1837 appears to have spread to Lower Canada from the United States and Great Britain. The origins of the crisis have been variously attributed to the British government's attempt to conserve specie by raising domestic interest rates in 1836, President Andrew Jackson's order to the United States Public Land Office in August of the same year to accept payments on frontier land transactions in specie only, and a loss of confidence in the American banking system accompanied by reduced public willingness to use paper currency in lieu of coins. (Lee and Passell, pp. 115-122) In May 1837, a financial panic induced American banks to suspend redemption of their notes for gold.

In comparison to many of the state-chartered institutions in the United States, the Lower Canadian banks enjoyed a reputation of relative stability at this time. Lower Canadian bank notes circulated in the United States effectively permitting the banks to borrow capital from American citizens. The demand for metal coins that followed the suspension of specie payments across the border resulted in a specie outflow from Lower Canada. In the apparent belief that this capital movement would undermine the stability of the monetary system, the banks, led by the Bank of Montreal, suspended specie payments one week after suspension occurred in the United States. As permitted by their charters, the banks acted without legal notice or the consent of the legislature.

The suspension of specie payments in Lower Canada lasted until June 1838. It was reintroduced by government ordinance for the period November 1838 to June 1839 as a result of renewed political unrest. Both periods of suspension produced contractions in the money supply. The interest rate on loans in specie increased to as much as 13 percent; the discount rate on suspended bank paper increased as well. (Breckenridge, 1895, p. 30) The shortage of currency resulted in a return to the use of merchants' *bons* and promissory notes. In addition, the incidence of bank note fraud increased and the legislature consequently introduced an ordinance that required unincorporated banks to obtain a license to issue paper currency in denominations of less than £5. The measure was designed to prevent fly-by-night operators from issuing irredeemable notes during the period of specie payments suspension. In contrast to banking history in the United States, none of the banks in Lower Canada failed during this period.

The Union of the Canadas

Until 1841 the currency and banking laws of Lower Canada evolved separately from those of Upper Canada. The union of the Canadas under one legislative body required the creation of a uniform monetary system in the two provinces. To this end, the Currency Bill of 1841 established a single set of exchange rates and reduced the number of coins acceptable as legal tender. Since all silver coins lost their status as legal tender, the market value of pre-revolutionary French silver coinage diminished to the level of its intrinsic worth. This resulted in a loss of net wealth to some Lower Canadians. The declassification of silver coins intensified the demand for small change and the Lower Canadian banks responded by issuing their own copper coins.

As a means of introducing greater uniformity into the currency system, and of raising additional government revenue, the newly appointed Governor-General of Canada, Lord Sydenham, proposed the creation of a government agency to exercise sole responsibility for the creation of paper money. As outlined in August 1841, the proposal involved the issue of paper currency in a fixed amount yearly with net revenues accruing to the government. In this way the paper money supply would be insulated from macroeconomic fluctuations that affected the chartered banks' note issues. Deposit, discounting, and foreign currency exchange servicing would remain the preserve of financial intermediaries in the private sector.

The Sydenham project for the central bank was defeated in the face of opposition from the chartered banks. The issue of paper money was a profitable activity for them.[8] Cash deposits did not play a sufficiently large role in total liabilities to allow the commercial bank to forego the issue of bank notes as a source of funds. (See

Table 7.2) Furthermore, argued the banks, a chartered bank had never failed in the Canadas, none had defaulted on its notes, and the flexibility provided by the bank note system was required to meet the seasonal business cycles characteristic of staple export economies.[9] Opposition to the Sydenham plan also developed because of its implications for the centralization of economic and political power in the colony. In lieu of the plan for a note-issuing agency as a source of government revenue, the legislature placed a tax of one percent per annum on the monthly average of bank notes in circulation.

Prior to the Act of Union, the Lower Canadian banks were not permitted to open offices to service banking needs in Upper Canada.[10] In 1841 the Union government enacted legislation to remove this limitation. The progressive standardization of regulations contained in all new and revised bank charters further contributed to the integration of provincial capital markets in the 1840s. With the rise of the wheat staple in Canada West, profitable importing and exporting opportunities abounded. The Montreal-based charter banks consequently extended their operations into the prosperous wheat exporting regions. In the belief that chartered banks failed to adequately service the Francophone community in Quebec, a number of banking institutions moved to fill the gap. Viger, DeWitt et Cie successfully applied for a corporate charter as the *Banque du Peuple* in 1843. An application for a legislative charter from the *Banque des Marchands* was approved in 1846.

Although the chartered banks were the largest financial intermediaries serving the capital market in Montreal and Quebec City, they were not the only ones. Numerous sectors of the market remained untapped and these opportunities were gradually exploited by specialized institutions. In a rural economy, such as that in the St. Lawrence Valley, land constituted the most valuable asset. But the legislature prohibited the chartered banks from mortgage lending. Long term financing by the banks was consequently a rarity. The chartered banks specialized in the short term servicing of international and interregional trade, that is, the issue of bank notes (an interest-free source of funds), the discount of commercial paper, and foreign exchange dealing.[11] The net rate of return on small savings deposits was not deemed profitable enough for them, and consequently, savings banks serviced this sector. Only when the federal government entered the market for paper money by issuing its own notes after Confederation did the chartered banks break into the savings deposit sector in a serious way.

With the Savings Bank Act of 1841, the Union government

attempted to standardize the regulations pertaining to trustee savings banks. The rapid growth of the Montreal Provident and Savings Bank between its opening in October 1841 and its foreclosure in 1848 indicates the extent to which the commercial banks failed to provide services to many depositors in the 1840s. As it happens, the Montreal Provident and Savings Bank was plagued with problems related to the nature of government regulation and the bank's own operating principles. The legal ceiling on the value of individual deposits was consistently violated by the bank: wealthy individuals, as well as low and middle income earners, found that interest-bearing savings deposits served their portfolio needs. The bank then invested in a wide range of securities, many ineligible under the Savings Bank Act, and ventured into the field of personally secured loans without adequate security or interest payment supervision. The early savings banks operated in a casual manner that reflected their voluntary, 'charitable' orientation and their need for adjustment in line with more rigorous management principles.

Perhaps Quebec savings banks learned from this experience. Of the three savings banks formed in Quebec in the 1840s, two of them, the *Banque d'Epargne* / Montreal City and District Savings Bank (May 1846), and the *Caisse d'Economie de Notre-Dame de Quebec* (May 1848) have survived, in one form or another, to the present day. But no new entrants appeared after mid-century. The abolition of trustee provisions and a substantial increase in the minimum capital requirements for new banks, as prescribed in the Savings Bank Act of 1855, raised the barriers of entry to the savings deposit market. A year later, the Bank of Montreal entered the scene by purchasing the Savings Bank of Montreal. In the 1860s the Union government enacted special legislation to remove the deposit ceiling for the *Banque d'Epargne* and the *Caisse d'Economie de Notre-Dame de Quebec*, and to allow the savings banks to make collateral loans to individuals.

The absence of new entrants to the savings deposit market after 1848 is also attributable to the competition provided by a new form of financial intermediary, the building society. Up to this time, members of the legal profession often acted as brokers in the market for mortgage credit. In 1845 the Montreal Building Society incorporated to become the first financial institution to service the mortgage market directly. Neufeld identifies several ways in which the building society competed with savings banks in the market for funds. "This competitor appealed to the small saver with overtones of charity, it pioneered the marvellous innovation of the contractual savings payment, it gave the saver a definite purpose for saving (the purchase of a house), and it could take full advantage of that important instrument, the real estate mortgage." (Neufeld, 1972, p. 151) As required by legislation in 1846, building societies became limited liability corporations belonging to twenty members or more. An important provision in the act permitted the societies to side-step existing usury laws. However, as temporary institutions, building societies were limited to one source of funds—an instalment system for share payment. The transition from temporary to permanent building societies did not occur until the legislation of 1846 was overhauled in 1859. The subsequent growth of building societies was related to the growth of capital formation in the form of non-residential construction and housing. Building societies appear to have played a more limited role in Quebec than in Ontario.

Money and Banking at Mid-Century

Subsequent to the rejection of the Sydenham plan for a central bank in 1841, the Union government successfully experimented with the issue of its own paper currency in the late 1840s. Designed as a source of revenue, the currency appeared in the form of 'debentures' in denominations of less than £10. The debentures came due in one year and carried an interest rate of 6 percent. Though not legal tender in private transactions, the debentures were payable on demand at the Treasury and accepted in payment of debts to the government (such as import duties). The chartered banks vigorously opposed the government's right to issue the notes and, after two years of experimentation, the issue was terminated in 1850. A government issue, in the name of the banks, reappeared under the provisions of the Free Banking Act of 1850. This aspect of the act proved to be of little consequence and it was repealed in 1866. In the same year the Union government signed an agreement with the Bank of Montreal, the government's financial agent, to take responsibility for the bank's note issue. The Provincial Notes Act of 1866 marked the beginning of a renewed effort to substitute a government-issued paper currency for chartered bank notes that continued after Confederation.

In the late 1830s, the structure of the banking industry in the United States had begun to change dramatically. As of 1838, free banking laws in New York and Michigan permitted the creation of new state banks with relative ease. By filing a notice of intent with the Secretary of State, any group of citizens could establish a new bank. The more restrictive procedure of obtaining a charter by legislative act was gradually abandoned throughout the United States. The ease of entry into the banking industry led to a dramatic increase in the number of banks in the United States and the aggregate size of the American commercial banking sector. In the Canadas, however, the banking system retained the practice of legislative charters and branch banking by a select few. The economic and political integration imposed by the Act of Union and the homogenization of banking regulations in the Canadas gave new life to the chartered banking system in Lower Canada. In 1841 this system comprised three charter banks and a small number of savings and private banks. In the United States, there were more than nine hundred banks by this time.

The Union government experimented with free banking in 1850 by enacting legislation along the lines of the free banking act in New York State. Individuals, general partners, or joint-stock companies could organize a bank to be operated at a single location provided they raise at least £25 000 ($100 000). To issue bank notes, bonds of at least this amount had to be deposited with the Receiver-General of the Canadas. The bank notes would then be printed by the government in the bank's name. In contrast to American practice, the Union government made no effort to phase out the system of commercial banking by charter. On the contrary, chartered banks did not have to meet the deposit minimum imposed upon the free banks. Of the three banks that met the requirements of the free banking act by 1855, all abandoned their status as free banks upon obtaining legislative charters. In 1880 the Free Banking Act was finally repealed.

* * *

Institutional innovations in the monetary system contributed to the growth of per capita income and wealth in Lower Canada. The increase in the use of money reduced uncertainty, the length of transaction chains, and the variance of price ratios that characterized economic exchange. By lowering transaction costs, the use of money encouraged specialization and the development of the market system.

In prevailing monetary theory, real money balances and all other financial assets are usually considered as substitutes. An increase in the aggregate holdings of one decreases the aggregate holdings of the other. In the economy of Lower Canada, however, no clear distinction can be drawn between the two. A wide array of debt instruments made important contributions to the production process as media of exchange. Growth in the use of paper currency also resulted in the creation of note-issuing financial intermediaries. Although the chartered banks rarely financed fixed capital formation, the gains from monetization of the economy almost certainly outweighed any losses from substitution between savings in the form of money balances and investment in physical capital.

The net impact of the usury laws on the functioning of the capital market in Lower Canada is difficult to estimate. The laws were imperfectly and unevenly enforced. Not all credit passed through the organized capital market. Because of their high public profile and financial reporting procedures, the banks may have found the laws more difficult to evade than did private capitalists and other intermediaries. (Neufeld, 1972, p. 545) In the desire to maximize the rate of return on their funds, the commercial banks turned to foreign exchange markets and the servicing of foreign trade.[12] Rapid economic growth in the neighboring United States also made the American capital market attractive. According to Bray Hammond, "By about 1857 or a little later the Bank of Montreal was larger than any American bank and probably the largest and most powerful transactor in the New York money market." (Hammond, p. 167) In 1858 the 6 percent ceiling on loans was raised to 7 percent for financial institutions and removed altogether in the case of most private contracts. The ceiling provision for financial institutions was dropped in 1867, though the banks remained unable to use the judicial system to recover interest payments exceeding 7 percent. It may be that the usury laws played as important a role in determining the "conservative" lending policies of the banks in Lower Canada as the concentrated structure of the banking industry itself.[13]

NOTES

[1]Colonial American paper money retained its status as legal tender in transactions with government, but the life of colonial government financial instruments was restricted to two years. The British Parliament's Currency Act of 1764 extended the restrictions on paper money to the remaining American colonies and (unsuccessfully) outlawed paper money in transactions with colonial governments as well.

[2]The excessive issue of paper money during the American War of Independence resulted in a similar suspicion of paper money in the United States.

[3]Duties on imports into Quebec remained payable according to exchange rates prevailing in England.

[4]*Select Documents in Canadian Economic History*, *1783-1885*, p. 369, by Harold A. Innis and A.R.M. Lower, eds., © 1933.

[5]The associated companies were Phyn, Ellis & Inglis of London, and Todd, McGill & Co. and Forsyth, Richardson & Co., both of Montreal.

[6]In their first few years of operation, all of the banks appear to have overextended themselves. The Bank of Montreal registered heavy losses primarily through its financing of timber merchants in Quebec City and Montreal. The

American-owned Bank of Canada effectively ceased operations in 1824 and its charter was not renewed in 1831.

[7]In addition to French coins minted before the Revolution of 1789, French coins minted in the post-revolutionary era became legal tender in Lower Canada in 1818.

[8]"As an economy grows, so does the demand for money. If the nominal money supply is fixed, this leads to deflation and appreciation in the stock of real cash balances. The real resources tied up in the increase in the stock of real balances, referred to as growth seigniorage, can be captured by the issue of new money. This money issue is a profitable economic activity. In addition, if money is a commodity then the real resources tied up in the commodity can be released by the substitution of a cheaper commodity paper." (*The Journal of Economic History*, p. 31 © March 1982, by Michael D. Bordo. Reprinted by permission.)

[9]The demand for money was greatest in the autumn and in the spring owing to the need to finance harvesting and transporting activities, and to meet the payment of duties on imported goods.

[10]The Bank of Montreal skirted the restriction by purchasing the 'Bank of the People' (not to be confused with *la Banque du Peuple*) and operating in Upper Canada under that name as of 1838.

[11]The commercial banks' preference for short term loans was not peculiar to the Canadas:
"The panic of 1837 and the depression of 1839-1842 placed considerable pressure on the banking system [in the United States], and the least liquid banks (those with the lowest reserve ratios) were placed under the heaviest pressure...For better or for worse, the experience of the 1840s convinced both bankers and the legislature that regulated their activities that long-term loans were "bad". In the 1840s that may have been so, but the policies that grew out of that period severely restrained the activities of the banks long after the conditions of the 1840s had disappeared. The 1840s were thus marked by a change in bank portfolios that saw banks' lending activities more and more restricted to short-term commercial credit. (*American Economic Growth: An Economist's History of the United States*, pp. 349-350, by Lance E. Davis, et al © 1972, by Harper & Row, Publishers, Inc. Reprinted by permission of the publisher).

[12]A financial analyst noted in the September 1859 issue of the *Canadian Merchants Magazine and Commercial Review*:

"[The] bank which has the largest number of exchange customers generally makes the most money. We have an instance of this in the Bank of Montreal, the most prosperous institution in the Province; its customers have been almost exclusively importing houses. The importers are generally men of good credit here and at home, the nature of the business requiring a fair amount of capital and credit...Now as the banks have always been limited by law to 6 per cent, and as money has generally been worth more than that rate, the banks to pay dividends that would be satisfactory to the stockholders, and offer inducements for further investments have been made it their particular business and interest to build up importing houses. (*The Financial System of Canada: Its Growth and Development*, pp. 545-546, by E.P. Neufeld. Reprinted by permission.)

[13]"Where loans are plentiful, high rates of interest for both lenders and

borrowers introduce the dynamism that one wants in development, calling forth new net saving and diverting investment from inferior uses so as to encourage technical improvement. In contrast, the common policy of maintaining low or negative rates of interest on financial assets and limited loan availability may accomplish neither. It is easy loans to small-scale enterprises that have low returns on existing investments. By comparison, established enclaves in export, or import-substitution, industries may seem more lucrative because of their historically freer access to domestic and foreign sources of external finance. However,... potential returns to the efficient deployment of finance in the indigeneous economy can be much higher than in the established enclaves. (*Money and Capital in Economic Development*, pp. 15-16, by Ronald I. McKinnon, reprinted by permission of The Brookings Institution.)

SELECT BIBLIOGRAPHY

Bordo, Michael D. "Monetary Innovation in America: Discussion." *The Journal of Economic History*. March 1982.

Breckenridge, Roeliff M. *The Canadian Banking System, 1817-1890*. New York: Macmillan & Co., 1895.

Breckenridge, Roeliff M. *The History of Banking in Canada*. Washington: Government Printing Office, 1910.

Davis, Lance E.,*et al. American Economic Growth: An Economist's History of the United States*. New York: Harper & Row, 1972.

Denison, Merrill. *Canada's First Bank: A History of the Bank of Montreal*. Toronto: McClelland and Stewart Ltd., 1966-67. 2 Vol.

Gwyn, Julian. "The Impact of British Military Spending on the Colonial American Money Markets, 1760-1783." *CHA Historical Papers*. Canadian Historical Association, 1980.

Hamelin, Jean and Yves Roby. *Histoire économique du Québec, 1851-1896*. Montreal: Editions Fides, 1971.

Hammond, Bray. "Banking in Canada before Confederation," in W.T. Easterbrook and M.H. Watkins, eds., *Approaches to Canadian Economic History*. Toronto: McClelland and Stewart Ltd., 1967.

Innis, Harold A. and A.R.M. Lower, eds. *Select Documents in Canadian Economic History, 1783-1885*. Toronto: University of Toronto Press, 1933.

Lee, Susan Previent and Peter Passell. *A New Economic View of American History*. New York: W.W. Norton & Co., 1979.

Marr, William L. and Donald G. Paterson. *Canada: An Economic History*. Toronto: Macmillan of Canada, 1980.

McIvor, R. Craig. *Canadian Monetary, Banking and Fiscal Development*. Toronto: Macmillan Co. of Canada, 1961.

McKinnon, Ronald I. *Money and Capital in Economic Development*. Washington: The Brookings Institution, 1973.

Neufeld, E.P. ed., *Money and Banking in Canada*. Toronto: McClelland and Stewart Ltd., 1964.

Neufeld, E.P. *The Financial System of Canada: Its Growth and Development.* Toronto: Macmillan of Canada, 1972.

Ouellet, Fernand. *Histoire économique et sociale du Québec, 1760-1850.* Montreal: Editions Fides, 1966.

Perkins, Edwin J. *The Economy of Colonial America.* New York: Columbia University Press, 1980.

Stevenson, James. "The Circulation of the Army Bills with some Remarks upon the War of 1812." *Transactions of the Literary and Historical Society of Quebec.* No. 21, 1891-2.

Stevenson, James. "The Currency of Canada after the Capitulation." *Transactions of the Literary and Historical Society of Quebec.* No. 12, 1876-7.

Tulchinsky, Gerald J.J. *The River Barons: Montreal Businessmen and the Growth of Industry and Transportation, 1837-53.* Toronto: University of Toronto Press, 1977.

8
Foreign Trade, Commerce and Transport

During the second half of the eighteenth century, the structure of the Quebec economy remained essentially unchanged. Quebec's comparative advantage in international trade remained about the same as before. Most export receipts flowed from the sale of fur pelts. The origin of imports and the destination of exports shifted in favor of the new metropole, but the composition of trade with Europe remained basically unaltered. Agricultural activity continued as the dominant sector in terms of aggregate output and employment.

At the beginning of the nineteenth century, an important restructuring of the colonial economy occurred. Fur pelt shipments from the St. Lawrence Valley declined and lumbering emerged as the primary source of Lower Canadian export receipts. By 1810 raw and manufactured forest products represented 75 percent of export value leaving the port of Quebec. The rise of the timber trade was not attributable to a new resource discovery or new patterns of consumption on the part of Quebecers. Timber cutting expanded as a result of relative price changes that altered the economic environment in the St. Lawrence Valley. The tariff reform that accompanied the revision of British colonial trade regulations induced capital and labor migration to the region. Technological innovations, such as the timber slide and the steam tug, also allowed for productivity increases. Continued increases in productivity raised profitability and contributed to the growth of the forest industries over time. While timber production expanded in Lower Canada and the Ottawa Valley, a wheat exporting region arose in the region now called southern Ontario.

ogether, these developments in the forestry and agricultural
ectors induced innovations in the banking and transport sectors.
This chapter will analyse changes in the volume and composition
f Quebec's foreign trade, and examine their effects on domestic
ommerce and transport.

The Navigation Laws

fter the Conquest, the British Navigation Laws regulated Que-
ec's international trade. Introduced with the Royal Proclamation
f 1763, the Navigation Laws replaced French mercantile restric-
ons of a similar kind. Quebecers were therefore obliged to adapt
 a new set of foreign trade regulations, in addition to the new
ystem of political and property rights. The Navigation Laws
nfluenced the volume and composition of colonial trade until
epealed by the British government in 1849.

The imperial government originally designed the Navigation
aws to tie American colonial trade to England by providing a
rotected economic environment for overseas market exchange.
nacted in the years 1651-1663, the Navigation Laws contained
ax incentives to encourage colonial specialization in the produc-
on of raw materials and a select number of processed goods. The
aws banned the colonial production of certain manufactured
ommodities such as wool textiles and fur hats. Exports of the
ost valuable colonial products, the 'enumerated' commodities,
ad to be shipped via English ports if they were destined for third
arty trading partners. The Navigation Laws also required most
nports originating outside the British empire to pass through
nglish ports. This regulation raised the transport costs of trade
xternal to the empire and provided a measure of protection for
nglish goods in the North American market. All international
ade was supposed to take place on British ships. The modern
merican literature on the Navigation Laws emphasizes, however,
iat the Laws were not consistently enforced during the American
olonial period.

The Navigation Laws embodied the general principles of British
nperial trade regulation and resulted in both costs and benefits to
olonial trading partners. After the British Conquest, the Naviga-
on Laws hampered Quebec's export merchants by obliging them
 sell to British buyers if they wished to remain in business. By the
ineteenth century, the Navigation Laws played a major role in the
ritish colonial system of protection of raw material imports and
strictions in favor of British and colonial owned ships.[1] Unfor-
inately, a detailed study of the overall burden of the Navigation

Laws for Quebec has never been undertaken. In a review of American literature on the impact of the Navigation Laws during the years 1763-1772, Susan Previent Lee and Peter Passell endorse the prevalent view that enforcement of the Laws had a relatively modest effect on colonial American welfare: at most, a 3 percent reduction in national income.

The Fur Trade

The fur trade continued to dominate Quebec's export sector during the first four decades after the Conquest. Many of the basic characteristics of the trade remained the same. The hunt for fur-bearing animals extended over a wide unsettled area in the north central and northwestern part of the continent. Canadian and American traders competed in the purchase of fur pelts, and shipments to Europe departed from American ports as well as the port of Quebec and the Hudson Bay posts. According to Fernand Ouellet, fur pelts represented 76 percent of the total value of Quebec's exports in 1770 and 51 percent in 1788. Almost all of these pelts came from regions west of the Ottawa River.

The rate of growth of fur trading activities by Quebec traders was regulated by British policy. Each change in the colony's institutional environment introduced new opportunities and constraints. Licencing and regulatory procedures applied in 1761, for instance, hampered Montreal merchants in their competition with entrepreneurs operating from Albany. Visits to Indian villages and the extension of credit, common practices among French speaking traders, were outlawed in favor of a more sedentary approach that obliged Indian hunters to travel to the trading posts. But this kind of favoritism faded as hostility developed between Britain and the American colonies. In 1768 the colonial administration in Quebec was granted the power to regulate the trade in accordance with the Montreal traders' demands.

As a result of the Royal Proclamation of 1763, the region west of the Appalachian Mountains and south of the Ottawa River became an Indian Reserve. The refusal of the British government to alienate land and permit agricultural settlement in this region created a protected fur trading environment. Aggregate fur pelt exports from the port of Quebec expanded until 1770. (See Table 8.1) Exports picked up again after the Quebec Act attached the lands west of the Appalachians to the administration at Quebec in 1774. During the American Revolutionary War period, aggregate fur pelt exports increased considerably as traders from Montreal filled the vacuum created by the suspension of American trading.

In the treaty of 1783, however, Britain abandoned the region south of the Great Lakes to the newly independent United States. Quebec traders subsequently encountered growing competition from American companies in this region. About the same time, Francophone outfitters, in the majority until the late 1770s, began to disappear from the North American fur trade.

During the years from 1774 to 1790, the average outlay per trading expedition increased as traders switched from transport by small canoe (*le canot du nord*) to large canoes (*le canot du maître*) and lake boats. The use of wilderness provision depots also expanded. As output increased, the industry gradually reorganized to achieve scale economies resulting in a reduction in the number of traders and trading companies. By 1790 the fur trade out of Montreal lay in the hands of a small group of capitalists associated with the North West Company.

Two phenomena characterized the spread of new techniques in the fur trade during the last quarter of the eighteenth century. One was the adoption of technologies that permitted economies of scale. The adoption of new transport methods that offered scale economies is usually attributed to an increase in unit transport costs associated with geographic expansion. The extension of the trade to the northwestern part of the continent raised the unit

Table 8.1

TOTAL FUR PELT EXPORTS FROM QUEBEC, 1764-1786, 1793

1764	215 422	1776	437 573
1765	223 210	1777	714 911
1766	247 155	1778	619 641
1767	249 546	1779	568 655
1768	351 348	1780	610 406
1769	430 497	1781	538 552
1770	347 305	1782	401 524
1771	366 303	1783	526 298
1772	378 746	1784	508 701
1773	466 702	1785	490 553
1774	417 707	1786	553 259
1775	574 230	1793	604 657

'Dualité Economique et changement technologique au Québec 1760-1790," by Fernand Ouellet, *Histoire Sociale*, pp. 259, 273, November 1976, reprinted by permission.

Chart 8.1

IMPORTS OF SQUARE TIMBER INTO GREAT BRITAIN

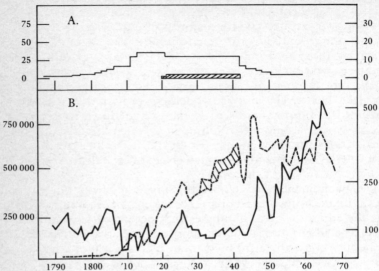

Imports of Square Timber into Great Britain from British North America and from the Baltic Countries before, during, and after the existence of the Differential Duties.

A. Scale of Duties
top line: from foreign countries
bottom line: from the colonies
left-hand scale: shillings per load
right-hand scale: dollars per
 thousand (M) board feet

B. Volume of Imports, 1789-1867:
 I from Baltic Countries
   (solid line)
 II from British North America
   (broken line)
 III wood other than pine
   (cross-hatched section)
left-hand scale: loads of 50 cubic feet
right-hand scale: board feet in
 millions

Great Britain's Woodyard: British America and the Timber Trade, 1763-1867, pp. 256, 259, by A.R.M. Lower, reprinted by permission of McGill-Queen's University Press.

costs of overland shipping and stimulated the search for cost-saving innovations. In an interesting argument, Ouellet attributes technological innovation in fur transport, not only to the search for economies of scale, but also to a change in the relative prices of capital and labor. The commercialization of Lower Canadian agriculture during the 1770s and 1780s, says Ouellet, raised average agricultural income and, consequently, the opportunity cost of labor in the fur trade. By this interpretation, the rise in net agricultural income per worker provoked an increase in the relative price of labor throughout the colony and thereby encouraged the

doption of labor saving techniques in the fur trade. The increase
n unit costs implied by these developments could not be covered
by the smaller, less competitive outfitters and they went out of
business.

Ultimately, changes in the institutional environment brought a
sudden end to the fur trade through the St. Lawrence Valley.
During the period immediately after the Revolutionary War, the
United States government enforced law and order west of the
Appalachians with some difficulty. The gains from trade in this
area accrued to efficient, sometimes lawless, companies irrespective of citizenship. Under the terms of Jay's Treaty, effective in
1796, Great Britain agreed to vacate western lake posts such as
Detroit and Michilimackinac. With the introduction of customs
duties in 1800, and the American acquisition of western lands in
the Louisiana Purchase of 1803, the North West Company was
obliged to move northwest of Lake Superior into the Hudson Bay
drainage basin. By 1810 fur pelts had fallen to 9 percent of total
export value from the port of Quebec. Barred from American
territory and facing growing transport costs, the North West
Company finally amalgamated with the Hudson's Bay Company
in 1821. The merger of the two companies marked the total eclipse
of the fur trade through the St. Lawrence Valley. By this time,
however, another staple industry had arisen to replace fur pelts as a
source of export income.

The Timber Trade

The rapid growth of the timber industry in Quebec is attributable
both to British colonial tariff policy and to Anglo-French warfare
in Europe. Tariffs, together with wartime trade restrictions, gave
rise to a 'hot-house' atmosphere in which the British North American timber industry mushroomed. In the short run colonial timber
cutters and merchants gained at the expense of British consumers,
including the Royal Navy, who were obliged to pay higher prices
because of protection. In the long run, however, timber prices fell
as the average costs of British North American timber production
diminished.

Tariffs tend to encourage domestic production and sales at the
expense of an overall loss in economic efficiency. But tariffs do not
lead to a loss in economic efficiency in all circumstances. The
presence of increasing returns to scale in production and marketing, for example, may justify protectionist policy for a given period
of time. This is the 'infant industry' argument for protection. In

the long run, however, trade restrictions are most appropriate for a few key industries necessary to international political survival or national defence. In the case of colonial timber, preferential tariff protection assured a steady and secure supply to the British navy.

During the eighteenth century, the high costs of Quebec timber on the British market kept colonial imports to a minimum. Because of the transport cost differential, Britain purchased most of its timber supplies from Baltic countries such as Norway, Sweden, Poland and Prussia. The outbreak of the Napoleonic wars in 1793 led the British government to rethink its naval timber policy from a strategic point of view. Two years later the British Parliament adopted a tariff structure that modestly favored colonial North American imports, and in the early years of the nineteenth century, the British government began contracting with colonial suppliers to purchase timber at subsidized prices. The first important contract for naval timber from Quebec was signed in 1804. During the years 1795 to 1813, Britain imposed increasingly discriminatory tariffs on timber imports from non-colonial sources. (See Chart 8.1A) The adherence of Russia, Denmark, and Prussia (1806-1808) to Napoleon's wartime blockade of British merchant ships in European ports further reinforced Britain's preferential tariff structure. Finally, in 1810, the British government abolished all duties on British North American timber imports entering British ports.

The net effect of a preferential tariff policy and the continental blockade was a substantial increase in timber prices on the British market. (See Chart 8.2) This rise in market prices had a spectacular impact on the timber industry in British North America. (See Chart 8.1B) Lumber and lumber products jumped to 74.5 percent of total exports by value from the port of Quebec in 1810.[2] Not only square timber (the log squared on four sides), but processed commodities such as deals (softwood planks), wooden casks, building materials, potash and wooden sailing ships emerged as export products. Through various industrial linkages, the lumber industry created a multiplier effect on commercial transactions, employment and economic activity in general. Consumers and merchants in both British North America and Britain obtained net gains from the growth of the colonial timber industry over the first three decades of the nineteenth century.

The spatial distribution of rivers and streams determined the location of the square timber industry in Lower Canada. Prior to mid-century, waterways provided the only efficient means of bulk transport. English common law assured that property rights in navigable rivers and streams stayed with the Crown so waterways remained common property. Rafts of square timber could there-

Chart 8.2

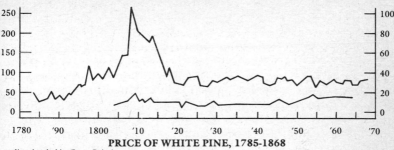

PRICE OF WHITE PINE, 1785-1868

top line: landed in Great Britain
left-hand scale: shillings per load
right-hand scale: dollars per thousand (M) board feet
bottom line: F.O.B. Quebec

Great Britain's Woodyard: British America and the Timber Trade, 1763-1867, pp. 256, 259, by A.R.M. Lower, reprinted by permission of McGill-Queens University Press.

fore be floated to the port of Quebec from points upstream in the St. Lawrence drainage basin at relatively low cost. During the first few decades of the nineteenth century, technical change played a small role in the growth of the industry; rough hewn square timber was brought down river over waterfalls and through rapids. The introduction of timber slides in 1829, allowed rafts or cribs to bypass waterfalls, improving the quality of the downstream product.

Forests, like fish and furs, are a renewable resource. If property rights are enforced, the forest resource owner has an economic interest in adhering to selective timber cutting and conservation to ensure a maximum sustainable yield over the long run. An exception to this rule occurs where deforested land has an alternative use, such as in agriculture. The deforested land can then be employed in another economic activity and rapid forest depletion may be economically appropriate. If property rights are not enforced, however, forested lands may be treated by woodcutters as a common property resource. Free access to forested lands can lead to rapid depletion from timber 'poaching' resulting in a loss of revenue to the resource owner and a loss of economic welfare to the society as a whole.

In a few regions of Lower Canada, rapid depletion of the forest occurred because cleared land offered competitive agricultural returns; the demand for agricultural land in seigneurial tenure increased steadily during the first half of the nineteenth century. But for the most part, extensive woodcutting was practiced in marginal agricultural areas where Crown property rights in timber stands went unenforced.

Colonial regulations, originating with the French regime in 1672, reserved 'naval timber' (oak forests) to the Crown. Similar regulations covering pine forests were promulgated by the British government in 1763. In principle, a licence was necessary to cut naval timber on either public or private lands, including most seigneuries. The British government issued such licences to contractors for the royal dockyards. Contractors were in turn authorized to issue timber-cutting permits to colonial merchants and lumbermen. In practice, however, the high costs of law enforcement in the wilderness resulted in widespread disregard for property rights in timber on both public and private lands. Many timber cutters obtained their raw material without licence. The Lower Canadian legislature attempted to regulate the quantity of 'merchantable' timber where no contract between buyer and seller existed, but these attempts appear to have been ineffective. Until the 1820s, says the historian A.R.M. Lower, the forests "were practically as open for cutting timber as the sea was for fishing." (Lower, 1973, p. 60) With the tacit approval of the legislative assembly, Quebecers treated Crown timber as though it was a common property resource, resulting in faster depletion and a transfer of income from the British Crown to the local population. In 1826 the Upper Canadian Executive Council began issuing licences to cut timber on Crown lands, collecting revenues without the consent of the colonial legislative assembly. A similar measure was subsequently undertaken in Lower Canada. Despite the low price of timber licences, entrepreneurs discovered the outright purchase of well-timbered tracts of land was a less costly option than buying a licence.

Exports of square timber from the port of Quebec climbed steadily during the 1820s and 1830s. (See Chart 8.3) Although a part of these exports originated in Upper Canada and the United States, the square timber industry appears to have provided a relatively stable source of income for Lower Canadians at a time of instability and falling income in the agricultural sector. Timber export income had a disturbing effect, however, on the regional distribution of income. Most of the actual timber cutting was accomplished by small independent operators, but the intermediary buyers were often branches of British companies formerly active in the Baltic trade. The flow of income to the English speaking community increased, particularly in Quebec City and Montreal where timber merchants typically engaged in few commercial and social relations with the local population. At the same time, spare capacity on timber vessels returning from Liverpool to Quebec lowered the price of an overseas passage and raised the rate of Anglophone immigration to the Canadas. The redistribution

Chart 8.3

THE RISE AND FALL OF THE SQUARE TIMBER TRADE: THE EXPORTS OF A CENTURY, 1810-1910

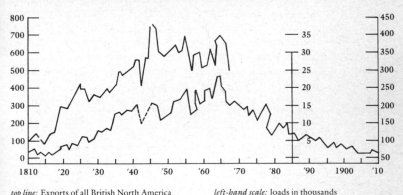

top line: Exports of all British North America
1810-1841—Pine
1842-1867—All timber

bottom line: Exports from Quebec
1810-1949—Pine
1850-1910—White Pine

left-hand scale: loads in thousands
centre scale: cubic feet in millions
right-hand scale: board feet in millions

Great Britain's Woodyard: British America and the Timber Trade, 1763-1867,
p. 258, by A.R.M. Lower, reprinted by permission of McGill-Queen's University
Press.

and spill-over effects from the growth of timber exports intensified
nationalist and anti-colonial sentiment in Lower Canada in the
1830s.

The British government granted preferential tariff protection to
the import of softwood planks as well as square timber. By 1832
the export of 'deals' from British North America to Britain
exceeded those coming from the Baltic region. The production of
deals required higher start-up costs, a larger proportion of fixed
costs, and more technically skilled labor than the production of
square timber. Prior to the completion of the Lachine Canal in
1824, the manufacture of deals was largely confined to the St.
Lawrence River region below Lachine. Of the 717 sawmills
enumerated in Lower Canada in 1831, for example, 47 percent
were located in the Quebec City area, 33 percent in the Montreal
area, and 18 percent in the Trois-Rivières area. (Ouellet, 1966,
p. 399) Until the completion of the canals on the upper St.
Lawrence in the late 1840s, Lower Canada enjoyed a margin of
natural protection from Upper Canadian competition. According
to Lower,

Transportation was probably the major factor in retarding the rate of
growth of the deal industry [in Upper Canada]. Square timber could be

Chart 8.4

WOODEN SHIPBUILDING IN THE ST. LAWRENCE VALLEY, 1800-1825
(tonnage per year)

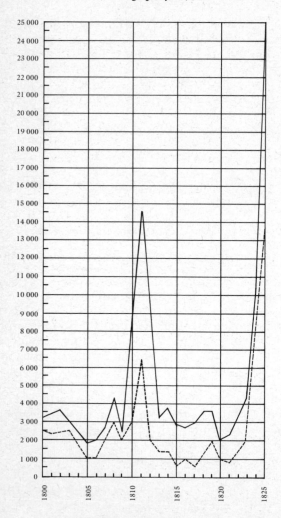

ST. LAWRENCE VALLEY _____
QUEBEC CITY _ _ _ _ _ _ _ _ _ _ _ _

Pierre Dufour, "La construction navale à Québec, 1760-1835: sources inexplorées et nouvelles perspectives de recherches," *Revue d'Histoire de l'Amérique française*, p. 247, September 1981, reprinted by permission.

brought down from infinite distances over the waterfalls and through rapids; sawn lumber could not, but had to wait for canals and railroads. Before they came, mills had to stick to water that provided a route to the seaport....there were few or no deals made on the St. Lawrence above the Lachine rapids or on Lake Ontario; the Ottawa River became the chief scene of the industry.[3]

Since the Navigation Laws required most colonial trade to take place on British or colonial ships, the laws provided a measure of protection favorable to Lower Canadian shipbuilding. First established during the French regime, shipbuilding in the St. Lawrence Valley appears to have received a short-lived boost from the continental blockade during the years 1808-1812. (See Chart 8.4) Unfortunately, reliable output data is not yet available for the years after 1825.[4] Employment in shipbuilding at the port of Quebec reached 3 355 workers in 1825, diminished to 1 155 in 1831, and increased to more than 4 600 by 1847. (Ouellet, 1966, pp. 403, 503).

The timber industry throughout British North America enjoyed a high degree of tariff protection from the early years of the nineteenth century until the 1840s. No tariffs were levied on colonial timber entering Britain between 1810 and 1821. In 1821,

the duty on Baltic timber was reduced from 65 shillings to 55 shillings a load, and a duty of 10 shillings a load was imposed on colonial timber. The schedule of sizes of deals was rearranged and new duties imposed paralleling the duties on timber and aiming at a preference for timber as supposedly the less manufactured article. American wood coming via Canada was to be charged full rates, and in order to prevent its entrance at colonial rates, certificates of origin were to be required. These certificates proved to be easily obtained.[5]

This preferential tariff structure remained intact until the 1840s. In 1842, under pressure from the British free trade movement, the import tariff on colonial timber was virtually abolished. At the same time the British Parliament initiated a series of tariff reductions on foreign timber, culminating in the abolition of all duties in 1866. The dismantling of the preferential tariff structure suggests that the gains to British consumers from the colonial timber industry had come to an end.

The narrowing of the tariff differential between foreign and colonial imports contributed to the sharp declines in the quantity of square timber exported from the port of Quebec in 1842 and again in 1848. (See Chart 8.1) Exports of lumber to the United States increased significantly during the 1840s, but the precise quantities involved are unknown. All in all, the British North American experience appears to provide a successful example of 'infant industry' tariff protection. Protection allowed for the development of a sizeable forest products industry. The withdrawal of protection, while making growth more difficult, did not lead to the industry's collapse because Quebec's forest products had attained a margin of comparative advantage on international markets.

Transport Innovations

From the beginning of colonization in the St. Lawrence Valley, Quebecers tended to settle within reach of domestic and overseas markets. Waterways provided transportation at lowest cost over all but short distances; most settlers chose to live near a navigable river. Away from waterways, the high costs of overland transport posed a barrier to economic exchange even among neighboring regions.[6] Any improvement in the transport and communications network lowered both transport and transaction costs—the costs of information concerning relative prices, institutional innovations, and new techniques.

The gradual development of an overland transport infrastructure facilitated economic exchange among previously isolated communities, increased economic specialization, and reduced price variations from region to region by breaking up local monopolies. The earliest overland transport improvements involved roads. Established long distance routes, such as the Montreal-Quebec and Montreal-Albany roads, permitted the creation of stage coach services to carry mail, passengers, and light freight in the 1760s. By 1811 the Montreal-Quebec coach ran twice a week in the winter and three times a week in the summer, taking at least two full days for the journey. Local roads often handled market exchange and communications between town and country. Local road building programs generally depended upon private economic initiatives; the slow growth of small towns and market transactions in rural Quebec consequently hampered the development of efficient surface transport. By 1851 the urban population, outside of Montreal and Quebec City, accounted for only 4 percent of the provincial population. As a result, the potential private returns to investment in surface transport improvement were correspondingly low.

Prior to the coming of railroads at mid-century, the transport and communications network continued to rely heavily on navigable waterways. A variety of innovations lowered the ton/mile costs of water transport during the first half of the nineteenth century. The advent of the paddle wheel steamboat to St.

Lawrence River transport in 1809, for example, lowered transport costs and improved communications between Quebec City and Montreal. In 1813 a steamboat could make the voyage from Montreal to Quebec in about twenty-four hours, and upstream from Quebec to Montreal in thirty-six to forty hours. By 1816, as many as nine hundred passengers could be accommodated in a single voyage. Steamboats were also used to tug ocean-going sailing vessels against the downstream current. The introduction of steamboats on the St. Lawrence River accelerated the development of Montreal as a seaport. The expansion of Montreal's docking facilities from 1 120 to 4 950 feet in 1832, and to 7 070 feet in 1840, further contributed to the eclipse of Quebec City as the province's chief port of entry.

By reducing the high costs of upstream water transport, steamboats increased the demand for canals as a means of circumventing rapids and waterfalls. Canals provided a means of by-passing rapid water without unloading and reloading cargo in transit. In the past, the unit transport costs of luxury items such as fur pelts had constituted a small proportion of total unit costs; the fur trade did not create a demand for cost reducing transport innovations until the second half of the eighteenth century. When the British government built four short canals on the St. Lawrence River south-west of Montreal during the years 1779-1783, it was to facilitate troop movements during the American Revolutionary War. These canals, a total of 1 700 feet, overcame the Cascades Rapids between Lake Saint-Louis and Lake Saint-François providing water passage at a depth of two-and-a-half feet. From the end of the eighteenth century until 1817, however, the St. Lawrence canals lay in a state of disrepair.

The high costs of canal construction continued to limit canal building on the upper St. Lawrence until the volume of bulk transport and the advent of steamboats justified a change. Both the lumber trade and the grain trade created a demand for transport innovations in the nineteenth century. As economic activity expanded in the Ottawa Valley and Upper Canada, the Lachine Rapids posed a costly obstacle to market exchange and communications between the Canadas. The opening of the Lachine Canal in 1824 permitted water transport on the St. Lawrence River as far upstream as the mouth of the Ottawa River. The Lachine Canal, eight-and-a-half miles long and five feet deep, was owned and operated by the government of Lower Canada. However, the success of the project was overshadowed by the opening of the Erie Canal south of the border.

The Erie Canal was completed through American territory from the Hudson River to Lake Erie in 1825. A branch of the three hundred and sixty-four mile long canal was constructed at Oswego, New York on Lake Ontario in 1829. In this way, farmers and merchants in Upper Canada obtained direct access by water to the port of New York, and European markets. The Montreal merchant community consequently lost its transport monopoly vis-a-vis upstream producers in the Great Lakes region.

The high rate of return to investors in the Erie Canal venture induced a host of similar canal projects throughout the northeastern part of the continent. The large scale and speculative nature of canal building generally discouraged private entrepreneurs from undertaking this form of transport investment on their own. The underdeveloped nature of banking and financial intermediary services further constrained the supply of private capital for large ventures. In both the Canadas and in the United States, canal building depended on government subsidies. In the United States, for example, 75 percent of all canal investment during the years 1815-1844 came from government coffers. (Davis *et al.*, p. 482) In Lower Canada, the colonial government began construction on the Chambly Canal in 1830, but the canal was not completed until 1843. Canal building on the St. Lawrence between the mouth of the Ottawa and Lake Ontario was also stalled until the 1840s. The benefits of further transport improvements, it was feared, would accrue to Upper Canadians and import-export merchants in Montreal, while the burden of costs would fall on Lower Canadian taxpayers. The Lachine Canal was the only major canal building project completed by the Lower Canadian government.

The political union of the Canadas in 1841 permitted the financial burden of government investment in canals to be passed along to the taxpayers and consumers of both provinces. In 1842 the Union government decided to use the proceeds of an imperial loan, not to redeem the provincial debt as had originally been planned, but to complete the St. Lawrence and Welland Canal systems. Import duties were raised from 2.5 to 5 percent as part of the financing package. Between 1842 and 1848, the Cornwall, Beauharnois and Williamsburg Canals were completed and the Lachine Canal enlarged to a depth of nine feet. By the end of 1848, the Canadas possessed canals on the upper St. Lawrence designed to compete with the successful Erie Canal system for the traffic from the continental interior. (See Chart 8.5)

The inability of the port of Montreal to rival the port of New York as a shipping point for Ontario's exports was clear by midcentury. During the years 1848-1851, annual shipments of wheat and flour from Ontario to overseas destinations were less than in 1841. The bulk of Ontario's wheat and flour shipments to Montreal were destined for Quebec and the Maritimes. By 1851 the

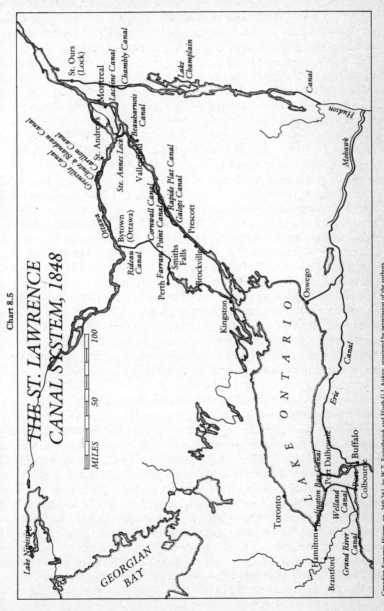

Chart 8.5

THE ST. LAWRENCE CANAL SYSTEM, 1848

MILES
50   100

St. Ours (Lock)
Montreal
Lachine Canal
Chambly Canal
Lake Champlain
Canal
Hudson
Mohawk
St. Andrew's
St. Annes Lock
Beauharnois Canal
Grenville Canal
Chûte à Blondeau Canal
Carillon Canal
Valleyfield
Cornwall Canal
Rapide Plat Canal
Galops Canal
Ottawa
Bytown (Ottawa)
Rideau Canal
Perth
Farran Point Canal
Prescott
Smiths Falls
Brockville
Kingston
Oswego
Lake Nipissing
GEORGIAN BAY
LAKE ONTARIO
Toronto
Hamilton
Burlington Bay Canal
Port Dalhousie
Welland Canal
Colbourne
Buffalo
Erie Canal
Brantford
Grand River Canal

Canadian Economic History, pp. 260-261, by W.T. Easterbrook and Hugh G.I. Aitken, reprinted by permission of the authors.

Erie Canal handled more of Ontario's overseas trade than the St. Lawrence canal system.

There are a number of elements that explain this situation. They add up to one overriding consideration: unit transport costs via the Erie Canal were lower. Although commodities from Ontario could travel more cheaply to Montreal than to the port of New York, lower transport costs from New York to Liverpool (less than one half the costs from Montreal) more than compensated for this difference. Ocean freight rates were cheaper from New York owing to more competition among carriers and a greater demand for return passages by immigrants coming to North America. Montreal did not become an ocean port until 1832; docking and entrepot facilities were therefore smaller and storage costs higher than in New York. Most importantly, the difficulty of navigation on the St. Lawrence River below Montreal resulted in substantial insurance premiums, pilotage fees, towing charges, and time lost. The depth of Lac Saint-Pierre, between Montreal and Trois-Rivières, fell to eleven-and-a-half feet in mid-summer and autumn. These additional costs rendered shipments to Europe via the St. Lawrence system more expensive than shipping via the Erie Canal system. International traffic on the St. Lawrence came to a standstill for at least five months every winter because of the ice, whereas the port of New York remained open year-round. The passage of the Drawback Acts by the American Congress in 1845-1846 permitted Ontario's exports to be shipped through the Erie Canal to the British market in bond, exempt from American duties. With the abolition of preferential tariffs for colonial imports into Britain, the economic advantage of shipping via the St. Lawrence disappeared as well.

The St. Lawrence canal system was predicated on trade with the British metropole. But at the same time as the unified government of the Canadas was building canals to reduce the costs of east-west trade with Europe, Britain was in the process of abandoning its preferential tariff policy. The removal of the old colonial tariff structure, together with the passage of the American Drawback Acts, lowered the costs of economic exchange with the United States. The abolition of the Navigation Laws in 1849, laws that required Canadian commerce on the Great Lakes and the St. Lawrence River to be conducted in British empire ships, removed another constraint on the growth of Canadian-American trade. Moreover, at the completion of the St. Lawrence canals, the diffusion of railroad technology had already influenced international trading patterns. By 1850, 9 000 miles of railway track had been laid in North America. The possibility of efficient overland transport opened new perspectives for economic exchange among producers and consumers in Quebec, Ontario, and the northeastern United States. The St. Lawrence canal system could not contribute to north-south trade in a substantial way.

In retrospect, the building of the St. Lawrence canal system in the 1840s may appear to have been uneconomic.[7] But this would be a severe *ex post* judgement. Even in the United States, where railroad building was considerably ahead of that in Canada, canal building continued in the 1840s and 1850s. Between 1844 and 1860, investment in American canals amounted to $57.4 million (of which two-thirds flowed from government). It is inaccurate, therefore, to say that the American canal building era was over by 1837. (cf. Easterbrook and Aitken, p. 294) Canal construction constituted a speculative venture; the financial success of the Erie Canal system in the United States proved to be the exception, rather than the rule.

* * *

At the time of the British Conquest, the settled regions in North America were largely independent of each other. International trading patterns depended upon regional resource endowments and comparative advantage in resource commodity production with respect to the metropolitan economies in Europe. The rise of interregional trade is attributable to changes in prices, costs, and metropolitan government regulation.

The cumulative impact of communications and transport innovations, rapid growth in the American mid-west and southern Ontario, and a decline in British colonial trade restrictions produced a restructuring of relative prices, incomes and opportunities throughout the northeastern part of the continent. Until the 1840s, trade and growth in Quebec had depended on economic and political signals emanating from Britain. In the 1840s colonial trade was substantially deregulated. The ensuing changes in international prices facing Quebec farmers and merchants produced a reallocation of mobile resources such as capital and labor. Changes in the volume and composition of market exchange with the United States and Ontario created new prospects and new problems for the Quebec economy in the second half of the nineteenth century. This is the subject of Part III.

NOTES

[1]The high costs of tariff administration along the American border, however, resulted in a form of inland free trade area with the United States until about 1812. (McDiarmid, pp. 23-24) In 1822, the port of Quebec was granted the status of a 'free port' and permitted to receive foreign goods in foreign ships, but Montreal never enjoyed the same concession.

[2]Exports from the port of Quebec included small quantities from the Upper Canada, Lake Champlain, and up-state New York regions.

[3]*Great Britain's Woodyard: British America and the Timber Trade, 1763-1867*, pp. 173-174, by A.R.M. Lower, reprinted by permission of McGill-Queen's University Press.

[4]In a recent article, P. Dufour has roundly criticized the traditional sources of information about the Lower Canadian shipbuilding industry, upon which the standard analyses (Faucher, Lower, Ouellet) have been based.

[5]*Great Britain's Woodyard: British America and the Timber Trade, 1763-1867*, p. 79, by A.R.M. Lower, reprinted by permission of McGill-Queen's University Press.

[6]In 1727 the Intendent Claude-Thomas Dupuy wrote, "there is no road by land from Quebec to Montreal. This is a great inconvenience and an obstacle to the establishment of the colony. It sometimes takes a month to and from Montreal, according to the wind." (Glazebrook, pp. 100-101)

[7]The St. Lawrence canal system appears to have generated fewer benefits than costs. The primary benefits appear to have flowed to consumers in Quebec and the Maritimes in the form of lower product prices. The costs of canal construction seem largely to have been paid by raising import duties on Canadian goods purchased overseas.

SELECT BIBLIOGRAPHY

Courville, Serge. "La crise agricole du Bas-Canada, Eléments d'une réflexion géographique (deuxième partie)." *Cahiers de Géographie du Québec*. December 1980.

Davis, Lance E. *et al. American Economic Growth: An Economist's History of the United States.* New York: Harper & Row, Publishers, 1972.

Dufour, Pierre. "La construction navale à Quebec, 1760-1825: Sources inexplorées et nouvelles perspectives de recherches." *Revue d'histoire de l'Amérique française*. September 1981.

Faucher, Albert. "La construction navale à Québec au XIXe siècle: apogée et déclin." *Histoire économique et unité canadienne.* Montreal: Editions Fides, 1970.

Faucher, Albert. *Québec en Amérique au XIXe siècle.* Montreal: Editions Fides, 1973.

Glazebrook, G.P. de T. *A History of Transportation in Canada.* Volume 1. *Continental Strategy to 1867.* Toronto: McClelland & Stewart Limited, 1964.

Government of Ontario. "A History of Crown Timber Regulations: From the date of the French Occupation to the Present Time." Report of the Department of Lands, Forests and Mines, 1907.

Graham, Gerald S. "The Origin of Free Ports in British North America." *The Canadian Historical Review.* March 1941.

Greer, Allan. "Fur Trade Labour and Lower Canadian Agrarian Structures." *CHA Historical Papers.* Canadian Historical Association, 1981.

Lee, Susan Previent and Peter Passell. *A New Economic View of American History.* New York: W.W. Norton & Company, 1979.

Lower, Arthur R.M. *Great Britain's Woodyard: British America and the Timber Trade, 1763-1867.* Montreal: McGill-Queen's University Press, 1973.

Lower, Arthur R.M. "The Trade in Square Timber," in W.T. Easterbrook and M.H. Watkins, eds., *Approaches to Canadian Economic History.* Toronto: McClelland & Stewart Limited, 1967.

Marr, William L. and Donald G. Patterson. *Canada: An Economic History.* Toronto: Macmillan of Canada, 1980.

McDiarmid, Orville J. *Commercial Policy in the Canadian Economy.* Cambridge, Mass.: Harvard University Press, 1946.

Nelles, H.V. *The Politics of Development: Forest, Mines and Hydro-Electric Power in Ontario, 1849-1941.* Toronto: Macmillan of Canada, 1974.

Ouellet, Fernand. "Dualité économique et changement technologique au Québec (1760-1790)." *Histoire Sociale-Social History.* November 1976.

Ouellet, Fernand. *Histoire économique et sociale du Québec, 1760-1850.* Montreal: Editions Fides, 1966.

Ouellet, Fernand. *Le Bas-Canada 1791-1840: Changements structuraux et crise.* Ottawa: Editions de l'Université d'Ottawa, 1976.

Ouellet, Fernand. "Colonial Economy and International Economy: The Trade of the St. Lawrence River Valley with Spain, Portugal and their Atlantic Possessions, 1760-1850," in J. Barbier and A.J. Kuethe, eds., *The North American Role in the Spanish Imperial Economy 1760-1819.* Manchester: Manchester University Press (forthcoming).

Tucker, N. Gilbert. *The Canadian Commercial Revolution 1845-1851.* Toronto: McClelland & Stewart Limited, 1964.

Tulchinsky, Gerald J.J. *The River Barons: Montreal Businessmen and the Growth of Industry and Transportation, 1837-53.* Toronto: University of Toronto Press, 1977.

Part III

QUEBEC AND CONFEDERATION 1850-1900

9

Institutional Change, Transport and Trade

Until mid-century, economic activity in Quebec relied heavily upon maritime transport on the St. Lawrence River. The river and its tributaries served both regional economic exchange and international commerce involving Great Britain. The withdrawal of preferential tariffs in the 1840s lowered British demand for colonial wheat and timber by reducing the price of non-colonial substitutes on the metropolitan market. The British North American colonies consequently turned elsewhere seeking new markets and means of transport on the continent. The introduction of railway technology in the 1850s promoted overland exchange by reducing transport and transaction costs among neighboring regions. Railways permitted cheaper access to previously isolated markets and raised the potential net benefits of colonization in unsettled areas. Railways also ended the slowdown of traffic on navigable waterways caused by winter ice. Although the St. Lawrence River remained of central importance to the Quebec economy, the river's proportion of total North American traffic steadily diminished after mid-century.

Transport innovations and the dismantling of colonial trade restrictions lowered the barriers to trade with the United States. In 1849, the year following the advent of responsible government, four of the principle Anglophone newspapers in Montreal declared themselves in favor of annexation to the United States. Though political integration did not occur, the Canadian and United States governments agreed on a limited form of free trade for the period 1855 to 1866. When the Reciprocity Treaty proved unsatisfactory, politicians in the British North American colonies devised another solution to the need for economic exchange within a broadly based common market.

Confederation was the product of diverse economic and political forces. Closer intercolonial ties stemming from railways, the termination of the Reciprocity Treaty, the American Civil War, and the desire of Canadian entrepreneurs and politicians to settle the northwestern part of the continent all played a role in shaping Canada's Constitution. The British North America (BNA) Act of 1867 represented a new venture in the search for an optimal domestic trading area. In creating a common market among the former colonies, the BNA Act established a new institutional environment for Quebec households and firms. Henceforth, government regulation of the Quebec economy occurred at two levels. Quebecers elected their own provincial government that possessed powers over matters of a local nature; however, most of the British government's former powers, such as those concerning trade and commerce, were transferred from London to the newly created central government in Ottawa.

When Confederation of the British North American provinces proved insufficient to attain a high rate of economic growth, the federal government adopted measures to increase immigration, settlement and industrial expansion. Narrowly conceived, the term 'National Policy' refers to the tariff policy that was enacted in 1879. More generally, however, the national policy strategy consisted of complementary policies involving free land grants in the Canadian west, subsidized transcontinental railways, and tariff protection for domestic manufacturing industries. Each of these policies produced benefits and costs that varied from region to region. The structure of the Quebec economy was unexpectedly altered by decisions taken in Ottawa aimed at stimulating the Canadian economy as a whole.

This chapter begins by examining two major innovations affecting Quebec's economic environment in the 1850s and 1860s. Railways lowered transport costs between Montreal and neighboring regions; the Reciprocity Treaty of 1854 removed tariff barriers on the exchange of unfinished products between the Canadas and the United States. The successes and failures of these two innovations help to explain the demand for new constitutional arrangements that culminated in the BNA Act of 1867. The BNA Act has provided the basis of the institutional environment on which the Quebec economy has relied to the present day.

Transport Innovations Before Confederation

The introduction of railways extended the frontier of profitable settlement, production, and economic exchange by reducing transport and transaction costs. Locational economic rents rose in the regions served by rail lines as the returns from *in situ* resource ownership increased. Rail transport served as an intermediate input into various final products so that the lower transport costs of shipping resource commodities created new employment and profit opportunities in resource processing and distributing. Railway entrepreneurs could not, however, capture all of the net returns to railway building unless they owned the lands affected by railway transport innovations. In settled regions, the aggregate social returns to transport improvements tended to be larger than the private profitability of railway investment suggested. Railway projects in settled regions often required cash subsidies in lieu of the land grants frequently associated with railway building in unsettled areas.

Railways constituted a distinctly nineteenth century technological innovation. The most important experiments with steam-powered locomotives and smooth rail surfaces occurred in England during the 1820s. In the following decade Great Britain and the United States became the leading nations in the adoption of railway technology. By 1840 railway mileage in the United States equalled canal mileage. In Quebec and Ontario, however, the diffusion of railway technology lagged behind development abroad.

As long as the Canadas reaped the fruits of British tariff protection, railway transport was not considered economically viable. Traffic moved efficiently along the St. Lawrence water route to the British Isles. The high capital/output ratio associated with railway services, the riskiness of the venture, and the underdeveloped state of the colonial capital market all constrained private investment in Canadian railway lines. Railway building required the import of foreign technology and a slow process of learning-by-doing. As the various barriers to trade with the United States diminished at mid-century, however, the expected profits from investment in rail transport attracted private investors. The divergence between private and social returns from railway building resulted in some government participation as well. But rather than trying to operate railways directly, as had been tried with canals, the Union government encouraged private companies to apply for lump sum subsidies.

In the beginning, railway entrepreneurs planned railways to service market-oriented producers rather than to open unsettled regions in anticipation of future transport demand. Given the uncertainty surrounding the new technology, investors preferred small scale, risk-averting projects. The earliest Quebec railways were therefore designed to complement the St. Lawrence River transport system. Two lines came into operation before mid-century. The Champlain and St. Lawrence Railway Company began operations between La Prairie and Saint-Jean in July 1836. The line ran for 16 miles between the St. Lawrence and Richelieu Rivers and circumvented the rapids on the Richelieu. The Montreal and Champlain Railway, on the Island of Montreal, was also a portage line. Opened in 1847, this line by-passed the Lachine Rapids and the Lachine Canal.

The idea of a rail link between southern Ontario and the Atlantic Ocean via Montreal was first entertained in the 1840s. Such a line would circumvent navigational difficulties on the St. Lawrence River below Montreal and overcome the winter shutdown due to ice. What is more, the railway would lower transport costs and hasten settlement in the Eastern Townships, an area poorly served by water transport facilities. In 1845 the Union government chartered the St. Lawrence and Atlantic Railway Company to build a rail line from Montreal to the American border by way of Longueuil, Saint-Hyacinthe and Sherbrooke. The Atlantic and St. Lawrence received a state charter to build from the Vermont border to the ocean port of Portland.[1] But the riskiness of the project discouraged private investors and by the end of 1848 construction was halted for lack of funds. On the Canadian side, only the thirty mile Longueuil/Saint-Hyacinthe section was complete. At mid-century, total railway mileage in the United States had risen to some 7 500 miles; but total track in all of British North America amounted to a mere 66 miles.

The completion of the Montreal-Portland line required additional funding and to this end the Guarantee Act of 1849 provided a government subsidy. The Guarantee Act offered assistance to several unfinished railway projects in the Canadas by guaranteeing the payment of interest on railway bonds held by private investors. The government guarantee covered the interest on half the value of authorized bonds issued by Canadian railway companies on lines over 75 miles in length, provided that at least half of the line had already been built. This form of government participation insured private investors against total loss in the event of bankruptcy and thus made eligible Canadian bonds easier to sell on the British capital market. The Union government plan amounted to risk sharing with private investors and effectively subsidized trunk lines already nearing completion.

In the autumn of 1851 the Champlain and St. Lawrence completed an extension from Saint-Jean to Rouse's Point, New York. This 42 mile line connected the Montreal region with New England's rail network to Boston and New York, offering a year-round transport and communications link with the Atlantic coast. In 1853 the Montreal and New York Railway was completed from Caughnawaga to Plattsburg, New York, parallel to the Champlain and St. Lawrence. Finally, due to the provisions of the Guarantee Act, the 120 mile St. Lawrence and Atlantic reached as far as Island Pond, Vermont. With the completion of the Portland railroad in later 1853, Montreal obtained a third rail link to the Atlantic coast. (See Chart 9.1)

In the early 1850s Canadian merchants began promoting the idea of building a trunk rail line from southwestern Ontario to a port in the British maritime colonies. The project gathered support for both political and economic reasons. The Ogdensburg Railroad in New York State, opened in 1850, effectively captured Ontario's export traffic to the detriment of the St. Lawrence canals and the port of Montreal. Running from Ogdensburg on the south shore of the St. Lawrence to Lake Champlain, the line fed into the Boston and New York City rail networks. A Canadian trunk line parallel to Lake Ontario and the St. Lawrence River, it was said, would lower transport costs and promote British American unity. For both reasons, the Union government chartered the Grand Trunk Railway Company of Canada in April 1853 to build from Toronto to Montreal.[2]

The Union government initially guaranteed the Grand Trunk's bonds to the extent of one half of the total cost of the line, though this was later modified to a flat £3000 per mile.[3] The Grand Trunk opened the Montreal-Toronto line for traffic in 1856. Through leasing arrangements the Company acquired the Montreal-Portland rail system, as well as the Quebec and Richmond Railway running from Richmond to Levis. The Grand Trunk extended the Quebec and Richmond line to Rivière du Loup. Following the completion of the Victoria Bridge across the St. Lawrence River at Montreal in November 1859, the Grand Trunk offered rail service to the winter port at Portland, Maine from as far west as Sarnia, Ontario and as far east as Rivière du Loup.[4]

In the desire to minimize the risks surrounding the new transport technology, railway companies built most of the early rail lines either to complement or compete directly with the St. Lawrence waterway. "Building ahead of demand" in isolated, unsettled regions was uncommon before Confederation. There is no doubt passengers appreciated the speed and efficiency of rail travel, but from a private profitability point of view, there was often room for either a canal system or a rail line, but not both. Railway building in Quebec took place in a less urbanized, less industrialized economic environment than the northeastern United States. Urban areas accounted for less than 15 percent of

Chart 9.1

RAILWAY CONNECTIONS OF MONTREAL 1853

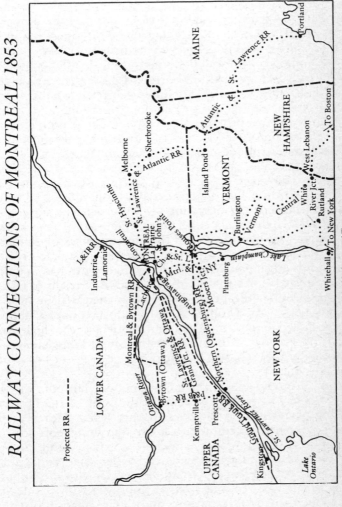

The River Barons: Montreal Businessmen and the Growth of Industry and Transportation 1837-53, p. 106, by Gerald J.J. Tulchinsky, reprinted by permission of University of Toronto Press.

the Quebec population in 1851, and average income depended heavily on self-sufficient agriculture. The comparatively low level of market exchange discouraged the construction of rail lines that did not serve interregional transport needs. Furthermore, Union government policy indirectly subsidized railway building in heavily populated, urbanized regions. The Municipal Loan Fund Acts of 1852 and 1854 pooled all Canadian municipalities' credit into a single fund—matched, though not legally backed, by provincial bond issues. The Loan Fund Acts facilitated the sale of municipal bonds for railway building. Quebec municipalities borrowed less than $1 million for railway building during the life of the fund while Ontario's municipalities borrowed more than six times as much. (Creighton, p. 69) This difference reflected the varying levels of urbanization, municipal incorporation, and market exchange in the two provinces. After a number of municipalities declared bankruptcy, the Canadian government terminated the fund and assumed about $12 million in municipal debt.

During the 1850s, total track mileage in the Canadas expanded by about two thousand miles, more than in any other decade in the nineteenth century. But owing to replication, almost all of the canals and rail lines in operation by 1860 failed to cover their costs. Certain individuals collected windfall gains from railway contracts, but the companies and their foreign investors generally incurred losses. Once constructed, however, variable costs were relatively low and it paid to keep railways in operation even if their costs of construction could not be covered. As a result of railway losses, total track mileage in the Canadas increased by only 77 miles during the years 1860–1867.[5] At Confederation, $33 million had been added to the Union government debt by the three major railway undertakings, $26 million by the Grand Trunk alone. The refinancing of this debt was a basic objective of the new constitutional agreement.

Technical innovation in pre-Confederation transport was not confined solely to railway building. Conscious of the obstacles impeding navigation on the St. Lawrence below Montreal, the Union government attempted to lower water transport costs by deepening and widening the channel. Between 1851 and 1865 the navigable passage on the St. Lawrence was deepened from 12.5 to 20 feet and widened from 75 to 300 feet. (Hamelin and Roby, p. 106) Navigation speed and security improved with the deployment of maintenance steamboats, and the installation of lights, buoys, and signals reduced the high costs of maritime insurance on the river. The government further agreed to subsidize the towing of sailing ships on the St. Lawrence. All of these improvements were designed to render the St. Lawrence River more efficient than he competing Erie Canal system in the transport of bulky commodities.

Tariff Policy Before Confederation

Tariff reform constituted the other major source of reductions in transaction costs associated with international trade. Quebecers had possessed a margin of influence over domestic import duties since the late eighteenth century. In effect, the Constitutional Act of 1791 allowed the Lower Canadian government to levy tariffs on imports in addition to those legislated by the British government. Various specific duties were applied until the two colonial governments agreed to place a single *ad valorem* duty of 2.5 percent on all imports in 1813. Most of Lower Canada's government revenues subsequently came from this source until 1839. Because Upper Canadian government revenues depended on tax remittances from Lower Canada, the two colonial governments quarreled over relative shares in the duties collected at the port of Quebec. The Act of Union of 1841 put an end to this conflict by ensuring the two Canadian provinces adopt a common tariff policy and act as a customs union.

The loss of preferential treatment on British markets and the expectations created by railway building induced Canadian merchants to seek new markets closer to home. Interregional economic integration involved both static (short term) and dynamic (long term) gains. In the short run, the abolition of tariff barriers stimulated trade and specialization. In the long run, economic integration provided firms with new opportunities to achieve economies of large scale production.

The Union government reacted to the dismantling of the British preferential tariff system by reducing tariffs on manufactured goods imported from the United States and raising the duties on British manufactures to a uniform level of 7.5 percent *ad valorem* in 1847. But the further development of trade relations with the United States was discouraged by American trade barriers. (In 1846 the United States government had placed a 20 percent *ad valorem* tariff on raw timber imports; two years later, it added a specific duty of two dollars per quarter on wheat.) The search for new markets therefore concentrated on closer ties with the other British North American colonies. The Union government raised the general tariff on manufactured goods from 7.5 to 12.5 percent in 1849, and in the following year, agreed with the governments of New Brunswick, Nova Scotia and Prince Edward Island to a limited form of free trade. In 1850 the British North American governments passed concurrent legislation establishing intercolonial free trade in specified resource and agricultural products. But they did not go so far as to abolish intercolonial duties on manufactured goods or establish a common tariff policy (customs union) with respect to external trading partners.

The intercolonial reciprocity agreement of 1850 served as a model for a reciprocal trade agreement with the United States in 1854. The Reciprocity Treaty, effective March 16, 1855, created a partial free trade area between the British North American colonies and the United States, that lasted until 1866. The most important tariff changes resulting from the Treaty involved:

(i)   the abolition of tariffs within the trading area on a specified list of 'natural' (resource-intensive) products;

(ii) an end to restrictions by the signatories on Atlantic coast fishing north of the 36° parallel, and reciprocal landing rights;

(iii) the abolition of trading restrictions on shipping and navigation on the St. Lawrence River and Lake Michigan.

Of these three changes, the free trade provision concerned Quebecers the most. Unfortunately, it is difficult to determine how much of the growth in trade that occurred in the years 1855-1866 is directly attributable to the Treaty itself. Of the commodities enumerated in the Treaty, the United States enjoyed an average tariff reduction of 6 percent on imports from Canada: British North America enjoyed an average reduction of 21 percent on goods from the United States. (Ankli, p. 10) But falling transport costs and the disruption of markets created by the American Civil War (1861-1865) resulted in changes that also favored Canadian-American trade. Because imports and exports rose during the Treaty period does not mean they rose because of the Treaty. Although the Treaty affected the pattern of trade, its net impact on growth and welfare in the Canadas (the available data does not distinguish between the two provinces) appears relatively small.

Officer and Smith have attempted to analyse the net static effects of the Treaty with the help of the economic theory of customs unions. Distinguishing between trade diversion (a switch in the source of imports from a low cost non-signatory party to a higher cost signatory party) and trade creation (a switch in source from a high cost domestic supplier to a low cost signatory trading partner), Officer and Smith conclude that trade creation took place only in the first year of the Treaty.

In 1855 trade creation appears to have increased British North American imports by some 35 percent. For the duration of the Treaty, any increase in exports or imports was attributable to trade diversion—the substitution of one trading partner for another—with no net welfare gain. Moreover, even the increase in imports of

1855 could be explained by the existence of smuggling prior to the operation of the Treaty, the recorded 'increase' in trade being attributable to merchandise previously undeclared.

Ankli comes to similar conclusions but with several nuances. Smuggling prior to the Treaty, says Ankli, may have accounted for an initial increase in recorded trade for some commodities with a high price/weight ratio. Bulky goods such as oats and lumber would not fall into this category. Proceeding on a commodity-by-commodity basis, Ankli's analysis suggests that barley, rye, and possibly forest product exports may have been modestly assisted by the Treaty. Imports rose during the Treaty period, but this increase was neither economically desirable, nor specifically attributable to the working of the Treaty. According to Ankli, "commercial policy did not alter the underlying 'real' forces in the economy at this time". (Ankli, p. 13)

The United States abrogated the Reciprocity Treaty in 1866 producing a return to the *status quo ante* tariff structure of 1854. Americans were unhappy with the Treaty. Sir Francis Hincks, the Canadian Inspector-General (Finance Minister), had promised the Canadian government would refrain from raising duties on manufactured goods during the life of the Treaty. His successors, William Cayley and Alexander Galt, reneged on this commitment arguing that Hinck's promise was not written into the Treaty. In 1858 and 1859 Canadian tariffs on manufactured goods increased to an average level of nearly 20 percent *ad valorem* where they remained until 1866. The American government, already angered by British and Canadian trading with the Confederacy, believed that higher Canadian tariffs on manufactured imports violated the spirit of the Treaty. Between 1861 and 1864, the average *ad valorem* tariff rate on dutiable goods entering the United States rose from 25 to 47 percent. Abrogation of the Reciprocity Treaty in 1866 therefore came as no surprise to Quebecers.[6]

The Canadian tariff increases of 1858 and 1859 reflected a conscious attempt by the Union government to accelerate the growth rate of manufacturing by means of tariffs. Despite some rhetoric to the contrary, the revised Canadian tariff structure promoted manufacturing at home, and was designed to do so.[7] Barnett has demonstrated the increasingly graduated nature of Canadian tariff changes at this time. (See Table 9.1) These tariff changes resulted from the 'rent-seeking' behavior of manufacturers in the major urban areas. The changes coincide with the rates proposed by the Association for the Promotion of Canadian Industry, a private employers' group. (Barnett, p. 392)

At the time of the tariff changes of 1859, the Inspector-General, Alexander Galt, also tried to promote the use of the St. Lawrence

Table 9.1

THE CANADIAN TARIFF STRUCTURE BY
DEGREE OF MANUFACTURE, 1858-1859
(Average Ad Valorem Rates)

	Primary	Intermediate	Tertiary
Prior to August 1858	2.30	5.24	12.81
August 1858-February 1859	0.26	6.28	16.50
February 1859-	0.13	7.18	19.62

"The Galt Tariff: Incidental or Effective Protection," Vol IX, No. 3, pp. 394-395, by D.F. Barnett, *Canadian Journal of Economics*, Copyright © August 1976, reprinted by permission.

River as a channel for international trade. By changing duties on items from the West Indies, such as tea, coffee, molasses and sugar, from a specific to an *ad valorem* level, and assessing them on their value at last point of departure, the Minister discouraged importing by way of the United States. According to D.C. Masters:

> As a further inducement to trade to follow the Canadian route, Galt in 1860 instituted the policy of refunding ninety percent of the tolls charged on a vessel passing through the Welland Canal on the down journey if it continued to the St. Lawrence, and of charging only ten percent of the tolls upon one which came from the St. Lawrence.[8]

These regulations provided additional incentives to use the ports and canals on the St. Lawrence River.

Confederation

Before Confederation, Quebec's external economic relations primarily involved Ontario, Great Britain, and the United States. Very little trading occurred with the British Maritime provinces or the scarcely populated Hudson Bay lands to the west. The high costs of intercolonial transport and the legacy of British mercantile policies contributed to the low degree of intercolonial trade. In the 1850s, all of the BNA colonies concentrated on developing ties with the United States. The government of the Canadas suggested broadening the intercolonial reciprocity agreement to create a general customs union but the Maritime governments, fearing a loss in tariff revenues, vetoed the idea in 1862. In fiscal year 1865-1866, exports from the Canadas to the Maritimes amounted to only 3 percent of total Canadian exports.

After several years of negotiation, the ruling colonial governments in British North America agreed upon complete economic and political integration within the framework of a federal system of government. The constitutional rules-of-the-game were laid down in 1867 by an act of the British parliament, the British North America Act. The BNA Act assigned powers to federal and provincial governments, and continues to serve today as the Canadian Constitution. The Act designated provincial governments to regulate matters of a "merely local or private nature" in four regions: Quebec, Ontario, New Brunswick and Nova Scotia. A federal government, elected by all Canadian voters, was given broad powers over all matters other than those "assigned exclusively to the provinces". Since Quebec members constituted a minority in the federal House of Parliament, their objectives often had to be accomplished by 'log-rolling' or vote trading.

Confederation was by no means conceived to serve economic objectives alone. The American Civil War, for instance, affected both the timing and nature of the Confederation pact. All the same, expectations concerning economic opportunities profoundly affected the assignment of powers in the Canadian Constitution. The expected economic advantages from uniform tariff barriers, free domestic trade, a federally subsidized interprovincial railway, settlement of the west, and an increase in immigration all played a role in the design of the British North America Act.

Greater economic integration constituted a primary objective of Confederation. British North American provinces already formed a limited free trade area. The creation of a veritable common market also involved a single tariff policy for all provinces, the removal of interprovincial barriers to the mobility of labor and capital, and common domestic commercial policies. The federal government became directly responsible for applying uniform standards in navigation and shipping, money and banking, and the fisheries, as well as activities that impinged directly on the economy such as immigration, the census and statistics, the postal service, weights and measures, patents and copyright, and criminal law. The move toward economic integration appeared feasible at the time because the British North American colonies had similar market sizes, a comparable degree of industrial development, and complementary resource advantages.

Greater economic integration in turn required lower barriers to interprovincial transport and economic exchange. Proponents of Confederation believed that interprovincial railways would lower transport and transaction costs, create larger markets, induce greater specialization and permit scale economies in the manufacturing sector. Advocates of Confederation in the Maritime colonies held out for an intercolonial railway as an essential part of the Confederation agreement. Advocates of Confederation in the Canadas, however, tended to accept the rationale for an intercolonial railway in terms of national defense. In Creighton's words, "Intercolonial railways were the necessary physical basis of Confederation; but, at the same time, Confederation appeared to be the necessary political basis for intercolonial railways". (Creighton, p. 59)

Confederation offered the hope of an improvement in Canada's credit rating on international financial markets. Canal and railway building in the 1840s and 1850s had substantially raised colonial indebtedness and the costs of foreign bond sales. By assuming the debt of the former colonies, some $90 million, the new central government would improve the credit rating of the provinces. Political unification, in creating an image of policical stability, would lower the costs of foreign bond issues and the costs of railway financing. At the same time, the government of the enlarged and independent political unit would enjoy more credibility and greater bargaining power in international economic relations, such as the expected renegotiation of the Reciprocity Treaty with the United States.

The acquisition of the Hudson's Bay Company lands by the new federal government was an implicit objective of Confederation. The purchase of the western lands, immigration, settlement, and the construction of transcontinental railways all formed part of a basic development package. American economic expansion and railway construction in the mid-west created an attitude of 'defensive expansionism' among Canadian capitalists and politicians.[9] Proponents of Confederation in the Canadas believed that a transcontinental railway to the Pacific Ocean would tie the west to central Canada and create profitable opportunities for eastern manufacturers.

The breakdown of the American federal system during the Civil War period favored arguments for a strongly centralized federation in Canada. Most of the British government's powers in the pre-Confederation era were assigned to the central government in Ottawa. The new federal government acquired all powers not specifically allocated to the provincial governments (the so-called 'residual' powers). Most Quebecers appear to have acquiesed to this arrangement, but not without an awareness of the BNA Act's potential impact on language, religion, and culture. In view of Quebec's special character, the BNA Act assigned powers over civil rights, civil law and education to the provinces.

The BNA Act was agreed upon in March 1867 and came into

effect on July 1. The colonial governments of the time ratified the provisions of the Act; it was not the object of a referendum or the result of a clear mandate from provincial electors. Opposition did not take long to manifest itself. In Quebec's first post-Confederation provincial election, the Parti Rouge elected twenty members to the sixty-seat assembly on a program to substantially revise the nature of the Constitution.[10]

In the years after 1867, several important changes altered the geographical shape of the new federation and the size of the domestic market in Canada. In 1869 the federal government purchased the territories between Ontario and British Columbia from the Hudson's Bay Company. One-twentieth of all lands in the region remained in the hands of the Company. Manitoba (1870), British Columbia (1871) and Prince Edward Island (1873) subsequently joined the Confederation pact. The negotiations with British Columbia resulted in a federal promise to build a transcontinental railway by 1881. Many French speaking Quebecers viewed these developments with trepidation. The admission of new English speaking provinces diluted Quebec's power of influence in the federal House of Commons and its relative importance in the new federation.

The restrictive nature of the constitutional arrangements, particularly with respect to government financing, soon led to Dominion-provincial conflict. The BNA Act effected an important transfer of regulatory powers from the provincial legislature of the Canadas to the new federal government in Ottawa. To finance the exercise of these powers and the burden of existing debts, the federal government received a major transfer of spending powers. This transfer included the power to collect customs and excise duties, an item that had provided 60 percent of Canadian government revenues during fiscal year 1866. To compensate for the loss of provincial revenue sources, Sections 118 and 119 of the BNA Act established an annual federal-provincial transfer of funds that has continued, in one form or another, to the present day. (See Chapter 16)

The slow pace of economic growth after Confederation, combined with the overwhelming power of the federal government in economic matters, provoked anger and frustration in several Canadian provinces. The recession of the years 1873-1896 was clearly international in scope, but it served to highlight the restricted nature of the economic powers assigned to the provinces by the Constitution.[11] During the provincial conference held at Quebec in 1887, the five participating provincial premiers recommended the abolition of the federal power to disallow provincial legislation, and insisted on the need for provincial approval of federal expenditures affecting overall Canadian economic development. These recommendations, though not accepted by the federal government, reflected provincial discontent at the time.

The move toward a more decentralized federation eventually resulted from a change in judicial interpretation rather than from constitutional amendment. In 1896, the Judicial Committee of the Privy Council in London, which acted as the Canadian Supreme Court, initiated an important swing toward greater provincial rights by upholding a broad interpretation of the "property and civil rights" clause (Section 92) in the BNA Act. In upholding the validity of the Ontario Temperance Act concerning the regulation of intraprovincial traffic in liquor, the Privy Council denied wide powers to the federal government concerning the "peace, order and good government" of Canada (Section 91). This judicial decision, the 'Local Prohibition Case', was one of several that strengthened the regulatory powers of the provinces at a time of considerable federal-provincial discord.

Tariff Policy After Confederation

After Confederation, the Quebec economy evolved within the institutional environment created by the BNA Act. The federal government defined tariff and commercial policy in accordance with both its revenue needs and development objectives. Customs and excise duties provided about 60 percent of federal government revenues between 1868 and 1878. The relative costs of customs administration favored the tariff over other instruments of revenue collection. Tariff duties also affected the growth rate and spatial distribution of manufacturing, even though these effects were not always recognized at the time. Canadian tariff policy produced both short term (static) and long term (dynamic) effects on economic growth and industrial structure in Quebec.

The expansion of (uncoerced) international trade generally confers benefits on both trading parties; but not every trading arrangement is equally satisfactory to both partners. Governments have often attempted to improve their country's terms of trade by taxing imports. As long as trading partners do not retaliate, one country may increase the annual value of its exports relative to its imports by means of tariffs. There are, however, both benefits and costs from higher tariff barriers even in the absence of retaliation. The protection of manufactured goods, for instance, attracts capital and labor into the manufacturing sector. An increase of employment in manufacturing may have a positive secondary effect on the rate of immigration. On the other hand, tariff protection of manufactured goods raises the costs of resource exploitation and the price of domestically produced exports. Resource owners, particularly owners of fixed resources such as land, must pay higher prices for their manufactured inputs—farm machinery, mining machinery, and so on. This cost increase reduces the competitiveness of domestic exports on international markets. Tariff protection in the short-to-medium run can be justified, however, if the tariff barriers will permit economies of scale in the long run. In terms of allocative efficiency, long run tariff protection is really justifiable only for those industries contributing to national defense. 'National defense', it should be added, has sometimes been interpreted broadly to encompass 'political and cultural autonomy' and to justify the protection of a wide array of industries. The costs of political autonomy through tariff protection are, of course, paid by consumers in the form of higher prices.

As indicated earlier in this chapter, tariff protection for manufactured products in Canada occurred before 1867. From a level of 7.5 percent in 1847, the average rate of duties on manufactured imports increased to 12.5 percent in 1849, and to 19.6 percent (on fully manufactured goods) by 1859. Although the average rate of protection was reduced to 15 percent as a conciliatory gesture toward the Maritime provinces on the eve of Confederation, it is fair to say that manufacturing industry in Quebec enjoyed a moderate degree of protection from the middle of the nineteenth century.

Between 1868 and 1887 the federal government raised the average rate of tariff protection on Canadian imports on a number of occasions. The average *ad valorem* rates on dutiable imports rose from 19.5 percent in the years 1869-1874 to 31.6 percent during the years 1888-1890, falling slightly in the 1890s.[12] (See Table 9.2) Tariff rates on dutiable imports entering the United States fluctuated between 39 and 48 percent during the same period. In both countries, the tariff structure was graduated to allow most raw materials to enter duty free. The central governments taxed manufactured goods according to the degree of manufacture, reflecting a conscious decision to favor the growth of domestic manufacturing industry.

The tariff increase of 1879 is the most prominent in Canadian tariff history. Together with subsidies to the building of transcontinental railways and an open door immigration policy, the tariffs of 1879 are remembered because of their part in the Conservatives' 'National Policy'. But, in fact, the tariffs of 1879 did not represent a radical departure from previous policy. Tariff protection, transcontinental railways, and immigration provided the basis of the

Table 9.2

**AVERAGE RATES OF DUTY ON CANADIAN IMPORTS,
1869-1897
(Percentages)**

Year of Legislation	Years Under Consideration	Ad Valorem Rate on Dutiable Imports	Ad Valorem Rate on Total Imports	Proportion of Imports Entering Free
1868	1869-1874	19.5	12.6	35.3
1874	1875-1879	21.2	14.2	33.4
1879	1880-1887	26.2	19.8	24.2
1887	1888-1890	31.6	21.7	31.2
1890	1891-1897	30.5	19.0	37.7

The Regional Impact of the Canadian Tariff, p. 6, by Hugh McA. Pinchin. Reproduced by permission of the Minister of Supply and Services Canada.

federal government's economic development strategy until the 1930s. The impact of the national policy on the growth of manufacturing industry in Quebec is examined in Chapters 12, 14 and 16.

Transport Innovations After Confederation

By 1860 the Quebec economy possessed a network of trunk rail lines connected with Ontario and the eastern seaboard of the United States, but very few branch lines. All of the lines east of Montreal lay on the south shore of the St. Lawrence River. The land nearest the railway reaped locational rents—extra income from reduced transport and transaction costs. The early railways often enjoyed a monopoly position on rapid transport in the province. The Grand Trunk, for example, attempted to minimize its losses by obstructing the construction of competing lines after Confederation. Municipal governments, on the other hand, used subsidies to encourage the construction of railways through their political unit. The Quebec government sought to redistribute income toward Francophone farmers and lower the costs of colonization in outlying areas by subsidizing new railways on the north shore of the St. Lawrence. The federal government occupied itself with interregional projects. In keeping with its promises, the federal government constructed the Intercolonial Rail Line to line

Central Canada with the Maritime provinces (1876) and subsidized the Canadian Pacific to link Central Canada with British Columbia (1885).

Meanwhile the Quebec government initiated a policy of cash subsidies for railway projects in 1873 that effectively ended the provincial subsidizing of railway companies with land grants. Two years later the government decided to take over the construction of the North Shore Railway (Montreal/Quebec City) and the Montreal Colonization Railway (Montreal/Saint Jerome and Montreal/Ottawa). Completed in 1879, the entire line, renamed the Quebec, Montreal, Ottawa and Occidental Railway, became the trunk operation for a series of branches running into the north shore hinterland. On the south shore of the St. Lawrence, the provincial government subsidized the construction of the Quebec Central from Sherbrooke to the Levis/Kennebec line running south from the Quebec City area. The Sherbrooke/Levis rail connection through the Thetford Mines region was completed in June 1881. (See Chart 9.2) The redistributive policy objectives of the provincial government coincided with the colonization efforts of the Roman Catholic Church aimed at slowing the rate of emigration of Francophone Quebecers.[13]

The subsidization of railways after Confederation dramatically influenced provincial finances. In 1873 Quebec did not have a provincial debt. During the fiscal year ending in June 1877, however, government expenditures on railways amounted to nearly 60 percent of total provincial spending. By 1882 the government of Quebec had spent some $12.5 million on the north shore railways. (Young, p. 140) There is no evidence these rail lines had an immediate impact on the rate of growth of provincial manufacturing. It seems likely, however, that they played a role in the diffusion of new agricultural techniques and the commercialization of the province's dairy products sector.

By 1901 the province of Quebec possessed some 3 481 miles of railway. Hamelin and Roby have constructed crude estimates of the sources of railway financing between 1832 and 1901. Government spending, they suggest, accounted for more than half of all railway financing in Quebec during this period.[14] Of the total, the federal government contributed about 34 percent, the provincial government about 20 percent, and the municipal governments about 5 percent. (Hamelin and Roby, p. 132) The close ties between elected politicians and railway entrepreneurs reflect the political nature of railway building at this time.

With Confederation, responsibility for navigation and shipping passed into the hands of the federal government. The most spectacular improvements in subsequent years affected the ports of

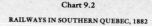

Chart 9.2

RAILWAYS IN SOUTHERN QUEBEC, 1882

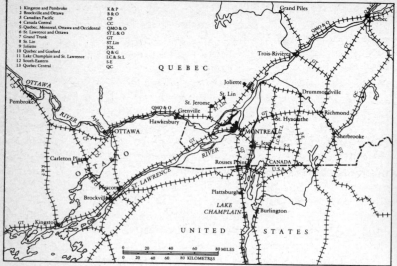

Promoters and Politicians: The North-Shore Railways in the History of Quebec 1854-85, Map A. by Brian J. Young, reprinted by permission of University of Toronto Press.

Montreal and Quebec City. By 1877 the port of Montreal possessed 20 585 feet of docking space. In an effort to improve the competitive position of the port of Quebec, docking facilities at Quebec were completely rebuilt between 1875 and 1890. Smaller docks, piers and jetties appeared along all of Quebec's major waterways. But these changes do no appear to have improved the relative importance of the St. Lawrence water route. In 1896, for example, the port of Montreal handled 52 percent as much cereal tonnage as that arriving at the port of New York. Rail lines handled less than a third of the total cereal traffic arriving in Montreal via the St. Lawrence.

* * *

During the first half of the nineteenth century, the direction of Quebec's trade with the outside world had depended heavily on colonial relations with Great Britain. In the second half of the century, institutional changes affecting trade barriers, the rapid growth of the American economy, a decline in overland transport and transaction costs, and the creation of the Canadian State permitted a relative increase in imports from the United States: business cycles in Canada exhibited a pattern similar to those of the

United States from about the time of Confederation. Except for the Reciprocity years, import duties on goods from the United States and Great Britain entered Canada at identical rates between 1849 and 1897, and by the end of the century the majority of Canada's imports came from the United States. (See Table 9.3) Although exports to Great Britain remained relatively high until World War I, the shift in the direction of Canadian imports occurred to the detriment of commerce on the St. Lawrence River and the level of activity in the transport sector of the Quebec economy as a whole. As economic activity moved westward, Montreal retained its status as the chief port of entry for Central Canada. But the relative contribution of the Quebec economy to the aggregate production and distribution of goods and services in North America diminished in importance.

Table 9.3

THE DIRECTION OF CANADA'S COMMODITY TRADE AS A PROPORTION OF TOTAL TRADE, 1870-1939
(Percentage)

Year	Great Britain		United States		Others	
	Imports	Exports[b]	Imports	Exports[b]	Imports	Exports[b]
1870[a]	57.1	37.9	32.2	50.0	10.7	12.1
1880	47.8	51.2	40.0	40.5	12.2	8.3
1886	40.7	47.2	44.6	44.1	14.7	8.7
1891	37.7	48.8	46.7	42.6	15.6	8.6
1896	31.2	57.2	50.8	34.4	18.0	8.4
1901	24.1	52.3	60.3	38.3	15.6	9.4
1911	24.3	48.2	60.8	38.0	14.9	13.8
1916	15.2	60.9	73.0	27.1	11.8	12.0
1929	15.0	25.2	68.8	42.8	16.2	32.0
1939	15.2	35.5	66.1	41.1	18.7	23.4

[a]Data for Quebec, Ontario, New Brunswick and Nova Scotia.
[b]Domestic product only.

Canada: An Economic History, p. 389, by William L. Marr and Donald G. Paterson, reprinted by permission of the authors.

NOTES

[1]In a controversial move, the Atlantic and St. Lawrence adopted wide (5'6") track in lieu of the narrower (4'8½") standard gauge. The wide track policy was pushed through by the Portland promoters to preserve the city's monopoly on Canadian traffic by preventing a hook-up with American standard gauge lines running to Boston and New York.

[2]Six of the Company's Canadian directors belonged to the Union cabinet.

[3]The subsidy to the Grand Trunk also included one million acres of land between Trois-Pistoles and the New Brunswick border.

[4]The use of wide track (5'6") instead of standard gauge (4'8½") protected the Grand Trunk rail system from competition at Ogdensburg and Montreal by imposing unloading and reloading costs on interline transfers. But it also raised the costs of transport for bulky goods coming by standard gauge rail from the American mid-west, to the advantage of the American rail system. Eventually, in 1870 the Grand Trunk began the costly process of converting its track and rolling stock to the standard gauge.

[5]In 1867 Quebec possessed 575 miles of railway, Ontario 1 393 miles. (Faucher, p. 48)

[6]The failure of the free trade experiment with the United States at this time confirms the experience of many countries today. Common markets and other forms of economic integration are most successful among partners at a relatively equal stage of industrial development, with similar market sizes, and possessing a desire to co-ordinate their growth patterns so as to share the net benefits of integration.

[7]Galt's tariff changes increased total net tariff revenue from $4.5 million (current) in 1856 to $4.7 million in 1860. (Barnett, p. 396)

[8]*The Reciprocity Treaty of 1854*, p. 66, by Donald C. Masters, reprinted by permission of The Canadian Publishers, McClelland and Stewart Limited, Toronto.

[9]The population of Minnesota, for example, increased from 6 000 in 1850 to 172 000 in 1860 and the territory became a state in the Union in 1858. The growth of trade between the Assiniboia settlement at Winnipeg and St. Paul, Minnesota worried the partisans of Confederation. "A bill providing for the absorption of all British North American territories into the American Union was introduced into the (U.S.) House of Representatives in 1866. It was defeated, but in 1867 Senator Ramsey of Minnesota moved that the Committee on Foreign Relations investigate the desirability of a treaty between the United States and Canada (sic) which, among other things, would provide for the annexation of all territories in North America west of the 90° "meridian". (*The National Policy and the Wheat Economy*, p. 43, by Vernon Fowke, © 1957, University of Toronto Press.)

[10]In Nova Scotia, adversaries of Confederation won thirty-six of the thirty-eight seats in the first post-Confederation provincial elections. But a petition requesting provincial withdrawal was rejected by the British government and a negotiated settlement eventually obtained.

[11]Between 1874 and 1896, total provincial government spending in Canada rose from $1.69 to $2.20 per capita.

[12]The ratio of duties collected to dutiable imports, as a measure of tariff protection, suffers from several weaknesses. If, for example, the duties are very high, they yield no revenue. The data necessary to calculate the average duties weighted by production, however, are not available.

[13]Prior to the takeover of the North Shore Railway by the provincial government, the Archbishop of Quebec was the company's largest shareholder.

[14]Hamelin and Roby's rough estimates include cash grants only. Between 1853 and 1886, millions of acres of provincial land were also alienated to railway companies. In 1886 the Quebec government decided to reacquire and resell some of these lands in order to accelerate their rate of development. (Hamelin and Roby, p. 131)

SELECT BIBLIOGRAPHY

Aitken, Hugh J.G. "Defensive Expansion: The State and Economic Growth in Canada", in W.T. Easterbrook and M.A. Watkins, eds., *Approaches to Canadian Economic History*. Toronto: McClelland and Stewart Ltd., 1967.

Ankli, Robert E. "The Reciprocity Treaty of 1854." *The Canadian Journal of Economics*. February 1971.

Barnett, D.F. " The Galt Tariff: Incidental or Effective Protection?" *The Canadian Journal of Economics*. August 1976.

Creighton, Donald G. *British North America at Confederation*. Ottawa: The Queen's Printer, 1963.

Davis, Lance E. *et al.*, *American Economic Growth: An Economist's History of the United States*. New York: Harper & Row, Publishers, 1972.

Faucher, Albert. *Québec en Amérique au XIXe siècle*. Montreal: Editions Fides, 1973.

Fowke, Vernon. *The National Policy and the Wheat Economy*. Toronto: University of Toronto Press, 1957.

Glazebrook, G.P. de T. *A History of Transportation in Canada*. Vol. 1. *Continental Strategy to 1867*. Toronto: McClelland and Stewart Limited, 1964.

Hamelin, Jean and Yves Roby. *Histoire économique du Québec, 1851-1896*. Montreal: Editions Fides, 1971.

Harley, C. Knick. "Transportation, The World Wheat Trade, and the Kuznets Cycle, 1850-1913." *Explorations in Economic History*. July 1980.

Latulippe, Jean-Guy. "Le Traité de réciprocité de 1854-1866." *L'Actualité Economique*. October-December 1976.

Marr, William L. and Donald G. Paterson. *Canada: An Economic History*. Toronto: Macmillan of Canada Ltd., 1980.

Masters, Donald C. *The Reciprocity Treaty of 1854*. Toronto: McClelland and Stewart Limited, 1963.

McDiarmid, O.J. *Commercial Policy in the Canadian Economy*. Cambridge, Mass.: Harvard University Press, 1946.

McDougall, David J. "The Shipbuilders, Whalers and Master Mariners of Gaspé Bay in the Nineteenth Century", in Lewis R. Fischer and Eric W. Sager, eds., *The Enterprising Canadians: Entrepreneurs and Economic Development in Eastern Canada, 1820-1914.* St. John's: Memorial University of Newfoundland, 1979.

Officer, Lawrence H. and Lawrence B. Smith. "The Canadian-American Reciprocity Treaty of 1855 to 1866." *Journal of Economic History.* December 1968.

Pinchin, Hugh McA. *The Regional Impact of the Canadian Tariff.* Ottawa: Economic Council of Canada, 1979, p. 6.

The Rowell/Sirois Report, Book I. Edited by Donald V. Smiley. Toronto: McClelland and Stewart Limited, 1963.

Tulchinsky, Gerald J.J. *The River Barons: Montreal Businessmen and the Growth of Industry and Transportation, 1837-53.* Toronto: University of Toronto Press, 1977.

Young, Brian J. *Promoters and Politicians: The North-Shore Railways in the History of Quebec, 1854-85.* Toronto: University of Toronto Press, 1978.

10
Agriculture and Emigration

During the first half of the nineteenth century, Quebec agriculture experienced growing competition from mid-continental grain and livestock exports. Inland canals and railways reduced interregional transport costs and opened up new, highly productive agricultural regions in the interior. In upland New England and upstate New York, where land productivity was lower than in the mid-west, as in Quebec, wheat production declined. In the American northeast, however, grain farmers adapted to the new environment by improving techniques and switching to the production of fresh fruits, vegetables and dairy products for urban consumption. In Quebec, changes in the structure of production and agricultural technique occurred more slowly. Uncertain of finding alternative marketable outputs, many Quebec farmers chose to minimize risks by diversifying their output and producing for home farm consumption.

Perhaps the single most important obstacle to the analysis of Quebec agriculture is the lack of information on prices. Regional variations and changes in the inflation rate inhibit intertemporal comparisons of output, income and welfare in the agricultural sector. Although the data necessary for a detailed study of agriculture in the nineteenth century are not available, output and income per farm worker appear to have diminished during the 1830s and 1840s. (See Chapter 6) This decline in the economic welfare of Quebec's agricultural population contrasts with a rise in the welfare of the agricultural population in Ontario, particularly after 1840. Precise interregional comparisons are difficult to make, but the average Quebec farm appears to have produced between two-thirds and nine-tenths of its Ontario counterpart at mid-century. Net agricultural output per worker amounted to about sixty percent of the estimated level of agricultural output per worker in the United States.

After mid-century, the British North American economies were subjected to a series of political and economic disturbances. The creation of the Canadian State, the adoption of protectionist commercial policies, and reductions in transport and transaction costs accompanied the rise of manufacturing in the east and the beginnings of settlement in the west. Because new economic opportunities were unevenly distributed, some regions benefited more than others. In response to new opportunities, population shifted from east to west, and within the older established regions from rural to urban areas. Confederation and the National Policy were designed to create the institutional environment necessary for extensive economic growth in Canada comparable to that observed in the United States. But although total population increased during the last three decades of the nineteenth century, fewer people migrated into Canada than migrated out.

As with other industrial sectors, Quebec agriculture adapted to economic growth and change beyond its borders. During the second half of the nineteenth century, net agricultural output and income per farm worker appears to have improved modestly as the composition of output shifted toward production for the market. In the 1890s a rapid increase in commercial dairy farming initiated an upward trend in sectoral output and income per capita that continued until World War I. This chapter examines the structure and growth of Quebec agriculture to the end of the nineteenth century. The discussion of agriculture is followed by a look at demographic movement. In the belief that migration was essentially an economic phenomenon, population movement is attributed to changes in the level of average income in Quebec agriculture relative to economic opportunities in other industries and regions.

Quebec Agriculture in 1851

Where did Quebec agriculture stand at mid-century? The most complete source of information available is the 1851-1852 census of Lower Canada. There are, however, numerous deficiencies in the published census data. Marvin McInnis has identified two potential pitfalls.

The published census tables for 1851-52 report land areas in an amalgam of acres and arpents and production in mixed units of bushels and minots. The French farmers in the seigneurial districts reported in arpents and minots; the English districts were reported in acres and bushels. It was presumably intended that an appropriate adjustment would be made in the tabulation of the returns [1 minot = 1.107 bushels, 1 arpent = 0.845 acres] but that was never carried out. The second problem concerns the definition of a farm. The number of "occupiers" of land includes many occupants of garden plots and other small plots. Unless these small holdings are excluded, any agricultural indicators expressed on a per farm basis will be seriously distorted.[1]

In their research on Quebec agriculture, Lewis and McInnis have adjusted the published census data to accommodate these pitfalls. Previous to their work, most analysis used the published census data for the years 1851 and 1860 (cf. Jones, Isbister, McCallum,...) and therefore underestimated output on seigneurial lands by about 10 percent, and yields on seigneurial lands by some 31 percent.

Using revised data from the 1851-1852 census returns, Lewis and McInnis have constructed estimates of net agricultural output, farm labor, and net output per agricultural worker for 1851. (Lewis and McInnis, 1981) They calculate annual net agricultural output per full-time worker in Quebec at \$102.[2] This amounts to about 60 percent of the estimated level of agricultural output per worker in the United States for 1850. About two-thirds of Quebec's agricultural output in 1851 consisted of animal products and only one-quarter of field crops, once animal feed crops are netted out. The estimated structure of production is therefore consistent with the hypothesis of considerable farm self-sufficiency in as much as the pattern of production resembles the pattern of final consumption. Agricultural output per worker varied considerably, however, from region to region.[3]

According to Lewis and McInnis, variations in land and capital equipment per worker account for some of the regional variation, but variations in total factor productivity account for about half of the regional differences. Very high levels of agricultural output per worker occurred in the Eastern Townships near the American border. (See Figure 10.1) Output per worker was also above average in the areas surrounding Montreal and immediately east of Quebec City. Proximity to markets would appear to have had some bearing on regional output per worker even though Lewis and McInnis, using crude proxy variables, could not capture this relationship statistically. (See Armstrong)

In a previous study, Lewis and McInnis compared Francophone

Figure 10.1

NET AGRICULTURAL OUTPUT PER FARM WORKER, LOWER CANADA, 1851

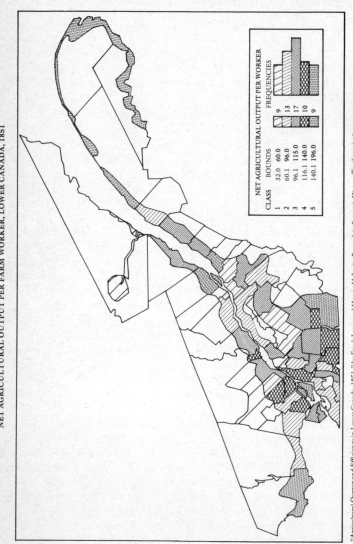

"Agricultural Output and Efficiency in Lower Canada, 1851," by Frank Lewis and Marvin McInnis, *Research in Economic History*, (Forthcoming).

and Anglophone farmers in a non-randon sample of Quebec parishes and townships. (Lewis and McInnis, 1980) The authors sought to test for the relative efficiency of the two linguistic groups in selected regions that were deemed roughly comparable. In other words, they tested for differences in output per unit of labor at the same (controlled) level of land and capital inputs.[4] Lewis and McInnis found that a relatively small proportion, at most 15.7 percent, of total agricultural productivity remained unexplained by differences in the level of inputs in their sample. This residual, they suggest, represents the upper limit on 'cultural-linguistic' differences among Quebec farmers in 1851. All other differences in output per unit of labor across the two linguistic groups resulted from initial disparities in non-human wealth. In their sample, the land/labor ratio was found to be 25.5 percent lower for French farmers than for English farmers. Francophones obtained lower output per agricultural worker, but slightly higher output per unit of land input. On the basis of the results from their pre-selected sample, Lewis and McInnis conclude that Francophone farmers were only slightly less efficient than their English speaking neighbors. According to the authors, the disparity in output between the two groups stemmed mostly from basic disparities in the distribution of land and capital.

The Abolition of the Seigneurial System

Shortly after mid-century a major institutional innovation reshaped the environment surrounding Quebec agricultural production. In 1854 the Union government passed legislation to end the seigneurial system in the St. Lawrence Valley. The legislation abolished all seigneurial dues in favor of an annual quit-rent that provided compensation to seigneurs for losses arising from former *cens*, *rentes*, *lods*, *banalités*, *journées de corvée*, and so on. Seigneurs acquired the status of landowners holding title as freehold owners. Censitaires became freehold tenants but were given the option to purchase their farmland. All vestiges of the seigneurial system did not disappear instantaneously, of course, but the system gradually dissolved in favor of the freehold land tenure system. Why the conversion of the seigneurial system occurred at this particular time has not been answered in historical literature. Recent economic analysis (McCallum, Lewis and McInnis) ignores the institutional environment altogether, as if the dual land tenure system in Quebec had no differential impact on agricultural output. Other writers, such as Serge Courville and Fernand Ouellet, argue that the seigneurial system seriously compounded the agricultural difficulties of the 1830s and 1840s. For them, the seigneurial system was impeding Quebec economy's ability to grow through capital accumulation at a time of rapid economic growth in much of the rest of North America. By this interpretation, the abolition of the seigneurial system resulted from a demand for institutional reform during the period of agricultural prosperity in the 1850s.

Field Crop Production

Although sectoral output and income per capita did not change dramatically after mid-century, the decade of the 1850s appears to have been a modestly prosperous period for Quebec agriculture. With the exception of wheat and hay production, the output of most field crops increased considerably during these years. (See Table 10.1) Ankli's analysis of the Reciprocity Treaty with the United States suggests that barley and rye were the only Canadian agricultural products to have been assisted by reciprocity. Most of the growth in this decade is probably attributable to reductions in domestic transport and transaction costs stemming from railway expansion. Despite the increase in aggregate field crop output, however, it is not certain the efficiency of farm workers improved. The rural population expanded by over 22 percent during the 1850s. (See Table 10.2) If farm labor increased at the same rate as the rural population over the decade (no precise data are yet available), then aggregate field crop output would have had to grow by 22 percent simply to maintain field crop output per agricultural worker at a constant level.

During the 1860s, wheat, barley, peas, and oats production decreased as producers switched to hay, buckwheat and potatoes. Judging from McCallum's index, the gross value of total crop production appears to have declined. (McCallum, p. 127) McCallum's estimates, based on the published census data, indicate the gross value of total crop production fell from $71.3 million to $63.8 million (current) between 1860 and 1870. Since the published census data underestimates Quebec's agricultural output for 1860, McCallum's estimates appear to understate the actual decennial decline.

For each census year from 1870 to 1900, André Raynauld has constructed a crude index of Quebec's aggregate field crop production.[5] (Raynauld, pp. 586-588) Valued at prices prevailing in 1900, the index indicates growth rates of 20.3, 14.5 and 37.9 percent for the three decades. Most of the growth occurred in animal feed crops: barley, hay, and oats. Labor, capital and land inputs also increased during this period so the growth in field crop

Table 10.1

FIELD CROP PRODUCTION AND FIELD CROP AREA IN PRODUCTION IN QUEBEC, 1851-1900

(Thousands of bushels except where indicated otherwise)

Year	Wheat	Barley	Hay (thousands of tons)	Peas	Oats	Buckwheat	Corn	Potatoes	Turnips and Other Root Crops	Area in Field Crop Production (thousands of acres)
1851*	3 269	509	756	1 488	9 531	558	422	4 659	476	1 849
1860*	2 799	2 423	690	2 792	18 569	1 301	353	13 461	1 475	2 571
1870	2 058	1 668	1 226	2 206	15 116	1 676	603	18 068	1 409	3 714
1880	2 019	1 752	1 615	4 170**	19 990	2 042	888	14 873	3 623	4 148
1890	1 647	1 580	2 243	1 912	17 819	2 118	826	15 862	2 657	4 065
1900	1 968	2 536	2 582	909	33 537	1 850	1 384	17 136	3 526	4 704

*Following R.M. McInnis's re-examination of the 1851-52 Census of Agriculture in Lower Canada, Normand Séguin has produced revised estimates of cereal output and area in production for 1851 and 1860. Séguin's estimates cover wheat, barley, oats, buckwheat and potatoes production. They suggest that the published census data underestimated "true" output by an average of 5.1 percent in 1851 and 5.9 percent in 1860. Séguin's estimates for 1851 and 1860 have been employed here, together with an adjustment of 5.1 percent in 1851 and 5.9 percent in 1860 to the published census data for peas, corn and turnips/root crop output.

**Includes a small quantity of beans.

"L'agriculture de la Mauricie et du Québec, 1850-1950," by Normand Séguin, *Revue d'histoire de l'Amérique française*, pp. 556-577, March 1982. Government of Canada, *Census of Canada*, 1851-1901.

Table 10.2

DEMOGRAPHIC CHANGE IN QUEBEC, 1851–1900

Year	Total Population	Urban Percentage*	Urban Population**	Rural Population**	Estimated Emigration to the U.S. over the previous decade
1851	890 261	14.9	132 649	757 612	35 000
1860	1 111 566	16.6	184 520	927 046	70 000
1870	1 191 516	19.9	237 112	954 464	n/a
1880	1 359 027	23.8	323 448	1 035 579	120 000
1890	1 488 535	28.6	425 721	1 062 814	150 000
1900	1 648 898	36.1	595 252	1 053 646	140 000

*Incorporated cities, tours and villages of 1 000 and over.

**Calculated from the first two columns in the table.

Urban Development in Canada: An Introduction to the Demographic Aspects, pp. 29, 269, by Leroy O. Stone. Ottawa: Dominion Bureau of Statistics, 1967. Reproduced by permission of Statistics Canada.

"Les mouvements migratoires des Canadiens entre leur pays et les Etats-Unis au XIXe siècles: étude quantitative," by Yolande Lavoie, in Hubert Charbonneau, ed., *La Population du Québec: Etudes Retrospectives*, p. 78, © 1973, reprinted by permission of Les Editions du Boréal Express.

output does not necessarily reflect any change in total factor productivity or efficiency. Some total factor productivity improvement probably occurred during the 1890s, however. The rural population declined by 0.9 percent over this decade (see Table 10.2), while the total quantity of land in field crop production increased by 15.7 percent. No information on total capital inputs is available, but it is doubtful the very large increase in aggregate field crop output, 37.9 percent, can be entirely attributed to increases in land and capital inputs. Some increase in total factor productivity must have occurred.

During the second half of the nineteenth century, new field cropping techniques originating in the United States gradually permeated the former seigneurial regions. Wooden ploughs gave way to cast-iron, and eventually steel plows. Mechanical threshing machines and the mechanical, horse-drawn reaper (harvester) extended the spectrum of available techniques and offered the possibility of substantially greater field crop output per unit of labor input. Yields per acre in the province increased for almost every crop. In those areas producing wheat and oats, farmers adopted mechanized means of production at a rapid rate. The number of threshing machines in Quebec rose from 469 in 1844 to 15 476 in 1870. (See Table 10.3A) In the overall North American context, however, Quebec's comparative disadvantage in wheat production was sufficiently great that mechanical reapers represented a relatively unattractive investment option. Small average farm size does not appear to have been the determining factor affecting the rate of adoption of new techniques. (See Table 10.3B)[6] The poverty of many Quebec farmers, however, hampered investment in costly mechanized techniques such as fanning mills, and in techniques requiring expensive complementary factors, such as horses and horse rakes. Less costly non-mechanized instruments, such as ploughs, harrows and cultivators, were employed at least as frequently in Quebec as in Ontario. A relatively low wage-rental ratio stemming from a comparatively high land-labor ratio in agriculture may also have slowed the rate of adoption of mechanized capital-intensive techniques. The most important technical innovations in nineteenth century American agriculture consisted of labor-saving, land-using mechanical devices that may have been inappropriate in Quebec agriculture.

Cattle and Dairy Products

Investment by Quebec farmers in animal stock expanded steadily over the second half of the nineteenth century. (See Table 10.4)

Table 10.3

A. QUANTITY OF FIELD CROP IMPLEMENTS IN QUEBEC AND ONTARIO, 1870

	Quebec	Ontario	Quebec average per farm*	Ontario average per farm*
Ploughs, harrows and cultivators	206 663	289 362	1.92	1.90
Reapers and mowers	5 149	36 874	0.05	0.24
Horse rakes	10 401	46 246	0.10	0.30
Threshing mills	15 476	13 805	0.14	0.09
Fanning mills	37 262	120 732	0.35	0.79

*Farms over 10 acres in size.

B. DISTRIBUTION OF FARMS IN QUEBEC AND ONTARIO BY TOTAL ACREAGE, 1870

	Quebec	%	Ontario	%
10 acres and under	10 510	8.9	19 954	11.5
11-50 acres	22 379	19.0	38 882	22.6
51-100 acres	44 410	37.6	71 884	41.7
101-200 acres	30 891	26.2	33 984	19.7
201 and over	9 896	8.4	7 574	4.4
Total	118 086		172 278	

Government of Canada, *Census of Canada*, 1871.

The 1860s and the 1890s were periods of particularly rapid growth. Since grass and animal feeds such as oats and hay grow at a lower temperature and have a shorter growing season than other field crops, cattle raising is less susceptible to winter conditions than the production of cash crops such as wheat. Growth in Quebec's animal stock reflected the region's comparative advantage on eastern Canadian and British markets.

Until mid-century most dairy products were consumed on the farm. The advent of rapid rail transport and the improvement of refrigeration techniques after 1850 accelerated the marketing of

Table 10.4

ANIMAL STOCK IN QUEBEC, 1852-1901
(Thousands of Head)

Year	Horned cattle	Milch cows	Horses	Sheep	Swine
1852	112	296	185	647	258
1861	201	328	249	683	286
1871	375	407	253	1 008	371
1881	539	491	274	890	329
1891	420	550	344	730	370
1901	598	734	321	655	404

Government of Canada, *Census of Canada*, 1852-1901.

Table 10.5

MISCELLANEOUS AGRICULTURAL PRODUCTION IN QUEBEC, 1851-1900
(Thousands of Pounds)

Year	Homemade butter	Homemade cheese	Wool	Maple products	Tobacco
1851	9 610	764	1 429	6 068	443
1860	15 907	686	1 967	9 325	n/a
1870	24 289	512	2 763	10 497	1 195
1880	30 631	559	2 731	15 688	2 357
1890	30 113	4 261	2 547	18 875	3 959
1900	18 357	n/a	2 773	13 565	7 656

Government of Canada, *Census of Canada*, 1852-1901.

dairy produce and locally slaughtered meat products. During the Reciprocity period, Quebec butter and cheese became exportable to the United States. At the end of the Treaty period in 1866, the Canadian government introduced modest tariffs on slaughtered meat, butter and cheese to protect domestic producers from American imports. The introduction of refrigerated rail car service lowered the costs of transporting fresh meat and dairy produce in the 1870s. Homemade butter output increased and factory production began to replace the homemaking of cheese. (See Table

10.5) W.F. Ryan, using Raynauld's data, has constructed estimates of the constant dollar growth in butter and cheese production. (Ryan, p. 321) For the last three decades of the nineteenth century, the percentage growth rates by decade are 35.8, 38.0 and 94.6. Factory production accounted for a growing proportion of total butter and cheese output, particularly in the 1890s. (See Chapter 12) Cheese production was largely directed to the export market in Britain while butter was consumed mostly in Canada.

Aggregate Agricultural Output and Income

Aside from inconsistencies in the census data, one of the major obstacles to analysing agricultural change in Quebec is the absence of relative price series and an aggregate farm price index for the nineteenth century. This is one reason for the frequency of Quebec/Ontario comparisons. Variations across regions and changes in the rate on inflation obstruct intertemporal comparisons of output, income and welfare in the agricultural sector. Raynauld has attempted to construct a rough index of Quebec's agricultural production for the years 1870-1925 to accompany his post-1926 data series. Unfortunately, as an index of aggregate agricultural output, Raynauld's index is unreliable. Raynauld restricts his analysis of the 1870-1910 data to a limited number of field crops plus butter and cheese. Livestock, orchard, market garden, and all other agricultural products are excluded. He then constructs an index of total output on the shaky assumptions that the structure of production in the nineteenth century mirrored that of 1926, and that the growth rate of total agricultural output was identical to the growth rate of field crops plus butter and cheese for the years 1870-1910. Raynauld's conclusions concerning the similarity of aggregrate agricultural output growth in Quebec and Ontario are not necessarily wrong, but they do not derive from a complete analysis of the available information.

In an interesting tabulation, J. Isbister has avoided the money price valuation problem by aggregating agricultural produce in terms of calorie equivalents. Isbister's index of total agricultural production remains dependent on the published census data for 1851 and 1860, but it avoids the problems arising from changes in the general price level.[7] With the aid of United States Department of Agriculture estimates of food calorie equivalents, and calorie requirements for comparable labor in modern Scotland, the author is able to estimate food production and food requirements in Quebec and Ontario.

Table 10.6

FOOD PRODUCTION, IN MILLIONS OF CALORIES PER DAY, QUEBEC AND ONTARIO 1850-1940

Year	(1) Calories Produced		(2) Requirements of Farm Population		(3) Farm Rate of Surplus Production [(1) − (2)] ÷ (2)		(4) Requirements of Provincial Population		(5) Provincial Rate of Surplus Production [(1) − (4)] ÷ (4)	
	Quebec	Ontario	Quebec	Ontario	Quebec	Ontario	Quebec	Ontario	Quebec	Ontario
1851	1 311	3 511	1 710	1 586	−0.2	1.2	2 289	2 488	−0.4	0.4
1860	1 897	6 939	1 866	2 094	0.0	2.3	2 858	3 648	−0.3	0.9
1870	2 133	5 623	2 108	2 734	0.0	1.1	3 063	4 235	−0.3	0.3
1880	2 360	9 158	2 461	3 132	0.0	1.9	3 492	5 035	−0.3	0.8
1890	2 410	8 859	2 588	3 107	−0.1	1.9	3 843	5 614	−0.4	0.6
1900	3 237	11 621	2 501	2 772	0.3	3.2	4 274	5 864	−0.2	1.0
1910	4 585	10 498	2 672	2 732	0.7	2.8	5 193	6 820	−0.1	0.5
1920	5 874	9 601	2 281	2 378	1.6	3.0	6 143	7 886	0.0	0.2
1930	4 210	9 592	2 000	2 157	1.1	3.5	7 563	9 332	−0.4	0.0
1940	4 656	12 113	2 193	1 920	1.1	5.3	8 941	10 465	−0.5	0.2

Reprinted from "Agriculture, Balanced Growth & Social Change in Central Canada: Since 1850: An Interpretation," in *Economic Development & Cultural Change*, Vol. 25, No. 4, p. 679, July 1977, by John Isbister, by permission of The University of Chicago Press.

Isbister's results suggest that Quebec's total agricultural output in terms of calorie equivalents, varied from one-quarter to one-half of Ontario's. (See Table 10.6) This result is not really surprising i differences in the volume of labor and arable land, the quality o land, and the length of the growing season are considered. (Ker and Smyth, p. 616) What is surprising is the apparent absence o surplus farm production in Quebec during the second half of th nineteenth century. Since many farms were making cash sale outside the agricultural sector, some others must have been buying 'imported' food with non-agricultural income or eating belov 'reference' nutritional standards. The absence of aggregate surplu production lends indirect empirical support to the hypothesis o widespread subsistence farming referred to by casual observers o the time. The increase in output and income associated with th commercialization of dairy farming in the 1890s is also evident ir Isbister's results. Stronger conclusions about real agricultura output and growth during this period must await more detailed study.

Demographic Movement

The demographic movement of Quebecers resulted from simple economic choice. As indicated in earlier chapters, potentia migrants evaluate the various labor market opportunities available to them and tend to select the option that maximizes expected ne income. The conditions that promote emigration are the same a those that discourage immigration. The expected net benefits from migration depend on income differentials across industries and regions, employment opportunities, and the costs (both mon etary and social) of moving. M.P. Todaro has demonstrated that rural-urban migration can be directly related to:

(i) the differential in real incomes as between rural and urban employment;

(ii) the probability of obtaining an urban job, a variable inversely related to the rate of urban unemployment.

In other words, the decision to migrate depends primarily or expected income in the future and the risk of urban unemploy ment or underemployment for a period of time to come. While the Todaro model was developed for application to rural-urban migra tion in contemporary underdeveloped countries, it is sufficiently general to apply to interregional migration in the nineteenth century.

The costs of moving discouraged migration from the Quebec countryside prior to the 1840s. Despite income differentials rela

ive to other North American regions, the net benefits of migra-
ion were insufficient to induce people to move in large numbers.
The costs of accurate labor market information in the French
anguage were probably too high to induce much searching in any
case. Gradually, however, the growth of per capita income in the
United States, together with decreases in the costs of information
and travel, raised the potential net benefits of emigration.[8] As
potential net benefits increased after mid-century, more and more
people began to leave the province. (See Table10.2) The growth
rate of domestic manufacturing employment simply could not
accommodate the number of people wishing to leave the countryside. Migrants to New England typically found employment in the
manufacturing sector and emigration to the United States may
therefore be considered as another facet of the urbanization phenomenon.

The social costs of leaving the province were high for French
speaking Quebecers but, in some cases, emigration was the most
viable option. For Francophone migrants, moving outside of the
province meant incurring high 'psychic' costs involving the potential loss of language and culture. Typically, older, less-educated
people benefited least from migration and were less likely to move.
For those Francophone Quebecers that did leave the province, the
availability of information concerning employment and living
conditions played an important role in the choice of destination.
Once Francophones began moving to the neighboring New
England states, the early migrants provided a stream of information to family and friends. The neighboring New England states
became the destination of most migrants; relatively few native-
born Quebecers migrated to western Canada. Even if the long run
of prospects of assimilation in New England were about the same
as in the Canadian West, New England was much closer to home.

Church and State were not oblivious to the emigration phenomenon in the nineteenth century. Their concern resulted in measures to stem the tide by encouraging the occupation of unsettled
areas in the province. Thus the 'colonization movement' emerged
out of attempts to find a domestic alternative to out-migration.
The origins of the colonization movement can roughly be dated
from a provincial law incorporating several colonization companies in 1848. During the second half of the nineteenth century, a
considerable quantity of public land was alienated to new occupants. (See Urquhart and Buckley, pp. 324-325) Between 1851
and 1900, improved farm land area in Quebec increased by 137
percent. (Séguin, 1982, p. 556) A substantial part of the new
territories occupied during this period was less productive than
territory already in cultivation. For this reason the colonization

movement proved unsuccessful in raising agricultural productivity or income per capita. The colonization movement did, however, result in settlement and the creation of public services in several previously unsettled regions: the upper Ottawa River, the Gatineau, Temiskaming, Saint-Maurice, Saguenay and Lac Saint-Jean regions. The existence of an economic infrastructure in these areas facilitated industrial growth during the early part of the twentieth century.

The Chicoutimi-Lac Saint-Jean region is one example of a peripheral region settled during the second half of the nineteenth century. A pioneer colonization company brought the first settlers to the Saguenay fjord in 1838 to cut pine timber. The timber entrepreneur, William Price, owner of two saw mills in the Lower Saguenay region, purchased the company sometime between 1841 and 1843. The absence of a log sluice at the head of the Saguenay River, however, reserved the Lac Saint-Jean area to pioneer settlement until the 1860s. The high costs of transport and external communications isolated the region and tied the population to the timber industry insofar as the marketing of agricultural produce was concerned. The entire region relied heavily on water transport until the arrival of the Quebec/Lac Saint-Jean Railway at Chambord and Roberval in 1888. The regional population expanded from 5 400 in 1851 to 23 500 in 1880, and 37 000 in 1900. (Ryan, p. 122) As communications gradually improved with the inauguration of regular steamboat service to Chicoutimi in 1869, a 140-mile road from Quebec City to Lac Saint-Jean in 1887, and the railway, the margin of regional monopsony power exercised by the Price family gradually diminished.

*   *   *

The level of net agricultural output and income per farm worker appears to have grown very little over the second half of the nineteenth century. Migration out of the agricultural sector therefore constituted a rational economic response on the part of rural Quebecers. Some moved to nearby urban areas in search of a new occupation. This migration involved a consideration of current and expected future income differentials, as well as some (implicit) probability calculation based on the fact that job searching in a new region was a risky undertaking. Rural-urban migration within the province was constrained, however, by the growth rate of urban employment in the manufacturing and service sectors. Many Quebecers emigrated to search for employment in neighboring New England. The rate of emigration reached its highest level during the 1880s and 1890s after which a narrowing of interregional income differentials associated with structural changes in Quebec agriculture gradually dampened the outflow of migrants.

NOTES

[1]"Some Pitfalls in the 1851-52 Census of Agriculture of Lower Canada", by Marvin McInnis, *Histoire Sociale*, pp. 220-221, May 1981, reprinted by permission.

[2]Women's labor is not included in this estimate. The estimate also excludes the production of poultry, eggs, garden vegetables, textiles, farm and forest products.

[3]Many farm workers earned supplementary incomes in other sectors: fishing, timber cutting, timber loading, shipbuilding, and so on.

[4]Lewis and McInnis exclude from their study land inputs for parcels of land less than ten acres in size (some 14 477 acres). They assume the lands included in their sample were uniformly productive. If, for example, the English speaking districts covered lower quality, less productive soils, then Anglophone efficiency would have been underestimated. The authors also assume that capital was uniformly productive and that land and labor earned the same rate of return on all farms. See Armstrong for a critical look at the Lewis and McInnis results.

[5]Wheat, barley, rye, oats, hay, corn and peas are included in the index, but not buckwheat, potatoes, or turnips.

[6]R. Pomfret argues that scale of operations was more important than factor prices in explaining the mechanization of reaping in Ontario. He estimates the threshold size for the self-rake reaper (that size of farm where the farmer is indifferent between purchase and no purchase) to have been 27.04 acres in 1870.

[7]Isbister uses the published 1851 and 1860 census data which underestimates Francophone output. (cf. McInnis, 1981) Before correction, this same error introduced an average underestimate of 5.4 percent per field crop in the 1890 census.

[8]Net national product per capita in the United States increased annually at a rate of 1.6 percent from 1840 to 1860 and at a rate of 1.9 percent from 1870 to 1910. "Over long periods, small differences in growth rates add up to big differences in living standards: 1.9 percent average annual growth increased per capita income by 110 percent between 1870 and 1910, while a 1.0 percent per annum rate would have increased real per capita income just about 49 percent." (*A New Economic View of American History*, p. 267, by Susan P. Lee and Peter Passell, © 1979, reprinted by permission of W.W. Norton & Company, Inc.)

SELECT BIBLIOGRAPHY

Ankli, Robert E. "The Reciprocity Treaty of 1854." *The Canadian Journal of Economics*. February 1971.

Armstrong, Robert. "The Efficiency of Quebec Farmers in 1851," Department of Economics, University of Ottawa, Research Paper No. 8304, June 1983 (forthcoming in *Histoire Sociale—Social History*).

Blanchard, Raoul. *L'Est du Canada Français.* Montreal: Librairie Beauchemin Limitée, 1935.

Bouchard, Gérard. "Introduction à l'étude de la société saguenayenne aux XIXe et XXe siècles." *Revue d'histoire de l'Amérique française.* June 1977.

Bouffard, Jean. *Traité du Domaine.* (Reproduction de l'édition originale de 1921). Quebec: les Presses de l'Université Laval, 1977.

Charbonneau, Hubert. *La Population de Québec: études retrospectives.* Montreal: les Editions du Boréal Express, 1973.

Courville, Serge. La crise agricole du Bas-Canada, éléments d'une réflexion géographique." *Cahiers de Géographie du Québec.* Part I, September 1980. Part II, December 1980.

Faucher, Albert. *Québec en Amérique au XIXe siècle.* Montreal: Editions Fides, 1973.

Greenwood, Michael J. "Research on Internal Migration in the United States: A Survey." *Journal of Economic Literature.* June 1975.

Hamelin, Jean, and Yves Roby. *Histoire économique du Québec, 1851-1896.* Montreal: Editions Fides, 1971.

Isbister, John. "Agriculture, Balanced Growth, and Social Change in Central Canada since 1850: An Interpretation." *Economic Development and Cultural Change.* July 1977.

Jones, Robert L. "The Agricultural Development of Lower Canada, 1850-1867." *Agricultural History.* October 1945.

Kerr, Donald and William J. Smyth. "Agriculture, Balanced Growth, and Social Change in Central Canada since 1850: Some Comments toward a More Complete Explanation." *Economic Development and Cultural Change.* April 1980.

Lee, Susan Previant and Peter Passell. *A New Economic View of American History.* New York: W.W. Norton & Co., 1979.

Letarte, Jacques. *Atlas d'histoire économique et sociale du Québec, 1851-1901.* Montreal: Editions Fides, 1971.

Lewis, Frank and Marvin McInnis. "The Efficiency of the French-Canadian Farmer in the Nineteenth Century." *The Journal of Economic History.* September 1980.

Lewis, Frank and Marvin McInnis. "Agricultural Output and Efficiency in Lower Canada, 1851." Institute for Economic Research, Queen's University, Discussion Paper No. 451, November 1981.

Little, J.I. "The Social and Economic Development of Settlers in two Quebec Townships, 1851-1870." *Canadian Papers in Rural History.* Vol. 1. 1978.

McCallum, John. *Unequal Beginnings: Agriculture and Economic Development in Quebec and Ontario until 1870.* Toronto: University of Toronto Press, 1980.

McInnis, Marvin. "The Changing Structure of Canadian Agriculture, 1867-1897." *The Journal of Economic History.* March 1982.

McInnis, Marvin. "Some Pitfalls in the 1851-52 Census of Agriculture of Lower Canada." *Histoire Sociale-Social History.* May 1981.

Ouellet, Fernand. "Le régime seigneurial dans le Québec, 1760-1854." *Eléments d'histoire sociale du Bas-Canada.* Montreal: Hurtubise HMH, Ltée., 1972.

Pomfret, Richard. "The Mechanization of Reaping in Nineteenth Century Ontario: A Case Study of the Pace and Causes of the Diffusion of Embodied Technical Change." *The Journal of Economic History.* June 1976.

Raynauld, André. *Croissance et structure economiques de la province.* Quebec: Ministère de l'Industrie et du Commerce, 1961.

Ryan, William F. *The Clergy and Economic Growth in Quebec (1896-1914).* Quebec: les Presses de l'Université Laval, 1966.

Séguin, Normand, ed. *Agriculture et colonisation au Québec.* Montreal: Boréal Express, 1980.

Séguin, Normand. "L'agriculture de la Mauricie et du Québec, 1850-1950." *Revue d'histoire de l'Amérique française.* March 1982.

Steckel, Richard H. "The Economic Foundations of East-West Migration during the 19th Century." *Explorations in Economic History.* January 1983.

Todaro, Michael P. "A Model of Labour Migration and Urban Unemployment in Less Development Countries." *The American Economic Review.* March 1969.

Urquhart, M.C. and K.A.H. Buckley. *Historical Statistics of Canada.* Toronto: Macmillan of Canada, 1965.

11
Forests and Mines

Quebecers first acquired influence over the management of public (Crown) resources under the provisions of the Act of Union. The British government delegated powers over Canadian resources to the Union government at the same time as it transferred the financial burden of colonial administration. From 1841 until Confederation, the Union government regulated the sale and leasing of *in situ* resources, such as agricultural lands, timber stands, and mineral deposits. These powers allowed the Union government to broaden the definition of resource property rights and tighten their enforcement. By the mid-1860s, however, agricultural settlement in the Canadas appeared to reach the margin of profitable production; the forest industries appeared to be on the decline. At Confederation, it seemed of little consequence if the new federal government possessed few administrative and licensing powers over natural resources. Consequently, the British government accorded full proprietary rights in on-shore resources to the newly formed provincial governments.[1]

The high degree of economic and political integration outlined in the BNA Act soon led to problems of regional self-interest, development, and sovereignty. Aside from taxation powers shared with Ottawa, the provincial governments possessed relatively little leverage in the economic domain. The most important economic powers proved to be the authority, in the form of property rights, to regulate resource development. The Canadian Constitution attempted to separate trade and commerce powers from rights and customs relating to lands and forests—its authors possessed little knowledge of mineral, oil, gas, and hydroelectric potential. As the resource industries emerged at a later date, they fell under provincial jurisdiction. However, the federal government obtained the power to influence resource industry growth rates by acquiring legislative authority over trade and commerce. In effect, the federal government retained a margin of influence over the market value of property rights in *in situ* resources, whether these rights were provincially or privately owned.

This chapter outlines the growth of the forest and mineral industries in the context of changes in the definition of natural resource property rights. The definition of property rights evolved as a result of constitutional change, provincial government legislation, and judicial decisions. Property rights in forests developed differently from property rights in minerals because forests were a renewable resource, while minerals were non-renewable.

Property Rights in Forests

The definition of property rights in natural resources governs the timing and rates of exploration, discovery, and production, as well as the functional distribution of resource incomes. Windfall gains are often available to private entrepreneurs who acquire unconditional property rights at their inception. Initial buyers of such rights will try to capitalize all future rents so that subsequent buyers will tend to earn normal returns. New windfalls are quite possible, however. A lease or rental agreement allows for the partitioning of rights on a conditional basis and permits the initial resource owner to participate in the capture of any future windfall gains. The nature and pricing of resource rights by governments are crucial factors affecting the benefits to the regional economy over time. Resource law ultimately affects the allocation of all economic resources and the distribution of income in the economy as a whole.

During most of the French regime, the metropolitan government withheld property rights in oak forests on lands granted in seigneurial tenure; oak timber was considered a strategic resource. At the Conquest, these oak timber rights accrued to the British Crown. After 1763, the metropolitan government in London retained property rights in pine forests on lands conceded in free and common socage. The timber rights in all unconceded lands also remained in the hands of the British government. A timber licensing system involving contractors for the British navy evolved early in the nineteenth century, but the high cost of property rights enforcement in the Laurentian backwoods meant the licensing system did not always function in practice. Owners of land conceded for agricultural purposes were permitted to cut timber for clearing purposes. But in most instances, farmers could set clearing fires that damaged crown forest resources without fear of penalty; in other instances, entrepreneurs acquired property rights in 'agricultural' lands for the express purpose of earning timber revenues.

With the Act of Union, the British government transferred responsibility for the management of property rights in lands and forests to the colonial government.[2] In 1842, the Legislative Council adopted a licensing system for all timber cutting in the colony. But the decline in timber exports to Great Britain in that year, and again in the years 1845-1848, resulted in a fall in government revenues and a subsequent move to revise the existing institutional arrangements. The Crown Timber Act of 1849 became the first statutory law to regulate Quebec's forest industry. The Crown Timber Act confirmed the basic principal of public ownership for provincial forests: timber cutting was permitted by license for a period of twelve months at a time, subject to prices and regulations set by the Union Cabinet. In the original regulations of 1849, permit holders paid royalties only on the timber actually cut and sold. But with the amendments of 1851, the government introduced supplementary annual rental payments that ensured a steady source of tax revenue. These annual rental payments impeded the acquisition of licenses for speculative purposes, thereby accelerating the rate of timber cutting and improving the regional allocation of resources.

At the time of Confederation, all of the British North American provinces effectively controlled their own resources. In the words of G.V. LaForest:

> The entire control, management, and disposition of the Crown lands, and the proceeds of the provincial public domain and casual revenues arising in these provinces were confided to the executive administration of the provincial governments and to the legislative action of the provincial legislatures so that Crown lands, though standing in the name of the Queen, were, with their accessories and incidents, to all intents and purposes the public property of the respective provinces in which they were situate.[3]

The BNA Act confirmed provincial ownership of natural resources in "all lands, mines, minerals and royalties" belonging to the provinces at the Union (Section 109), and the right to legislate in matters concerning "the management and sale of the public lands belonging to the province and of the timber and wood thereon" (Section 92). Since provincial government revenues were limited to licensing and rental fees, direct taxes, and the sale of Crown lands, the economic rents available from provincial forests became a basic source of Quebec government income. In July 1868, the Quebec government doubled the annual rental price of forested land to one dollar per square mile, initiated a system of license sales by public auction, and introduced a charge for the transfer of licenses from one party to another. In October of the same year, the government decided to extend the duration of timber licenses from twelve months to twenty-one years; all of the other fees and charges remained in place. In 1889, however, the licensing system reverted to an annual basis. Throughout this time, property rights in forests on public lands remained in the hands of the Quebec provincial government.

The Timber Industry

Until 1842 forests on Crown lands were often treated as a common property resource. (See Chapter 7) When the Union government introduced regulations to clarify and enforce existing property rights in colonial forests, timber poaching by small operators diminished. Under the timber licensing system, wealthy operators ('lumber lords') could hold exclusive rights to timber stands even if current prices did not justify immediate exploitation. The year-to-year variance in international timber prices favored those who could tie up their savings and afford to wait. Pressed as it was for tax revenues, the Union government organized the timber leasing system on the basis of willingness-to-pay.

Imprecisions in the census data, the numerous small ports shipping to the United States, and the volume of exports originating in Ontario make it difficult to arrive at a precise analysis of Quebec timber exports during the second half of the nineteenth century. Exports of squared white pine from the port of Quebec, for instance, increased irregularly until the mid-1860s even though the degree of preferential tariff protection accorded to colonial imports by the British government decreased over this period. (See Chapter 8, Charts 8.1, 8.3) The last vestige of colonial protection was removed in 1866. Then, from the time of Confederation until World War I, square timber exports from the port of Quebec diminished steadily. The slow growth of Quebec City after mid-century was related to the decrease in employment opportunities associated with the decline of the timber trade. Several distinct phenomena account for this decline.

Exports to Great Britain, after a lag in time, began to suffer from Baltic competition. Prior to the 1840s, preferential duties (discriminatory tariffs) had raised the relative price of Baltic imports in the British market, to the advantage of Canadian exports. The gradual abolition of preferential duties lowered the relative price of Baltic imports on the British market, to the disadvantage of exports from the port of Quebec. In addition, the growth of lumber processing and manufacturing in Quebec reduced the proportion of unprocessed lumber in total provincial exports in favor of semi-finished wood products exports. Furthermore, owing to reductions in the relative prices of coal and iron, the demand for wood as a fuel and a building material in the construction of transport and capital equipment diminished in favor of iron and steel. In the construction of both ships and rail transport equipment, for example, manufacturers turned to iron and steel as substitutes for wood products. Finally, the overall importance of the port of Quebec diminished as a result of competition from the port of Montreal. Increased trade with the United States, the widening and deepening of the St. Lawrence River above Quebec City, and the relative improvement of port facilities at Montreal had a decentralizing effect on shipping points in Quebec as a whole.

The composition of the raw forest products industry changed significantly after mid-century. (See Table 11.1) The square timber industry had emerged in the protected environment of British preferences. After the removal of this protection, the forest products industry adapted gradually to the demands of economic growth closer to home. The decline in the production and export of raw forest products was accompanied by increased demand for semi-finished wood products. Urbanization and industrialization

Table 11.1

PRINCIPLE RAW FOREST PRODUCTS IN QUEBEC, 1870-1900
(Thousands of cubic feet, except logs and firewood)

	Square Pine	Square or Sided Tamarack	Square or Sided Birch and Maple	All Other Square or Sided Timber	Pine Logs (units)	Other logs (units)	Firewood (cords)
1870	9 224	3 995	501	10 590	5 012	3 629	3 122
1880	5 495	2 708	2 784	14 680	5 400	8 182	3 639
1890	1 983	2 596	959	11 803	2 560	10 757	3 380
1900	1 133	n/a	637	3 751	n/a	n/a	3 070

Government of Canada, *Census of Canada*, 1852-1901.

Table 11.2

SELECTED MISCELLANEOUS FOREST PRODUCTS IN QUEBEC, 1870-1900
(Thousands of units except lathe-wood and pulpwood)

	Masts and Spars	Staves	Lathe-Wood (cords)	Fence Posts	Railway Ties	Telegraph Posts	Pulpwood (cords)
870	94	1 184	7	n/a	n/a	n/a	n/a
880	104	3 585	32	n/a	n/a	n/a	n/a
890	50	44 628	173	10 670	2 405	97	131
900	7	n/a	n/a	8 662	2 704	82*	527

*Poles for electric wires

overnment of Canada, *Census of Canada*, 1871-1901.

reated a demand for new residential and non-residential construc-
ion. To the established production of spars, masts and staves,
Quebec lumber manufacturers added fence posts, railway ties,
elegraph posts, shingles, pulpwood and paper. (See Table 11.2)
Unfortunately, the present state of research does not allow for an
xtended discussion of forest products output. The development
f wood products manufacturing is discussed in Chapter 12.

roperty Rights in Minerals

he sudden rise of the mineral industries in North America during
ie second half of the nineteenth century caught local communi-
es and governments unaware. Many of the initial discoveries
ere accidental and did not result from investment in exploration.
small number of entrepreneurs made substantial gains by means
f their access to markets and technical information, their existing
ealth and credit worthiness, their risk-taking, and their ability to
xercise political power. The pattern of mineral rights alienation
flected considerable imprecision in mining legislation. Greater
efinition of property rights in minerals developed in response to
ie growing economic rents that mineral industries offered and
overnment recognition that a potential source of income was
ipping out of Quebec hands.

The distinction between possession of surface rights and the
wnership of underground minerals in Quebec was a legacy of

both French and English colonialism. French mining law had its origins in a series of general ordinances dating back to 1413 that established a royal prerogative in matters relating to underground resources. In 1627 full ownership of underground minerals in New France was vested in the fur-trading monopoly, the *Compagnie des Cent Associés*, which in turn conceded mining rights in most seigneurial titles granted, on condition of payment of a royalty tax. From 1664 to 1674 the *Compagnie des Indes Occidentales* enjoyed the same concession, and likewise conceded mining rights in some titles, but without imposing a tax. Thereafter, mining rights apparently reverted to the Crown and its colonial agents, and most concessions included the clause "*donner avis des mines au roi*", without making further mention of mining rights. In the controversial case of Regina vs. DeLery *et al*, the Quebec Court of Appeal decided in 1883 that this clause effectively reserved all mining rights to the Crown in the seigneury of Rigaud-Vaudreuil. The Quebec government thereby claimed the minerals in all seigneurial lands, except those seigneuries for which underground rights had specifically been mentioned in the original title. Théodore Denis has estimated that mining rights granted to seigneurs in this way affected about 10 percent of the eleven and one-half million acres granted during the French regime. (Denis, p. 591)

The Treaty of Paris, signed in 1763, implicitly extended the British practice of reserving precious metals (gold and silver) to the province of Quebec. In 1789 the British government issued guidelines to the Quebec Land Office to prevent individuals from "monopolizing such spots as contain mines, minerals, fossils and conveniences for mills and other singular advantages of a common and public nature, to the prejudice of the general interests of the settlers." (Nelles, p. 6) More specific instructions sent to the Governor of Lower Canada, published in Quebec on February 7, 1792, provided for the reservation of gold, silver, coals, copper, tin, iron and naval timber on lands granted in free and common socage. Five years later the British government amended the list of minerals to include gold and silver alone. From 1797 to July, 1866, all letters of patent in colonial agricultural lands contained a clause reserving gold and silver to the Crown. The regulations concerning gold and silver mines adopted by the Union government in 1854, and the 1864 Gold Mining Act, introduced administrative changes. But neither of these changes affected mining rights generally. Because no general mining law existed, the majority of mineral rights could be obtained by purchasing surface properties.

When the BNA Act came into effect in 1867, the Quebec government acquired responsibility for the management of all natural resources, including minerals. As the expected value of mineral deposits increased, the nature of mineral rights became more and more important to mining entrepreneurs and the public. In 1874, regulations approved by the Lieutenant-Governor in Council established rules to govern the alienation of surface lands in non-agricultural regions. Under the regulations, the price of mineral-bearing lands in non-agricultural areas was set at one dollar per acre—the price of government land in most unoccupied agricultural regions. By requiring proof of a mineral find, the regulations required investment in prospecting prior to mineral land purchases. This proviso improved the regional allocation of resources by encouraging greater search activity and generating more information about the province's mineral deposits while limiting the accumulation of mineral reserves by a wealthy few.

Rising resource rents from the nascent phosphate industry attracted the attention of the provincial government and the Joly administration enacted the Phosphate Mines Act in 1878 to regulate the sale of property rights in phosphate. In addition to establishing the conditions of sale of 'phosphate lots', the Act specified that lands sold for agricultural purposes could not be worked for phosphate of lime without paying an additional amount sufficient to raise the price of such lands to two dollars per acre. This form of reservation of a non-precious mineral by the provincial government established an important precedent; two years later it would be extended to all minerals.

The economic development policies pursued by Quebec governments in the 1870s accelerated the process of defining property rights in minerals. In 1873 the province of Quebec did not have a provincial debt. But the railroad building and colonization programs of the 1870s led the provincial government to near bankruptcy. By 1880 Quebec's debt charges amounted to 23 percent of the province's total expenditures. The deficits incurred as a result of this development policy stimulated the search for new sources of public financing. The sudden increase in economic rents flowing from the phosphate and asbestos industries attracted attention to the low rate of social return from mining industries. By enlarging the definition of property rights in minerals, the Quebec government sought to secure a greater share of the rents flowing from the province's mineral resources.

The General Mining Act of 1880 introduced by the Conservative government of Premier Chapleau clearly distinguished between surface and underground property rights. This distinction gave rise to a new source of public financing through the separate sale of mineral rights. The General Mining Act defined 'ores' to include gold, silver, copper, phosphate of lime (apatite), amianthus, asbestos, and "any other mineral substance having an appreciable value." Henceforth, no special mention of such mining rights in letters patent for agricultural purposes was required to reserve these minerals to the Crown. Mining rights had to be purchased separately from surface rights and provision was made for 'royalties', and put into effect in the case of gold, silver and phosphate of lime, but not asbestos.

There was considerable uncertainty regarding the interpretation of the law of 1880 and numerous litigations arose in the years that followed. The aforementioned Regina vs. DeLery *et al* (1883) established a precedent for provincial ownership of all minerals in lands granted during the French regime, except those explicitly conceded in the original title. This judicial decision considerably limited the windfall gains that would otherwise have accrued to surface proprietors of former seigneurial lands. The decision awarded mineral rights in 90 percent of all seigneurial lands to the provincial government and allowed for the rapid alienation of these rights to whosoever paid the government-administered price.

The legislation of 1880 had permitted the mining of underground minerals upon the paying of a fee, but without clearly specifying to whom such mineral rights actually belonged. To clarify this issue, the Quebec government passed an Act of amendment to the General Mining Act on June 10, 1884. One article specified that mineral rights constitute:

> ...property separate from the soil covering such mines and minerals...and shall constitute a property under the soil which shall also be public property, independent from that of the soil which is above, unless the proprietor of the soil has acquired it from the Crown as a mining location or otherwise, in which case both the soil and the property under the soil form but one and the same private property.[4]

The evolution of mineral law toward well specified statutes and court verdicts during the 1880s occurred in response to the increase in rents flowing from the mineral industries. By 1890 the annual value of raw asbestos shipments alone had grown to over $1 million. To bolster government revenues and redistribute income in the province, the Parti National government of Honoré Mercier extended control of mineral rights to those regions in which lands had been alienated between 1791 and 1880, effectively making the General Mining Law of 1880 retroactive. The Quebec Mining Law of 1890 thereby levied a charge on certain mineral resource owners to the advantage of all other taxpayers in the province. This provision moved asbestos and phosphate mine owners to form an action group to oppose the legislation. The activities of the mine owners' group were a direct function of the economic rents expected from political lobbying. Under pressure from this group, the reform measure of 1890 was rescinded two years later.

In the spring of 1901, the Parent government abandoned any claim to property rights in asbestos and other minerals underlying lands alienated prior to the legislation of 1880. Article 1425 of the 1901 amendments declared that:

> All mines belonging to the Crown under the law or titles of concession in the property under the soil, conceded before the 24th July, 1880, in the townships, with the exception of gold and silver mines, are abandoned by the Crown and belong exclusively to the owner of the surface, provided the latter has not divested himself of his right of pre-emption preserved by the former provisions of the Law.[5]

Thus mining entrepreneurs in the Eastern Townships whose surface lands had been conceded prior to the proclamation of the 1880 Mining Act could henceforth exploit their mines as unfettered owners of the minerals underground. Another important change in government policy in 1901 concerned the option available to surface owners to acquire mineral rights. This option was dropped in the amendment of 1901, reflecting a tighter governmental hold on unalienated minerals. The change was plainly favorable to mining companies and other parties with specialized information, for whom the cost of mineral rights fell to the government administered price.

With the passing of the amendments of 1901, the long debate engendered by the legislation of 1880 was over. The framework of ownership within which mineral exploitation would be conducted during the first half of the twentieth century was established. Changes would be made, but these changes would affect the administration of mineral rights sales, and revenue raised through taxation, rather than the more fundamental issue of mineral rights ownership.

The Mineral Industries

The growth rate of Quebec's mineral industries was influenced by a variety of social and political parameters: the supply of geological information, accidental discoveries, the legal definition and enforcement of property rights, and so on. Exploration and surveying, the first step toward mineral extraction, resembled investment in other economic activities except that exploration and surveying of underground minerals was a particularly risky undertaking: even after a mineral find, the exact location, size and quality of the deposit was uncertain until the mineral had actually been removed from the ground. To reduce uncertainties in exploration and foster the development of mineral extraction, the government supplied geological information in the form of mineral surveys.

Systematic geological mapping of Quebec's underground resources did not begin until the Act of Union transferred responsibility for the administration of natural resources to the colonial government. In 1842, William Logan, the first director of the Geological Survey of Canada, initiated a series of studies that laid the foundation for geographical information about Quebec for the next century. The Geological Survey published its first comprehensive inventory of provincial resources, "Geology of Canada", in 1863. Iron, copper and gold deposits attracted detailed attention, but various other minerals and building stones also received mention. The Geological Survey continued its work as a federal government agency after Confederation even though regulation of the mineral industries became a provincial responsibility. In Quebec, the supervision of the mineral industries fell to the Commissioner (Minister) of Crown Lands who delegated his responsibilities to a 'Mine Inspector'. The Mine Inspector supervised the issue of gold mining licenses and dues, and collected royalties on the small quantity of gold being mined in the county of Beauce. But the provincial government produced no new geological information until the 1880s. After the passage of the first General Mining Act in 1880, a technically qualified engineer, Joseph Obalski, was nominated to the position of 'Mining Engineer of the Province of Quebec'. Provincial mineral surveys and annual reports began to appear in 1883.

The discovery of mineral deposits did not always result in immediate attempts to start production. The decision to mine is an economic decision like any other; the rate of extraction depends on market prices and mining costs.

> Minerals are like the juice in an orange. The total amount extracted depends on how hard the orange is squeezed, and there is always a little left behind...this relates to the definition of reserves, the known amounts of a mineral than can profitably be recovered at current prices. An increase in prices, a new discovery, technical progress - all can result in an increase in reserves...The decision on when and how hard to squeeze the orange depends on conditions in the future as well as the present.[6]

Sustained efforts at mineral extraction in the St. Lawrence Valley began in the 1730s near Trois-Rivières. Over the next century and a half, the St. Maurice forges smelted locally recovered bog iron ore in response to the domestic demand for household articles.[7] In a similar way, lime and building stone quarries supplied the local demand for building materials from the early years of the colony. Apart from these operations, however, mining activity retained a low profile until the 1860s. In 1863, a modest gold rush to the Beauce region led to a flurry of small discoveries and claims. But litigation over the definition of mineral rights in lands conceded in seigneurial tenure impeded gold mining operations until the air was cleared by the Regina vs. DeLery *et al* decision of 1883.

The demand for metals stemming from the American Civil War raised the market price of iron and copper ores. In 1860 the Radnor Forges in the seigneury of Cap-de-la Madeleine started smelting, forging and rolling operations, and the owner of the St. Maurice Forges established a blast furnace under the name of the 'Islet Forges'. Rising copper prices, that reached a peak in 1864, stimulated a copper mining boom in the Sherbrooke region of the Eastern Townships. After the American Civil war, new sources of domestic demand partially offset the decline in American demand associated with the reimposition of tariff barriers. Growth in the Canadian manufacturing and transport sectors stimulated the demand for mineral products of all kinds. The census of 1871 reported mining operations for iron (St. Maurice, Trois-Rivières, Champlain, Ottawa West), copper (Megantic, Sherbrooke, Brome), gold (Beauce), graphite (Ottawa), mica (Argenteuil) and fuel peat (Laprairie, Chambly, Champlain).

In the 1870s and 1880s, low average ore grades and the high cost of transport from the mines to the embryonic railway system discouraged further development of the iron and copper mining industries.[8] (See Table 11.3) At the same time, market prices declined. The deflated American dollar price of copper, for example, diminished steadily from 1872 to 1887. (Potter and Christy, Jr., p. 38) However, the expanding phosphate and asbestos industries compensated for the slow-down in iron and copper production. The phosphate deposits in the Lièvre River Valley had been discovered in 1829, but systematic attempts at mining did not begin until about 1875. The demand for apatite, the crystalline variety of phosphate found in Quebec, resulted from its use as an agricultural fertilizer. Market competition from richer deposits in the United States eventually slowed the rate of extraction at the Quebec mines; phosphate production in Quebec reached a peak in 1889-1890. (See Table 11.4)

The demand for asbestos fibre was two-fold. The longer fibres could be woven for use in fire-resistant cloth and textile products, while the shorter fibres were combined with other building materials in roofing compositions, paints, millboard and paper. A 25 percent *ad valorem* American tariff on manufactured asbestos

Table 11.3

OUTPUT OF THE PRINCIPAL MINERAL INDUSTRIES IN QUEBEC, CENSUS YEARS, 1851-1880
(Tons, except gold)

Year	Total number of miners	iron ore	copper	gold (ounces)	phosphate of lime	asbestos & asbestic
1851	23	n/a	n/a	—	—	—
1860	138	17 877	3 292	—	—	—
1870	151	92 001	11 326	3 411	—	—
1880	391	74 242	6 007	2 192	8 924	380

Government of Canada, *Census of Canada*, 1851-1880.

Table 11.4

OUTPUT OF THE PRINCIPAL MINERAL INDUSTRIES IN QUEBEC, 1886-1900

Years	iron one production tons	copper production		production of phosphate of lime		shipments of asbestos	
		tons	value($)	tons	value($)	tons	value($)
1886	n/a	1 670	367 400	19 435	288 603	n/a	n/a
1887	13 404	1 469	330 514	19 589	264 452	4 219	220 976
1888	10 710	2 781	927 107	20 396	219 779	4 404	255 007
1889	14 533	2 658	730 813	27 552	287 400	6 113	426 554
1890	22 305	2 355	741 920	27 172	309 980	9 860	1 260 240
1891	14 380	2 701	695 469	20 244	206 416	9 279	999 878
1892	22 690	2 442	564 042	10 231	134 964	6 082	390 462
1893	22 076	2 234	480 348	7 650	60 076	6 331	310 156
1894	19 492	1 088	208 067	6 861	41 166	7 630	420 825
1895	17 783	1 121	241 288	1 822	9 596	8 756	368 175
1896	17 630	1 204	261 903	570	3 420	10 892	423 066
1897	22 436	1 237	279 424	908	3 984	13 202	399 528
1898	17 873	1 050	252 658	632	3 160	16 124	475 131
1899	19 420	816	287 494	1 279	7 674	17 790	468 635
1900	19 000	1 110	359 418	1 270	6 090	21 621	729 886

The Canadian Iron and Steel Industry: A Study in the History of a Protected Industry, by W.J.A. Donald. Boston: Houghton Mifflin, 1913.

The Copper Smelting Industries of Canada, by Alfred W.G. Wilson, p. 162, © 1913. Reprinted by permission of Energy, Mines and Resources Canada.

Phosphate in Canada, p. 24, by Hugh S. Spence, © 1920. Reprinted by permission of Energy, Mines and Resources Canada.

Chrysotile Asbestos in Canada, Chap. IV, Table 2, by James G. Ross, © 1931. Reprinted by permission of Energy, Mines and Resources Canada.

goods encouraged the export of unmanufactured asbestos fibres to the United States. Despite the introduction of a comparable Canadian import duty amounting to 20 percent *ad valorem* in 1879, the general pattern of raw material exports and manufactured imports was established by the 1880s. The United States became the most important market, taking some 70 percent of all exports (by value) during the years 1888-1930. (Ross, Chap. IV, Table VI)

The growth of Quebec railways in the second half of the nineteenth century was the major element in the transport revolution that led to the breakdown of small unintegrated regional markets and the creation of a continental market. The Quebec Central Railway permitted the rapid and efficient transport of asbestos from isolated areas in the Eastern Townships to seaports such as Levis and Portland, Maine. By 1890 total shipments of asbestos by Quebec producers were valued at four times the value of phosphate production. (See Table 11.4) The Quebec Central Railway moved not only the raw product, but labor, machinery, raw materials, and information as well. The increase in the quality and rate of flow of information lowered transaction costs to asbestos producers in their dealings with buyers. Reductions in transport and transaction costs increased the expected value of asbestos deposits and raised the stakes involved in any further definition of provincial mineral rights. The growth of asbestos output was also accompanied by a transition from pick and shovel technology to mechanized mining and milling processes. During the first decade of production, labor intensive hand cobbing and constant returns to scale characterized asbestos mining technology. The adoption of mechanical processes and steam power in the late 1880s introduced increasing returns to scale. Lower unit costs of production, coupled with higher market prices, raised the present value of asbestos mineral deposits.[9] The increase in the value of rents flowing from the ownership of mineral rights in asbestos created a demand for a wider distribution of the income flowing from provincial mineral resources.

A structural change in the market for raw asbestos fibre occurred in 1891 when all of the leading manufacturers of asbestos in the United States amalgamated to form the H.W. Johns' Manufacturing Company. Although the new American company did not own a significant portion of Quebec asbestos mines, it was able to exercise a margin of monopsony power on raw fibre prices during the early 1890s. The resulting fall in asbestos prices had the effect of eliminating the smaller, less economic operations and stimulating the adoption of new techniques. Henceforth, the financial capacity to hold idle mines, in addition to the economies of physical scale, became an important determinant of firm size.

During the next few years, the switch to mechanized milling processes permitted the recovery of very short asbestos fibres known as "asbestic" that had previously been discarded. Fibres previously considered waste material became an important by-product of the milling process. This re-evaluation of existing dumps revitalized the asbestos industry during the last few years of the nineteenth century.

* * *

The contribution of forest and mineral products to output, employment and income in the nineteenth century Quebec economy should not be exaggerated. Square timber, lumber and raw asbestos certainly contributed to provincial export receipts; the following chapter indicates how the domestic supply of wood, iron and copper helped to shape the structure of Quebec's manufacturing sector. But as the century drew to a close, mineral extraction and timber cutting contributed relatively little to aggregate employment. Together, lumbering, mining and quarrying employed no more than one percent of the gainfully employed labor force in Quebec at the end of the nineteenth century. (See Chapter 15, Table 15.1) The history of forest and mineral exploitation between 1840 and 1900 is primarily of interest because of the way in which primary resource commodity production shaped the definition, distribution and enforcement of resource property rights and resource development in the twentieth century.

NOTES

[1]Following the acquisition of the Hudson's Bay Company lands in 1869, however, the federal government withheld property rights in natural resources from the prairie provinces until 1930.

[2]Because the extent of the rights transfer was unclear, the British government formally agreed, in 1846, that the Union government had the same control over provincial land sales revenues as the British Parliament exercised over British land sales revenues. (LaForest, p. 13)

[3]*Natural Resources and Public Property Under the Canadian Constitution*, p. 14, by Gerard V. LaForest, © 1969.

[4]An Amendment to the *General Mining Act of 1880*, 47 Victoria, Chapter 22. Reprinted by permission of Energy, Mines and Resources Canada.

[5]An Amendment to the *General Mining Act of 1880*, I Edward VII, Chapter 13. Reprinted by permission of Energy, Mines and Resources Canada.

[6]"The Exploitation of Extractive Resources: A Survey", by Frederick M. Peterson, Anthony C. Fisher, *The Economic Journal*, pp. 692-693, December 1977, reprinted by permission of Cambridge University Press.

[7]These bog ores are hydrous peroxides of iron, relatively free of phosporous or sulphur, but containing a large proportion of organic matter.

[8]In 1889, reported Obalski, "The working of these [bog iron ore] deposits is primitive; the ore is simply removed with pick and shovel, and then washed... The average theoretic yield is 50% of metallic iron, but at the furnace the practical yield is from 30 to 40%." (Obalski, p. 24).

[9]Said *The Monetary Times*, "The profits of some of these [Quebec asbestos] mines are said to be very large. Thus, the Johnson-Irvine mine at Thetford, which some years ago might have been bought for $5000, now returns to its owners—Judge Irvine, of Quebec and Mr. Johnson, M.P.P.—an annual profit of $100,000." (The Asbestos Industry," *The Monetary Times*, August 14, 1891).

SELECT BIBLIOGRAPHY

Armstrong, Robert. "L'industrie de l'amiante au Québec, 1878-1929." *Revue d'histoire de l'Amérique française*. September 1979.

Armstrong, Robert. "Le dévelopement des droits miniers au Québec à la fin du dix-neuvième siècle." *L'Actualité Economique*. September 1983.

Bouffard, Jean. *Traité du Domaine*. (Reproduction de l'édition originale de 1921). Quebec: les Presses de l'Université Laval, 1977.

Denis, T.C. "Mining Rights in Seignories in the Province of Quebec." *Journal of the Canadian Mining Institute*. Vol. XIV (1911).

Donald, W.J.A. *The Canadian Iron and Steel Industry: A Study in the Economic History of a Protected Industry*. Boston: Houghton Mifflin, 1915.

Dufresne, A.O. "Mining in Quebec: An Historical Sketch." *The Canadian Mining Journal*. October 1948.

Faucher, Albert. *Québec en Amérique au XIXe siècle*. Montreal: Editions Fides, 1973.

Hamelin, Jean and Yves Roby. *Histoire économique du Québec, 1851-1896*. Montreal: Editions Fides, 1971.

Hardy, René, Normand Séguin, Alain Gamelin, André Miville, and Guy Trépanier. *L'exploitation forestière en Mauricie. Dossier statistique: 1850-1930*. Trois-Rivières: U.Q.T.R., 1980.

Jones, I.W. "Progress of Geological Investigation in Quebec." *The Canadian Mining Journal*. October 1948.

LaForest, Gerard V. *Natural Resources and Public Property under the Canadian Constitution*. Toronto: University of Toronto Press, 1969.

Lower, Arthur R.M. *Great Britain's Woodyard: British America and the Timber Trade, 1763-1867*. Montreal: McGill-Queen's University Press, 1973.

Nelles, H.V. *The Politics of Development: Forest, Mines and Hydro-Electric Power in Ontario, 1849-1941*. Toronto: Macmillan of Canada, 1974.

Obalski, J. *Mines and Minerals in the Province of Quebec*. Quebec: Government of Quebec, 1889.

Peterson, Frederick M. and Anthony C. Fisher, "The Exploitation of Extractive Resources: A Survey." *The Economic Journal.* December 1977.

Potter, Neal and Francis T. Christy, Jr. *Trends in Natural Resource Commodities: Statistics of Prices, Output, Consumption, Foreign Trade, and Employment in the United States, 1870-1957.* Baltimore: Johns Hopkins Press, 1962.

Ross, James G. *Chrysotile Asbestos in Canada.* Ottawa: Department of Mines, 1931.

Spence, Hugh S. *Phosphate in Canada.* Ottawa: Government Printing Bureau, 1920.

Thomson, Normand and Major J.H. Edgar. *Canadian Railway Development from the Earliest Times.* Toronto: Macmillan Company of Canada, 1933.

Wilson, Alfred W.G. *The Copper Smelting Industries of Canada.* Ottawa: Government Printing Bureau, 1913.

12
Manufacturing Industry and Labor Organization

About mid-century, manufacturing industry began to emerge in the St. Lawrence Valley. The rise of manufacturing belongs to a wider phenomenon known as 'industrialization'. Industrialization refers to the substitution of artisal production by mass production, that is, a change from home and workshop production by skilled craftsmen to the division of labor, specialization, and factory production by unskilled workers often drawn from the countryside. The industrial 'revolution' occurred first in Britain at the end of the eighteenth century and spread to the United States during the early decades of the nineteenth century. In Quebec, capitalists did not really begin to adopt factory methods until about 1850. By this time, industrialization also involved the adoption of mechanical devices, the deployment of power sources such as the steam engine, and the intensified use of metals such as iron and copper. The adoption of large and costly power-driven machines in manufacturing production led to the concentration of manufacturing jobs in central places. Because many of the factory's specialized processes required fewer work skills, industrialization accelerated rural-urban migration and encouraged higher labor market participation rates, especially among women and children.

There is no evidence that Quebec's manufacturing sector experienced a spectacular take-off at one specific point in time. Manufacturing industry expanded gradually over the nineteenth and twentieth centuries. The growth of Quebec's manufacturing sector will be divided into two phases: the initial phase will be discussed here and the second in Chapter 14. The first phase, 1850-1900, involved the primary processing of raw materials destined for final consumption by households. A growing number of consumer goods industries provided manufactured living essentials: food, clothing, and housing. This phase of industrial growth generally resembled early manufacturing growth in Great Britain, 1760-1840, the northeastern United States, 1800-1860, and southern Ontario, 1850-1900. In the beginning, Quebec's manufacturing section turned out relatively few producer goods, transportation equipment being something of an exception. In contrast to the sophisticated applied science and engineering technology that typified industrial expansion between 1900 and 1940, the first phase of Quebec's manufacturing growth involved rather simple mechanized processes, if any at all.

Census data on Canadian manufacturing output, reclassified on the basis of the Standard Industrial Classification (SIC) of 1948, are available from the year 1870. Discussions of the problems that hinder intercensus comparisons are contained in Bertram, McDougall, Pomfret, and Ryan. The census data indicate moder-

Table 12.1

GROWTH RATES OF CANADIAN AND QUEBEC MANUFACTURING, COMPOUND RATES OF GROWTH PER YEAR IN CONSTANT DOLLARS, 1870-1910

Period	Gross Value of Canadian Manufacturing Output in 1935-1939 Dollars	Gross Value of Quebec Manufacturing Output in 1900 Dollars*	Total Value Added in Quebec Manufacturing in 1900 Dollars*
1870-1880	4.4	4.0	3.5
1880-1890	4.8	4.2	5.4
1890-1900	2.4	2.3	2.2
1900-1910	6.0	5.7	6.5

*Calculated from the growth rates by decade as given by Ryan. The data for the years 1900 and 1910 have been adjusted to compensate for the incomplete coverage of the 1901 and 1911 censuses.

G.W. Bertram, "Economic Growth in Canadian Industry, 1870-1915," *Approaches to Canadian Economic History*, p. 82, eds. Easterbrook and Watkins, reprinted by permission of Carleton University Press.

The Clergy and Economic Growth in Quebec, 1896-1914, p. 320, by William F. Ryan, (c) 1966, reprinted by permission of Les Presses de l'Université Laval.

ate growth in the value of total manufacturing output over the last three decades of the nineteenth century, with a slowdown in the 1890s. Manufacturing output in Quebec followed this same trend reflecting the extent of interprovincial trade and economic integration already present in the nineteenth century (See Table 12.1)[1]. W. F. Ryan's estimates of growth in Quebec manufacturing value added indicate somewhat wider variations than his estimates of total output. The high average growth rate in the 1880s is especially noteworthy.

Regions tend to specialize in the production of those goods and services they can produce at relatively low cost. The manufacturing industries that located in Quebec between 1850 and 1900 usually did so because of some comparative cost advantage relative to a location in other regions. In this chapter, the focus will be on four sources of comparative advantage: domestic demand and transport costs, the resource endowment, government taxes and subsidies, and wage rates. The last part of the chapter is devoted to related changes in labor organization. Industrialization provoked a defensive response on the part of many urban workers that led to the formation of new institutional arrangements to increase wages and improve working conditions. The growth of the manufacturing sector accelerated the rate of diffusion of trade unionism.

An Overview of Manufacturing Growth

Quebec's manufacturing sector played a major role in supplying the aggregate Canadian demand for manufactured products in the nineteenth century. In 1870, the first year of reliable census data on manufacturing output and employment, only the province of Ontario's manufacturing output and value added per capita stood at a higher level than Quebec's. The structure of manufacturing industry was very similar in both provinces. Six of the seven leading manufacturing industries, by value added, produced similar commodities in 1870. (See Table 12.2) After 1870, growth in the total value of manufacturing output occurred at about the same rate in both Quebec and Ontario (Raynauld, p. 44); faster population growth in Quebec resulted in a slightly lower manufacturing growth rate per capita than in Ontario.

Domestic Demand and Transport Costs

The expansion of manufacturing industry is typically based on the expansion of local demand for manufactured products; the rise of

Table 12.2

LEADING MANUFACTURING INDUSTRIES IN QUEBEC AND ONTARIO BY VALUE ADDED, CURRENT DOLLARS 1870

Quebec Industry (SIC)	% of Total Value Added	Ontario Industry (SIC)	% of Total Value Added
Leather products	20.5	Food and beverages	21.0
Wood products	19.2	Wood products	19.3
Iron and steel products (secondary)	13.9	Iron and steel products (secondary)	19.2
Food and beverages	13.3	Leather products	10.0
Clothing	7.9	Clothing	6.6
Transportation equipment	5.9	Transportation equipment	5.1
Non-metallic mineral products	3.4	Textile products	5.0
All others	15.9	All others	13.8
Total	100.0	Total	100.0
Total primary	29.3	Total primary	42.0
Total secondary	70.7	Total secondary	58.0

Gordon W. Bertram, "Historical Statistics on Growth and Structure in Manufacturing in Canada, 1870-1959," in J. Henripin and A. Asimakopolous, eds., *Conference on Statistics 1962 and 1963 Papers*. Toronto: University of Toronto Press, 1964.

manufacturing production exclusively for export is uncommon. The regional demand for manufactured products is related to such variables as the total size of the regional population, the average level of regional income, and the degree of urbanization. Urban areas are often associated with the demand for manufactured goods because the costs of transporting and distributing products are lower in regions with a high population density. Furthermore, agricultural populations are often self-sufficient in the supply of basic commodities that manufacturers wish to produce. A shift in the population from rural to urban areas will normally increase the regional demand for manufactured commodities. In Quebec the urban population increased by three-and-a-half times during the second half of the nineteenth century. (See Chapter 10, Table 10.6) This urbanization was heavily concentrated, however, in a small number of cities and towns. By 1900, Ontario had 30 towns with a population of over 5 000 while Quebec had only 10. Montreal accounted for more than 40 percent of the total urban population in the province and was by far the largest city in Canada.

The slow growth of small and medium-sized towns in Quebec discouraged the development of rural transport infrastructure and impeded the diffusion of manufactured consumer goods in the countryside. The small size of the market hindered interindustry linkages associated with specialization,[2] and inhibited potential economies of scale. Despite these disadvantages, many manufacturing industries chose to locate in Quebec. The province encompassed a large part of the Canadian population (just under a third of the total), and manufacturers minimized the costs of transporting raw materials and finished products by locating in the Montreal region. The canal construction of the 1840s endowed Montreal with the double advantage of waterways to the Great Lakes region and ocean port facilities; by 1853 Montreal also possessed three rail links with the eastern United States. (See Chapter 9) This basic transport infrastructure lowered the costs of raw material imports and offered an avenue for the sale of lightweight manufactured products in Ontario. Raw materials such as wheat, sugar, rubber, silk and cotton could be procured more cheaply outside of Quebec than domestically. Manufacturers 'imported' these materials and processed them for domestic consumption, shipment to the rest of Canada and, in the case of flour, export abroad.

As long as Ontario remained Canada's primary wheat producer, a flour milling industry operated in the Montreal region. But as the locus of wheat shifted west to Manitoba in the 1880s, so too did the milling industry. Montreal continued, however, as the centre of Canadian sugar refining; the raw sugar originated in the West Indies. From the United States, animal skins and raw cotton were imported to feed the leather tanning, boots and shoes, clothing and textile industries. All of these industries enjoyed tariff protection across Canada, but transport cost advantages and urban population density attracted many to the region surrounding the port of Montreal. By 1900 manufacturing industry in the Montreal area employed about half of all manufacturing workers in the province.

The Resource Endowment

Raw materials constituted a major item in the total costs of manufactured products in the nineteenth century. Access to domestically produced raw materials was therefore a major competitive advantage affecting the location of manufacturing industries. Over the second half of the century, Quebec possessed relatively abundant supplies of forest, mineral, and cattle resources. The comparatively low cost of these resources offered manufacturing opportunities in the wood products, paper, transportation equipment, iron products, butter and cheese industries. (See Table 12.3) The wood products industries constituted a forward linkage from the development of timber cutting. Wood products included sawn lumber, furniture, doors, frames, staves, shingles and matches. During the first half of the century, these secondary industries had expanded with the aid of cheap raw material supplies from the tariff-advantaged square timber industry. The demand for urban housing accelerated with the begin-

Table 12.3

PERCENTAGE OF TOTAL GROSS VALUE OF MANUFACTURING OUTPUT IN QUEBEC BY INDUSTRY GROUP, CURRENT DOLLAR VALUE, CENSUS YEARS 1870-1900

Industry Group (SIC)	1870	1880	1890	1900*
Food and beverages	26.1	23.1	23.0	20.7
Leather products	19.0	20.7	13.5	14.8
Wood products	17.1	13.9	13.3	11.1
Clothing (textile and fur)	7.8	10.2	10.1	10.7
Iron and steel products	9.3	9.2	11.1	8.8
Textile products	3.4	4.9	5.6	7.3
Transportation equipment	3.9	3.5	7.2	5.2
Tobacco and tobacco products	1.9	1.7	2.6	4.9
Paper products	1.3	1.6	2.8	3.8
Chemical products	3.0	3.5	3.0	3.3
All Others	7.2	7.2	7.8	9.4
Total	100.0	100.0	100.0	100.0

*The data for the year 1900 has been adjusted to compensate for the incomplete coverage of the 1901 census.

The Clergy and Economic Growth in Quebec, 1896-1914, pp. 318-319, by William F. Ryan © 1966, reprinted by permission of Les Presses de l'Université Laval.

nings of the trend toward urbanization. Wooden carriage construction and shipbuilding had also attained an important place in the Quebec economy by mid-century.

The decline of wooden shipbuilding in Quebec after 1860 provides an interesting example of the general substitution of industrial minerals for wood products in response to relative price changes. The gradual disappearance of shipbuilding throughout North America in the second half of the nineteenth century, and the concentration of the industry in Great Britain resulted from the adoption of metals in place of wood as the basic structural material in the construction of ship frames and hulls. As of the 1850s the North American price of sailing ships was determined by the British iron shipbuilding industry. The supply of wooden ships from various regions differed in its elasticity of response to price decline, depending on the regional availability of alternative employment. British wooden shipbuilding disappeared in the early 1870s while the North American industry continued into the mid-1880s. The Canadian industry remained in existence the longest.

The revival of timber cutting toward the end of the nineteenth century (see Chapter 11) resulted from technological change in paper manufacturing methods. At the beginning of the century, paper had been considered a luxury product; paper-making required scarce raw materials such as cloth rags. Over the course of the century new paper-making technology permitted the manufacture of paper from woodpulp. The rise of the North American pulp and paper industry in the last quarter of the century gradually revalued Quebec's abundant timber stands, though rapid growth in pulp and paper production did not occur until after 1900.

The location of iron smelting and iron products manufacturing in Quebec similarly reflected the domestic availability of the industry's basic raw material inputs. Given the state of technology at mid-century, these material inputs consisted of iron ore and charcoal fuel. To minimize transport costs, the iron smelting industries tended to locate near the principal source of fuel—forests accessible to major waterways. Quebec enjoyed the advantages of both accessible forests and locally mined bog iron ore deposits. Charcoal blast furnaces and iron forges consequently developed along the St. Lawrence River, particularly in the St. Maurice and Sorel regions. These installations produced cast and wrought iron products for domestic consumption. During the 1850s, the demand for iron nails, rails and cast iron railway car wheels created a rail transport manufacturing sector centred in the Montreal area.

New resource discoveries and technical innovations subsequently reduced the role of iron smelting in Quebec's manufacturing sector. The North American industry shifted toward the mid-continental region with the development of bituminous coal deposits west of the Allegheny Mountains. At the same time, the substitution of steel for iron, initiated by the introduction of steel rails to the North American continent during the American Civil War, diminished the demand for charcoal. (Steel could not be efficiently produced using charcoal as a fuel.) The locus of North American iron and steel production consequently moved toward the Great Lakes region as bituminous coal and its gasless derivative, coke, replaced charcoal. Owing to the deposits of high grade iron ore north of Lake Superior, southern Ontario eventually emerged as the cost-minimizing location for the primary iron and steel industry in Canada. (See Table 12.4) In spite of tariffs on imported coal, Hamilton's proximity to American coal fields gave the city a privileged position in primary smelting operations by the end of the century. Quebec's older iron smelting operations, based on charcoal as a fuel, lost their competitive edge. Two small charcoal furnaces operated at Drummondville from the early 1880s, but the St. Maurice forges near Trois-Rivières closed in 1883. Although a secondary iron products manufacturing industry remained in the province, it depended on wrought iron, scrap iron, and coal 'imports' from Nova Scotia and Great Britain.

Over the last two decades of the nineteenth century, the manufacturing and marketing of butter and cheese became a major activity in the Quebec countryside. Along with other processed food products (flour, meat, and refined sugar), butter and cheese enjoyed tariff protection from American imports after the termination of the Reciprocity Treaty in 1866. But rapid growth in manufactured butter and cheese production did not occur until 1880. (See Table 12.5) Even then, many 'factories' were very small, employing only two operatives. The introduction of Commonwealth tariff preferences in 1897 reduced the trade barriers facing agricultural exports to Great Britain and butter became a major export to the United Kingdom. By 1901 Quebec accounted for two-thirds of all butter produced in Canada.

Government Taxes and Subsidies

The federal, provincial and municipal governments intervened in the Quebec economy in various ways that influenced the growth rate and structure of the manufacturing sector. At the federal level, tariff policy and railway subsidies affected the size and location of manufacturing industry. The regional impact of tariffs, for instance, varied from product to product tending to favor those areas that already possessed some form of comparative advantage.

Table 12.4

PRODUCTION OF PIG IRON IN CANADA BY PROVINCES, 1887-1912

Calendar Year	Nova Scotia (tons)	Ontario (tons)	Quebec (tons)	Total (tons)
1887	19 320	—	5 507	24 927
1888	17 556	—	4 243	21 799
1889	21 289	—	4 632	25 921
1890	18 382	—	3 390	21 772
1891	21 353	—	2 538	23 891
1892	40 049	—	2 394	42 443
1893	46 472	—	9 475	55 947
1894	41 344	—	8 623	49 967
1895	35 192	—	7 262	42 454
1896	32 351	28 302	6 615	67 268
1897	22 500	26 115	9 392	58 007
1898	21 627	48 253	7 135	77 015
1899	31 100	64 749	7 094	102 943
1900	28 133	62 387	6 055	96 575
1901	151 130	116 371	6 875	274 376
1902	237 244	112 688	7 970	357 902
1903	201 246	87 004	9 635	297 885
1904	164 488	127 845	11 121	303 454
1905	261 014	256 704	7 588	525 306
1906	315 008	275 558	7 845	598 411
1907	366 456	275 459	10 047	651 962
1908	352 642	271 484	6 709	630 835
1909	345 380	407 012	4 770	757 162
1910	350 287	447 273	3 237	800 797
1911	390 242	526 635	658	917 535
1912	424 994	589 593	—	1 014 587

The Canadian Iron and Steel Industry: A Study in the History of a Protected Industry, p. 327, by W.J.A. Donald, © 1915.

Higher tariffs on tanned leather products favored Quebec manufacturers, higher tariffs on agricultural implements favored producers in Ontario, higher tariffs on pig iron and coal imports encouraged iron smelting in Nova Scotia. Tariff policy induced manufacturing growth in several, if not all of the provinces, but local market size, resource endowments, and proximity to American resources and markets generally favored Ontario.

In the iron and steel sector, for example, tariffs and subsidies do not appear to have played the major role in industrial location. As

Table 12.5

BUTTER AND CHEESE FACTORIES IN QUEBEC, ONTARIO AND CANADA, CLASSIFIED ACCORDING TO THEIR FIRST YEAR OF OPERATION, 1855-1900

Provinces	1855-1860	1861-1870	1871-1880	1881-1890	1891-1900	Not specified
Factories making butter only						
Quebec	—	1	9	65	355	15
Ontario	—	—	6	11	71	15
Canada	—	1	15	78	505	30
Factories making cheese only						
Quebec	—	4	39	167	955	42
Ontario	5	52	148	289	453	114
Canada	5	57	188	472	1510	157
Factories making butter and cheese						
Quebec	—	5	32	109	175	19
Ontario	—	20	41	56	46	9
Canada	—	25	73	168	264	28

Government of Canada, *Census of Canada*, 1901, Vol. II, p. xlviii.

of 1858, rolling mill producers in the Canadas benefited from duties of 20 percent *ad valorem*; pig iron, scrap iron, coal and coke were given duty-free status. The following year, bar iron, cast iron and wrought iron received protection amounting to 10 percent. The modest level of these duties reinforced the position of domestic manufacturers without sheltering them from all competition. After Confederation, in 1868, rolling mill products were placed on the duty-free list and most other iron products taxed at 5 percent (Donald, p. 336).

Following the tariff revisions of 1879, the iron manufacturing sector experienced another period of expansion. The tariff on most iron products increased by 10 to 15 percent; coal and coke importers were also taxed. Between 1879 and 1887, the tariff schedule underwent various amendments to meet specific criticisms and pacify various lobbies. In 1883, for example, as an alternative to revising the schedule, the federal government introduced subsidies ("bounties") for pig iron produced from Canadian ore. Finally, in 1887, a general revision of duties again raised tariff rates on most iron and steel products; but public oppostion to higher prices for final products subsequently led to modest reductions in 1893.

It is difficult to separate the impact of greater tariff protection on industrial location from the effects of other economic changes occurring at the same time. The building of the government subsidized CPR in the 1880s may have done as much for the iron and steel industry in Quebec as tariffs and direct subsidies. Despite high tariff barriers and some $781 000 (nominal) in subsidies to pig iron producers in Canada, more than half of Canadian pig iron consumption between 1883 and 1897 was imported. (Donald, p. 103) For forty years, attempts to build economically viable blast furnaces in Ontario failed. Only in 1895, with the help of municipal subsidies, did Hamilton attract its first modern blast furnace. Donald suggests that tariffs and subsidies partially succeeded in promoting the secondary iron and steel sector, but had little impact on the growth of primary smelting.

Apart from tariff policy, a number of independently designed measures to promote manufacturing increased the size of Quebec's manufacturing sector. Patent laws and government subsidies to manufacturers (bounties, bonuses, and municipal tax exemptions) were perhaps the most important of these. Unfortunately, no studies have yet been published indicating the quantitative impact of these measures on the size, structure or location of manufacturing industry in Quebec (or Canada). Patent laws and subsidies had some positive effect on the sector, but how much is unknown. Ultimately, it is difficult to establish a comprehensive balance sheet indicating the costs and benefits of a particular federal government policy to one region such as Quebec. (See Chapter 16)

Wage Rates

It is tempting to suggest comparatively low wage rates attracted certain types of labor-intensive manufacturing industries into the province. There are frequent references to "cheap and abundant" labor in the historical literature. (eg. Donald, p. 110; McCallum, Chap. 7) Average rural incomes were relatively low and emigration heavy during the second half of the century. A relative abundance of labor with respect to other factors of production may have resulted in lower wage rates and more labor-intensive manufacturing industry than in Ontario. Urban wage rates in the larger Quebec and Ontario towns, appear to have been about the same in comparable occupations (See Buckley and Urquhart, pp. 94-95); but regional cost of living differences may have been large enough to discredit the use of nominal wage rates as an index of comparative economic well-being in the two provinces. The inter-provincial income differential (as opposed to the wage differential) may have been attributable to lower labor participation rates and a less educated, less skilled work force.[3] Popular opinion notwithstanding, there is little direct evidence that wage rates played a determining role in the size or composition of Quebec's manufacturing sector in the nineteenth century.

Labor Organization

The industrialization and urbanization of the Quebec economy caused major changes in social structure and the occupational distribution of the work force. The factory system of production gradually replaced various forms of artisanal production, and gave rise to a new social class, the urban proletariat. The new urban labor force was variously drawn from the agricultural population, from declining resource-based industries such as lumbering, from the ranks of skilled craftsmen and artisans whose production was underpriced by factory methods, and from new immigrants from abroad. During the second half of the nineteenth century, urban workers banded together in order to improve working conditions and increase their share of the national income.

The economic and social dislocation that accompanied the rise of industrial capitalism and the expansion of urban labor markets accelerated the rate of diffusion of new institutional forms such as the trade union. The earliest Quebec unions were 'trade' unions in the narrow sense of the word—associations of skilled tradesmen or craftsmen. A tailors' union founded in Montreal in 1823 is sometimes taken to be the first union organized in the province. Over the next decade, shoemakers, tailors, printers, and various building trades organized unions in Montreal and Quebec City. These workingmen's associations had no status in law and their ability to standardize working conditions depended entirely on their members' willingness and ability to co-operate among themselves. Most of the early associations were relatively short-lived. Not until 1840 did a shipbuilders' association in Quebec City, *la Société amicale et bienveillante des charpentiers de vaisseaux*, risk attempting to exercise the right to strike.

The absence of documentation and data concerning the labor movement is a major constraint on research in labor history. Newspapers and chronicles of the times focused on business conditions rather than working conditions. What is more, the founding of a trade union or workingmen's association, with no status in law, received little or no attention in the press compared to labor strikes and parades. Consequently, research in the labor history of the nineteenth century often focuses on industrial conflicts rather than labor organization *per se*.

The firms and industries most susceptible to labor unrest are often those earning excess profits or economic rents. As far as the timing of labor/management conflict is concerned, firms tend to be more tractable to union demands during periods of full employment, and more resistant during periods of economic recession. During periods of full employment (ie. rapid growth and full capacity utilization), the labor demand curves of firms tend to become more inelastic because the individual firm can pass along price increases to consumers more easily. In the 1850s, for instance, work stoppages and walk-outs occurred with considerable frequency. Rapid growth sectors, such as railway construction, were often affected by labor/management conflict. During these years, strikes often occurred spontaneously, usually outside the trade union framework and without much formal organization. Short-lived work stoppages also occurred in industries subject to a sudden drop in output, employment, and wages. The naval construction yards at Quebec experienced this kind of walk-out during the years 1865-1867.

The introduction of American trade union institutions and practices in the 1860s was associated with the higher levels of commercial exchange that accompanied the Reciprocity Treaty and the American Civil War. Iron molders, typographers, cigar workers, and locomotive firemen and enginemen joined locals of American union federations in the years immediately prior to Confederation. The greater experience of American union organizers, their established institutional framework, comparable working conditions, and the growing extent of labor market integration between Quebec and the United States all contributed to the growth of the 'internationals'.

Despite this development, the trade union movement remained a small and fragile force in the Quebec economy; the degree of unionization of the labor force inevitably reflected the size of the manufacturing sector. Many fledgling trade unions and labor associations, like the firms to which they were attached, disappeared at the time of the economic recession of 1873-1879. During most of the nineteenth century, trade unionism was restricted to the organization of skilled tradespeople, artisans and craftspeople. Beginning in the 1880s, however, unionism began to spread from workshops to factories, and union organizations of the inter-industrial type began to appear. Inter-industrial unionism constituted a lagged response to the change in the nature of production from small workshops employing craftspeople to large factories employing unskilled as well as skilled workers. The industrial union organization known as the 'Knights of Labour' was a creation of the American labor movement and, though it did not have a general assembly in Canada, proved popular in Quebec because of its social and political objectives. Unlike the established craft organizations, the Knights of Labor admitted workers' wives and the unemployed to its membership, and lobbied to improve workers' education and living conditions outside the workplace. The decentralized, often secretive, nature of Knights of Labour local assemblies, however, weakened their influence on local employers and government.

The development of inter-industrial unionism in the 1880s also led to the formation of the first durable inter-industry union federations. Trades and labor councils were formed in Montreal in 1885 and in Quebec City in 1890. A pan-Canadian federation, the Trades and Labour Council of Canada, appeared in 1886. The Canadian Trades and Labour Congress (as it was renamed in 1892) consisted mostly of subsidiary branch locals of the American Federation of Labour (AFL) in the United States. The AFL favored 'bread and butter' unionism and, though often very militant, generally aimed for higher wages and better working conditions, eschewing political and social action such as that practiced by the Knights of Labour. Many of the longest and most bitter strikes by Quebec workers occurred outside of the mainstream trade union movement.

* * *

The first phase of industrialization in Quebec coincided with the coming of interprovincial railways. By lowering the costs of economic exchange, railways accelerated the commercialization of Quebec agriculture, the transition from raw timber to sawed lumber production, and the growth rate of mineral extraction. The increase in cash incomes flowing from resource commodity production in turn created a demand for manufactured products: machinery, equipment, and consumer goods. Railways created a demand for iron rails, railway ties, and rolling stock. At the same time, the urbanization of central Canada created a demand for food products, clothing, and housing. Within the common market shaped by uniform tariff barriers, Quebec and Ontario developed relatively similar manufacturing industry structures.

Capital accumulation, the rise of manufacturing industry, and the expansion of the urban labor market resulted in the diffusion of new institutional arrangements such as the trade union. First, skilled workers, and later unskilled workers banded together to maintain or improve wage rates and working conditions. The trade union provided a forum for exchange of labor market information, a means of adopting a common code of behavior among members, and an instrument for the exercise of power through collective action. Many of the institutional arrangements adopted by Quebec workers were initially borrowed from the United States. By comparison with Ontario, however, the rate of diffusion of trade unionism occurred more slowly because of the language barrier. (Rouillard, p. 20) Many urban workers declined to participate in trade unions because of harassment by employers and the union's uncertain status in law. Most apparently believed the costs of membership outweighed the potential net benefits (the free rider problem). The growth of the trade union movement in the nineteenth century was therefore accompanied by slow growth and instability.

NOTES

[1] A crude compilation of the current dollar value of manufacturing output in Quebec for census years 1851 and 1860 is given in Hamelin and Roby. (p. 267)

[2] On the question of specialization in the iron smelting industry, Donald writes, "American furnace-men could purchase raw material, such as ore and charcoal in the open markets, but Canadian companies had to provide workmen for the entire cut of wood, had to transport the wood to the charcoal kilns, and the charcoal to the furnaces, to mine the full supply of ore, and quarry all the limestone." (*The Canadian Iron and Steel Industry: A Study in the History of a Protected Industry*, p. 110, by W.J.A. Donald © 1915.)

[3] According to participation rates from the census data of 1910, the earliest available, rates for both males and females aged 15-64 years were lower in Quebec than in Ontario. (Raynauld, p. 568) A. Greer's estimates of cohort literacy from the 1891 census indicate the enormous differential in literacy rates between Quebec and Ontario. (Greer, p. 327)

SELECT BIBLIOGRAPHY

Bertram, Gordon W. "Economic Growth in Canadian Industry, 1870-1915: The Staple Model," in W.T. Easterbrook and M.H. Watkins, eds., *Approaches to Canadian Economic History*. Toronto: McClelland and Stewart Ltd., 1967.

Burgess, Joanne. "L'industrie de la chaussure à Montréal: 1840-1870 - le passage de l'artisanat à la fabrique." *Revue d'histoire de l'Amérique française*. September 1977.

Caves, Richard E. and Richard H. Holton. *The Canadian Economy: Prospect and Retrospect.* Cambridge: Harvard University Press, 1961.

150 ans de lutte: histoire du mouvement ouvrier au Québec (1825-1976). Montreal: Centrale de l'enseignement du Quebec, 1979.

Coehlo, Philip R.P. and James R. Shepherd. "The Impact of Regional Differences in Prices and Wages on Economic Growth: The United States in 1890." *Journal of Economic History.* March 1979.

Davis, Lance, E. *American Economic Growth: An Economist's History of the United States.* New York: Harper & Row, 1972.

Donald, W.J.A. *The Canadian Iron and Steel Industry: A Study in the History of a Protected Industry.* Boston: Houghton Mifflin, 1915.

Faucher, Albert. *Québec en Amérique au XIXe siècle.* Montreal: Editions Fides, 1973.

Field, Alexander J. "Sectoral Shift in Antebellum Massachusetts: A Reconsideration." *Explorations in Economic History.* April 1978.

Firestone, O.J. *Canada's Economic Development, 1867-1953, With Special Reference to Changes in the Country's National Product and National Wealth.* London: Bowes and Bowes Publishers Ltd., 1958.

Greer, Allan. "The Pattern of Literacy in Quebec, 1745-1899." *Histoire Social-Social History.* November 1978.

Hamelin, Jean and Yves Roby. *Histoire économique du Québec, 1851-1896.* Montreal: Editions Fides, 1971.

Harley, C.K. "On the Persistance of Old Techniques: The Case of North American Wooden Shipbuilding." *Journal of Economic History.* June 1973.

Harvey, Fernand, ed. *Aspects historiques du mouvement ouvrier au Québec.* Montreal: Boréal Express, 1973.

Linteau, Paul-André, René Durocher, and Jean-Claude Robert. *Histoire du Québec contemporaine: de la Confédération à la crise (1867-1929).* Montreal: Boréal Express, 1979.

Mackintosh, W.A. *The Economic Background of Dominion-Provincial Relations.* Toronto: McClelland and Stewart Ltd., 1964.

McCallum, John. *Unequal Beginnings: Agriculture and Economic Development in Quebec and Ontario until 1870.* Toronto: University of Toronto Press, 1980.

McDiarmid, O.J. *Commercial Policy in the Canadian Economy.* Cambridge: Harvard University Press, 1946.

McDougall, Duncan M. "Canadian Manufactured Commodity Output, 1870-1915." *The Canadian Journal of Economics.* February 1971.

Naylor, R. Tom. *The History of Canadian Business, 1867-1914.* Toronto: James Lorimer & Co., 1975.

Pomfret, Richard. *The Economic Development of Canada.* Toronto: Metheun Publications, 1981.

Raynauld, André. *Croissance et structure économiques de la province de Québec.* Quebec: Ministère de l'Industrie et du Commerce, Province de Québec, 1961.

Rouillard, Jacques. *Les syndicats nationaux au Québec de 1900 à 1930.* Quebec: les Presses de l'Université Laval, 1979.

Ryan, William F. *The Clergy and Economic Growth in Quebec (1896-1914).* Quebec: les Presses de l'Université Laval, 1966.

Urquhart, M.C. and K.A.H. Buckley, eds. *Historical Statistics of Canada.* Toronto: Macmillan Co. of Canada, 1965.

Part IV

THE PROVINCE OF QUEBEC 1900-1940

13

Resource Industries

At the turn of the twentieth century, industrialization in North America entered a new phase. Changes in technology affected almost every sector of economic activity. In place of trial-and-error methods of innovation, technical change resulted increasingly from science-based knowledge involving abstract reasoning. In the nineteenth century, new inventions had been largely mechanical in nature. The principles of mechanical engineering had inspired innovations in agriculture and mining as well as the manufacturing and transport service industries. The study of chemical, biological and electronic processes, however, required more advanced methods of scientific observation. In the twentieth century, chemistry, biology, electronics and physics all contributed to the development of new products and techniques: synthetic raw materials; alternative energy sources; more efficient machinery, plant and equipment; improved means of communication; and new consumer durables. These innovations affected technology and the costs of production in the resource sector, as well as the structure of resource commodity demand and relative prices.

In agriculture, modern genetics and biochemistry contributed to technological changes in plant cultivation and cattle breeding. The introduction of herbicides, insecticides and commercially produced fertilizers, together with new farm machinery, influenced agricultural prices and output throughout North America. In the forestry sector, the development of a commercially viable process for transforming woodpulp into paper in the second half of the nineteenth century paved the way for the rapid growth of the paper industries after 1900. The development of the electric motor, electric lighting, electrolytic processes, and the central electric station combined to create the modern hydroelectric industry. By providing a relatively cheap source of energy, hydroelectricity accelerated the rate of exploitation of *in situ* resources. For example, the application of power to the process of mineral extraction contributed to lower costs per unit of mineral output and a shift toward the more intensive use of minerals in the manufacture of building materials and transport equipment.

Technological change also influenced resource commodity production on the demand side. Growth in resource commodity output was related to increased demand for raw materials. In the United States, Canada and Great Britain, aggregate resource commodity consumption expanded rapidly. In the United States, Quebec's principle buyer, growth was particularly high in the minerals sector. Chart 13.1 indicates American resource commodity consumption growth rates in per capita terms. Although the per capita consumption of forest products diminished, domestic production of forest products declined at an even faster rate. Overall, the United States became a net importer of resource commodities about 1920, though net imports of some products, such as woodpulp, newsprint and asbestos, began in the nineteenth century.

Agriculture

Quebec agriculture adapted to the long term behavioral trends that characterized the North American economy during the first four decades of the twentieth century. A slowdown in the growth rate of aggregate agricultural output accompanied continued industrialization and urbanization. Diminishing income elasticity characterized the aggregate demand for food products with the result that the growth rate in the per capita demand for food declined. No aggregate index is available for Quebec or Canada, but the per capita consumption of agricultural commodities in the United States expanded by 0.5 percent between 1870 and 1905, and decreased to zero between 1905 and 1939. (See Chart 13.1) In other words, the aggregate demand for food increased at about the same rate as population after 1905. The per capita demand for individual food products varied, of course, from commodity to commodity. In Canada, the data available on per capita 'disappearance' of food products prior to 1940 (i.e. without allowance for losses in transport and handling) appear to indicate trend increases for certain products such as poultry, milk, butter and ice cream and trend decreases for others such as lard and potatoes. (Urquhart and Buckley, p. 380)

Chart 13.1

PER CAPITA CONSUMPTION OF RESOURCE COMMODITIES IN THE UNITED STATES, BY SECTOR, 1870-1957

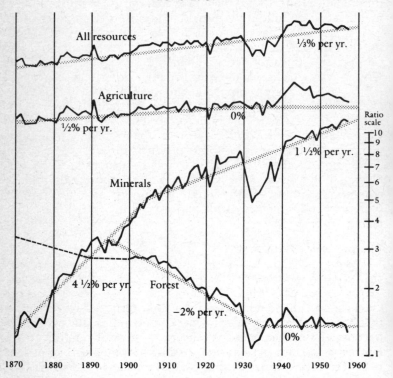

Trends in Natural Resource Commodities: Statistics of Prices, Output, Consumption, Foreign Trade, and Employment in the United States, 1870-1957, p. 9, by Neal Potter and Francis T. Christy, Jr. © 1962, reprinted by permission of The Johns Hopkins University Press, A Publication of Resources for the Future, Inc.

Technological progress lowered the average costs of agricultural production. The demand for farm labor per unit of output tended to diminish as a result of increases in agricultural productivity per worker. Although Quebec's farm labor force expanded slightly, the proportion of the total labor force employed in agriculture decreased from 38.2 percent to 21.5 percent between 1901 and 1941.

The problem of agricultural price instability continued to trouble producers in the twentieth century. Both producers and consumers are relatively slow to respond to food price changes in the short run. The price elasticities of supply and demand tend to be low for many agricultural products. Small changes in output resulting from random shocks, such as bad weather, often lead to considerable fluctuations in price. The price inelasticity of supply and demand curves for agricultural products means that total income to producers can decline in years of good harvest, and rise in years of bad harvest. Given the relative instability of prices and incomes in the agricultural sector, it is not surprising the number of farms and farm operators fluctuated widely. Although the total number of occupied farms in Quebec reached a twentieth century peak in 1941, it failed to attain the level of 1891.

The composition of farm output in Quebec remained relatively stable over the first two decades of the twentieth century. But after World War I, the structural changes that characterized Quebec agriculture before 1900 reappeared: field crop production diminished in favor of meat and dairy production. (See Table 13.1) As the continental integration of markets proceeded, soil quality and the length of the growing season continued to influence the region's agricultural vocation.

The production of livestock played a central role in determining the kind of field crops cultivated. Except for the vegetables (potatoes, corn and peas), all of the field crops listed in Table 13.2 were used primarily for animal feed. Even the diminishing volume of wheat production was destined predominantly for livestock feed, as cracked wheat for poultry and bran for cattle. The cultivation of hay expanded from 53 percent of total field crop acreage in 1901 to 62 percent in 1941. Most of this increase occurred during the first decade of the century. After 1910, the replacement of animal power by the tractor slowed the growth in the demand for horses, hay and oats. Hay and oats production temporarily recovered in the 1930s, however, when the rate of diffusion of mechanized implements declined as a result of relatively high fuel and repair costs. Among the vegetable crops, peas and corn production diminished in the face of continental specialization stemming from more favorable climatic conditions and mechanization in southern Ontario and the United States corn-belt. Quebec's largest potato output increase occurred in the 1930s as Quebecers switched to low priced foods during the Depression. On the whole, field crop acreage increased between 1900 and 1920; but as indicated below, this acreage increase may have been offset by lower yields. There was little change in field crop acreage under cultivation between 1920 and 1940.

Table 13.1

**ESTIMATED DISTRIBUTION OF GROSS ANNUAL
AGRICULTURAL REVENUE IN QUEBEC,
1919, 1929, 1939 (Percentages)**

	1919	1929	1939
Field crops	69.6	49.0	43.4
Dairy products	15.4	27.6	27.8
Farm animals	8.5	13.1	15.5
Fruits and vegetables	1.8	2.5	4.9
Poultry products	1.1	4.6	4.8
Maple products	1.4	1.5	1.3
Tobacco	1.5	0.4	0.8
Fur farming	—	0.7	0.6
Flax fibre	—	—	0.4
Wool	0.8	0.4	0.2
Honey and Wax	—	0.1	0.2
Total	100.0	99.9	99.9

Government of Canada, *The Canada Year Book*. Ottawa: King's Printer, 1925, 1931, 1941. Reproduced by permission of the Minister of Supply and Services Canada.

While the output of meat and dairy products continued to expand between 1900 and 1940, the farm processing of food was progressively replaced by factory production. The output of home-made cheese, for example, diminished from 358 625 pounds in 1910 to 12 250 pounds in 1940. (Government of Canada, p. 430) Total homemade and processed cheese output declined in favor of butter. Milk deliveries, particularly from the Montreal and Eastern Township regions, expanded to accommodate the aggregate demand for dairy products. Quebec producers often favored livestock that could be raised by pen feeding: dairy cows, swine and poultry. (See Table 13.3) These animals could be kept on small farms near urban centres, unlike beef cattle and sheep herds that required pasture feeding and larger farms. Such land intensive activities tended to locate in more outlying areas. The spatial distribution of livestock varieties reflected the tendency to economize on highly priced farm land near urban markets.

The farm production of wood products also contributed to aggregate farm output. In 1941, about one third of all occupied

Table 13.2

FIELD CROP PRODUCTION AND FIELD CROP AREA IN PRODUCTION IN QUEBEC, 1900-1940

(Thousands of bushels except where indicated otherwise)

Year	Wheat	Barley	Hay (thousands of tons)	Peas	Oats	Buckwheat	Corn for Husking	Potatoes	Turnips (thousands of tons)	Area in Field Crop Production (thousands of acres)
1900	1 968	2 536	2 582	909	33 537	1 850	1 384	17 136	n/a	4 704
1910	932	2 340	3 831	414	33 804	2 366	575	15 452	3 329	5 266
1920	1 576	2 321	3 259	388	36 837	1 501	296	17 746	4 403	5 905
1930	554	1 948	3 844	176	32 861	1 487	136	15 201	7 129	5 997
1940	271	2 506	3 970	125	35 100	1 094	99	22 418	11 118	6 026

Government of Canada, *Census of Canada, 1941*, Vol. V., p. 427. Reproduced by permission of the Minister of Supply and Services Canada.

Table 13.3

ANIMAL STOCK IN QUEBEC, CENSUS YEARS, 1901-1941
(Number of farm animals in thousands)

Year	Milk Cows	Other Cattle	Horses	Sheep	Swine	Poultry
1901	734	632	321	655	404	3 112
1911	754	699	372	637	794	4 833
1921	811	784	333	856	691	5 252
1931	892	816	301	734	728	7 862
1941	1 001	754	333	526	808	8 063

Historical Statistics of Canada, p. 369, by M.C. Urquhart and K.A.H. Buckley, © 1965, reprinted by permission.

Table 13.4

FIELD CROP YIELDS IN QUEBEC, ALTERNATE CENSUS YEARS
(bushels per acre except where indicated)

	1851	1870	1900	1920	1940
Wheat	9.2	8.5	14.1	13.8	15.0
Barley	13.8	n/a	24.3	21.5	22.5
Hay (tons per acre)	n/a	1.0	1.0	0.9	1.0
Oats	19.2	n/a	24.8	23.9	23.1
Buckwheat	12.0	n/a	18.0	16.6	14.9
Potatoes	71.9	141.0	134.7	120.9	150.7

"L'agriculture de la Mauricie et du Québec, 1850-1950," by Normand Séguin, *Revue d'historie de l'Amerique française*, p. 557, March 1982.

farm land in Quebec remained forested; by comparison, less than a fifth of occupied farm land in Ontario was wooded. Wood served for firewood, fence posts and rails, bridge-building and to repair farm buildings. The value of marketed wood per Quebec farm was consistently higher than in Ontario. Some Quebec producers, particularly in the Beauce and Megantic regions, also specialized in the production of maple products.

There is as yet no firm evidence concerning changes in total factor productivity or productivity per farm worker in Quebec agriculture before World War II.[1] Some indication of trends in land productivity is available on a crop-by-crop basis. (See Table 13.4) Field crop yields fluctuated from year to year, but yields appear to have remained about the same between 1900 and 1940. Yields were generally higher than in 1850, but most of the land productivity increase appears to have taken place before the turn of the century. Some of this improvement resulted from the simple elimination of inefficient activities such as wheat production, as well as from technical improvements.

Quebec farmers employed a range of equipment and techniques that suited the province's resource endowment and factor prices. In census year 1931, for example, the percentage of Quebec farms using threshing machines and gasoline engines was higher than in Ontario, but the percentage of Quebec farms using grain binders, automobiles, motor trucks and farm tractors was much lower. (Haythorne and Marsh, p. 235) The comparative scarcity of grain production, the greater incidence of rural poverty, the prevalence of unpaid family labor[2] and a lower wage-rental ratio all contributed to a slower rate of mechanization in Quebec agriculture. (See Table 13.5) Although the co-operative marketing of produce was common, the co-operative use of farm machinery was a rarity among Quebec farmers. The employment of small threshing machines powered by stationary gasoline engines was conse-

Table 13.5

MACHINERY PER OCCUPIED FARM*, QUEBEC, ONTARIO AND CANADA, CENSUS YEARS, 1901-1941

Year	Implements and Machinery (current dollars)			Farm Tractors (units per 1 000 farms)		
	Quebec	Ontario	Rest of Canada	Quebec	Ontario	Rest of Canada
1901	193	258	213	—	—	—
1911	347	367	377	—	—	—
1921	813	858	935	7.0	36.2	66.7
1931	715	791	893	17.8	98.8	144.6
1941	551	844	813	37.9	199.0	218.0

*Farms of less than one acre excluded.

Historical Statistics of Canada, pp. 351, 353, 354, 381, by M.C. Urquhart and K.A.H. Buckley, © 1965, reprinted by permission.

quently greater than in Ontario. The relative absence of automobiles and motor trucks in Quebec is attributable to the lower level of market sales per farm.

Agricultural producers relied heavily on markets within the province. The location of urban areas influenced the spatial distribution of production. Not only milk, poultry and pork production, but also fruit and vegetable production tended to locate in the regions surrounding Montreal. The co-operative movement played an active part in the marketing of all types of agricultural produce, especially milk. The *Coopérative fédérée de Québec*, founded in 1910, became the movement's central co-ordinating agency after World War I. By 1941, total membership in agricultural co-operatives represented 21 percent of all farm operators. Quebec producers did succeed in exporting a modest quantity of select agricultural products. For example, cheese and bacon was exported to Great Britain. Until the rise of American tariff barriers in the 1930s, farmers in the Eastern Townships shipped a sizeable volume of milk to the United States. Good roads, railway connections, and geographical proximity all played a role in this trade. But overall, Quebec's agricultural sector produced a relatively small surplus above and beyond the needs of the farm population. Isbister's calculations support the contention that Quebec agriculture never enjoyed a large surplus to feed the province's entire population. (See Chapter 10, Table 10.6) Throughout the first four decades of the twentieth century, Quebec required net food 'imports'.[3]

Many of the factors explaining the long run differential in average farm income between Quebec and Ontario have been discussed in previous chapters. Soil quality, precipitation, and the length of the growing season played a major role in determining the level of output and income per farm worker. Ontario enjoyed a more favorable resource endowment for agricultural production than Quebec. In 1941 Quebec possessed 18 million acres of occupied farm land and 9 million acres of improved land; Ontario possessed 22 million acres of occupied farm land and 13 million acres of improved land. (Urquhart and Buckley, p. 352) The interprovincial distribution of lands with 150 or more days of growing season is indicated in Figure 13.1.

Haythorne and Marsh have estimated that net agricultural output per Quebec worker was highest in the Montreal region. Using data for 1931, Haythorne and Marsh calculate the gross value of all products raised on the farm and deduct an allowance for produce fed to livestock.[4] According to their admittedly crude results, net agricultural output was lowest in the Gaspé-Saguenay, Bas du Fleuve and Abitibi regions. Income from fishing also

Figure 13.1

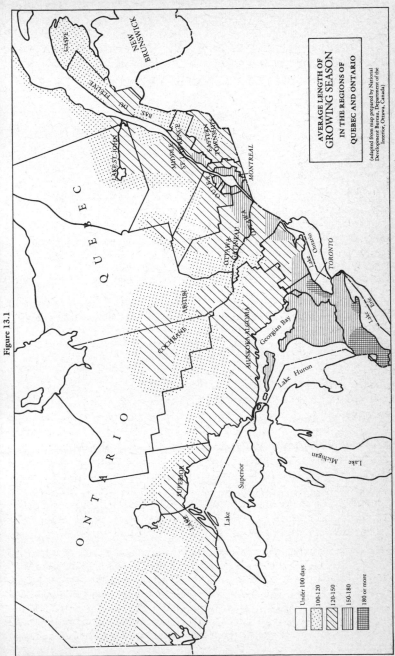

AVERAGE LENGTH OF
GROWING SEASON
IN THE REGIONS OF
QUEBEC AND ONTARIO

(adapted from map prepared by National
Development Bureau, Department of the
Interior, Ottawa, Canada)

Under 100 days
100-120
120-150
150-180
180 or more

Land and Labour: A Social Survey of Agriculture and the Farm Labour Market in Central Canada, p. 92, by George V. Haythorne and Leonard C. Marsh. Toronto: Oxford University Press, 1941.

Table 13.6

AGRICULTURAL PARTICIPATION INCOME PER WORKER IN QUEBEC, ONTARIO AND CANADA, CENSUS YEARS, 1910-1940*

	1910-1911	1920-1921	1930		1940	
			McInnis	DBS	McInnis	DBS
		Current Dollars				
Quebec	398	779	374	322	368	378
Ontario	556	845	452	498	487	515
Canada	509	952	400	374	453	494
		Relative Level				
Quebec	78	82	94	86	81	77
Ontario	109	89	113	133	108	104
Canada	100	100	100	100	100	100

*McInnis's estimates are given for each of the benchmark years from 1910-1911 to 1940. For 1930 and 1940, estimates by the Dominion Bureau of Statistics are also presented for comparison.

"The Trend of Regional Income Differentials in Canada," By Marvin McInnis, *Canadian Journal of Economics*, pp. 459-462, Copyright © May 1968, reprinted by permission.

provided a source of income for some farms in these areas. Five of the nine agricultural regions in Ontario equalled or exceeded the level of net agricultural output per worker in the Montreal region.

R.M. McInnis has estimated agricultural participation income per worker in 1910-1911 and 1920-1921 for the Canadian regions. Participation income is defined as the net income of proprietors plus wages and salaries. McInnis's estimates for Quebec, together with the results of the application of his method to subsequent census years, are presented in Table 13.6. Except for 1930, the relative level of farm income per worker in Quebec hovers around eighty percent of the Canadian average. Drought and the decline in the world price of wheat explain why prairie farm income diminished and the relative position of Quebec farm income increased during the 1930s.

In addition to differences in output per worker, farm family size played a role in determining agricultural income per person. Quebec's average farm size was smaller than Ontario's in 1941, larger in 1931 and 1921, and about the same in 1911 and 1901. However, the average Quebec farm (farms of less than one acre excluded) continuously supported more people than its Ontario counterpart: 5.4 persons in 1941 as opposed to 4.0 in Ontario. (Urquhart and Buckley, pp. 350-351) Quebec's farms were less productive than Ontario's, and their net income was distributed over a larger number of family members.

The Timber Industry

The abundance of forest resources played a significant role in determining the level and composition of provincial output and income. Square timber was the most important Quebec export during most of the nineteenth century. Wood products constituted the second largest manufacturing industry in the province in 1870, and the largest in 1900. As the stock of accessible forest resources diminished relative to iron, coal and water power resources in most of the industrializing nations, relative prices induced a shift away from the consumption of wood as a building material and as a fuel. The deflated price of lumber in the United States more than tripled between 1870 and 1940 as American forests were depleted. (Potter and Christy, Jr., p. 30) American lumber consumption per capita reached a peak during the first decade of the twentieth century and then declined. Both per capita and total fuel wood consumption decreased steadily between 1870 and 1940.

Although the available data does not give a clear indication, the per capita consumption of lumber products may have declined in Quebec as it did in the United States. The place of wood products in provincial manufacturing decreased steadily between 1900 and 1940. The consumption of pulpwood and paper provided the only significant exception to the shift away from wood products. In the United States, the per capita consumption of pulpwood increased six-fold between 1900 and 1940 even though the deflated price of pulpwood showed little or no trend. (Potter and Christy, Jr., p. 31) By 1939, wood and paper accounted for 44 percent of Canada's total exports to the United States. Quebec produced about one half of Canada's woodpulp and paper.

The absence of consistent time series data hampers empirical analysis of Quebec's forestry sector. For census years 1871-1901, the federal government collected data on timber cutting using a variety of measures that have not yet been translated into a satisfactory index of total volume. (See Chapter 11) As of 1911, the census takers restricted themselves to forest products cut on occupied farm lands. The Forestry Service and the Forest Products Branch of the federal government published information on provincial forest activities after 1900, but their documents often specify that no effort was made to cover all activities or to prevent double-counting. Beginning in 1913, the Quebec government published annual data on forest operations; a few series extend back to 1870. The overall divergence in magnitudes reported by the two levels of government is disconcerting.[5] The task of consistently sorting out the published information remains to be accomplished. The data that appears in Tables 13.7 and 13.8 should not be taken as more than an indication of trends.

About 26 percent of the occupied forest land in Quebec was privately owned in 1940. (Angers, p. 352) Most of these lands had

Table 13.7

ESTIMATED VOLUME OF TOTAL TIMBER PRODUCTION IN QUEBEC, ONTARIO AND CANADA,
1922-1940 (millions of cubic feet)

Year	Quebec	Ontario	Canada
1922	795	656	2 378
1923	868	725	2 671
1924	883	761	2 809
1925	841	779	2 839
1926	845	740	2 838
1927	856	698	2 865
1928	877	771	2 988
1929	811	776	3 091
1930	1 001	719	3 057
1931	645	604	3 306
1932	706	402	1 882
1933	717	440	2 028
1934	810	467	2 300
1935	850	514	2 441
1936	932	559	2 702
1937	1 050	630	2 996
1938	891	576	2 652
1939	953	589	2 824
1940	1 115	662	3 345

"Documentation Statistique" by François-Albert Angers, in *La Forêt*, p. 353, ed. by Esdras Minville, © copyright 1944, reprinted by permission.

Table 13.8

ESTIMATED DISTRIBUTION OF TIMBER PRODUCTION IN QUEBEC, BY END USE, 1938-1940 (Percentages)

	1938	1939	1940
Pulpwood	52.1	32.8	45.3
Fuel wood	29.1	42.5	32.0
Lumber sawed in Quebec	16.2	20.8	19.3
Singles	0.7	1.1	0.9
Other	1.9	2.8	2.5
Total	100.0	100.0	100.0

"Documentation Statistique" by François-Albert Angers, in *La Forêt*, pp. 354-355, ed. by Esdras Minville, © copyright 1944, reprinted by permission.

originally been conceded as part of an agricultural concession; some had been conceded in lieu of cash subsidies to nineteenth century railway builders. Property rights to the rest of Quebec's forest resources were available from the provincial government by lease. As determined in the nineteenth century, provincial leasing policy resulted in two types of charges: fixed charges irrespective of the volume of timber cut, and a charge per cord of wood removed. By order of the provincial Cabinet, the latter varied in line with timber prices. In this way some of the economic rents flowing from the industry could be appropriated by the provincial government.

Owing to the distribution of forest species in Quebec, the rise of the pulp and paper industry influenced the location of timber cutting in the province. During the nineteenth century the demand for pulpwood was limited; timber cutting was concentrated in the Ottawa Valley where pine forests prevailed. At the turn of the century, increased demand for pulpwood shifted the focus of timber cutting toward the St. Maurice and Saguenay regions where spruce and balsam fir predominated. The parallel development of hydroelectric power installations that supplied low cost energy to pulpwood producers provided an added inducement to timber cutting in these regions. As indicated in Table 13.8, pulpwood emerged as the most important source of demand for timber in Quebec.

The Mineral Industries

In the nineteenth century, iron, copper, gold, phosphate and asbestos operations successively dominated Quebec's mineral sector. Mining occurred primarily in the Eastern Townships, but also in the lower St. Maurice, Beauce and Ottawa Valleys. Pick-and-shovel extraction methods and constant returns to scale characterized mining technology until the 1890s. About this time mining exploration began to employ more sophisticated techniques that involved high fixed costs and increasing returns to scale. Many of the province's most valuable mineral deposits gradually passed into the hands of American residents.

American capital and technology played an active role in the development of Quebec's mining sector in the twentieth century. No aggregate data on American investment in Quebec is available, but the largest mine operators in most regions came from the United States. Of the six asbestos mining companies operating in Quebec by the late 1920s, four were affiliates of American asbestos manufacturers.[6] American financing and mining expertise fostered the creation of Noranda Mines Ltd. in 1922, though majority control of the company may have passed into the hands of Toronto financiers in the late 1920s. (Marshall, *et al*., p. 94) Noranda's Horne mine accounted for more than ninety percent of Quebec's copper production and more than fifty percent of Quebec's gold production during the years 1930-1935.

The production of asbestos fibre expanded through the first four decades of the twentieth century. (See Table 13.9) The United States accounted for more than 70 percent of Quebec's asbestos exports during this time. The demand for asbestos resulted from the variety of characteristics possessed by the mineral: fire resistance, low conductivity, durability, tensile strength, non-corrosiveness, acid resistance, weaving possibilities, and others. These characteristics found application in the production of industrial clothing and textiles, paper and millboard, tiles and cement. Until World War I, the demand for asbestos was closely associated with the demand for new building construction. During the war years, the demand for asbestos in the war industries compensated for the decrease in its demand as a building material. Following the sharp decline in asbestos demand during the recession of 1920-1921, output expanded in line with new building construction and motor vehicle production. Asbestos served as the basic component in automobile brake linings and clutch facings.

The development of Quebec's Rouyn-Noranda district originated with the spillover of mineral prospecting and mining from across the provincial border in Ontario. In 1898 the federal

Table 13.9

OUTPUT OF THE PRINCIPLE MINERAL INDUSTRIES IN QUEBEC, SELECTED YEARS, 1900-1940

Year	Iron Ore Production	Copper Production		Gold Production		Shipments of Asbestos*	
	tons	tons	value ($000)	thous. ounces	value ($000)	thous. tons	value ($000)
1900	19 000	1 110	359	nil	nil	22	729
1905	12 681	811	253	0.2	4	51	1 486
1910	4 503	439	112	0.1	3	78	2 556
1915	nil	2 099	725	1.2	23	111	3 553
1920	nil	440	154	0.9	19	179	14 735
1925	nil	1 314	277	1.8	38	274	8 978
1930	nil	40 155	10 426	141.7	2 930	242	8 390
1935	nil	39 526	6 162	470.5	16 558	210	7 055
1940	nil	67 080	13 530	1 016.2	39 122	347	15 620

*Asbestic excluded.

The Canadian Iron and Steel Industry: A Study in the History of a Protected Industry, p. 328, by W.J.A. Donald © 1915.

Government of Canada, *The Production of Copper, Gold, Lead, Nickel, Silver, Zinc and other Metals in Canada during the Calendar Year 1920*, p. 18. Ottawa: Department of Mines, 1921.

Gold in Canada, p. 114, by A.H.A. Robinson. Ottawa: Department of Mines, 1935.

Chrysotile Asbestos in Canada, Chap. IV, Tables 2-3, by James G. Ross, © 1931. Reprinted by permission of Energy, Mines and Resources Canada.

Government of Quebec: *L'industrie minière de la province de Québec pour l'année 1940*. Quebec: Service des Mines, 1941.

government extended Quebec and Ontario's northern borders by virtue of its acquisition of the Hudson Bay lands some twenty-nine years earlier. (See Linteau, *et al*, p. 19) Mining exploration in this region dates from the construction of the Temiskaming and Northern Ontario Railway in 1902. But in the years that followed, the high costs of overland transport to the rail line impeded the growth of mineral extraction in Quebec.[7] The renaissance of copper and gold mining in Quebec began in 1920 with a major discovery of gold on the northwest side of Lake Temiskaming. Development in Quebec's northwest depended entirely on rail transport in Ontario until the Rouyn Railway Company completed a branch from Rouyn to Taschereau on the Transcontinental line in 1926. Copper production at Noranda's Horne mine began in the following year. Despite falling copper prices,[8] production expanded steadily thereafter. (See Table 13.9)

On the gold market, the deflated gold price in the United States declined between 1895 and 1920, and then increased until 1940. (Potter and Christy Jr., p. 45) In Canada, federal government monetary authorities fixed the nominal price of gold so that mild deflation over the 1927-1929 period increased gold's constant dollar price. The abandoning of the gold standard as the basis of the international monetary system, an increase in consumer demand for gold as an asset, and price deflation all contributed to the rise in gold's relative world market price. The higher price illicited more output. (See Table 13.9) Gold constituted Quebec's most valuable mineral product between 1931 and 1945.

Hydroelectricity

The abundance of forests and rivers explains the preponderance of wood and water power energy sources in the eastern region of North America during the first half of the nineteenth century. In the United States, 91 percent of aggregate energy consumption involved fuel wood in 1850. (Schurr and Netschert, p. 36) But the industrialization of production and exchange required enormous quantities of energy. As a result of changes in technology and relative prices in the second half of the nineteenth century, fuel wood constituted only 21 percent of American energy consumption by 1900. Coal contributed 71 percent. By 1940, fuel wood constituted a mere 5 percent of the United States energy consumption and coal had diminished to 50 percent. In their place, oil and natural gas accounted for 41 percent and hydropower for 4 percent. Comparable data are not available for the Quebec economy, but in 1937 coal accounted for 53 percent of the energy consumed in Quebec and Ontario together (excluding fuel wood consumption), oil and natural gas for 13.5 percent, and water power for 34 percent. (Burley, p. 172) The high proportion of water power in Quebec's total energy consumption reflected the province's water resource endowment.

Growth in the demand for electricity accompanied the diffusion of new products that required electrical power: the electric motor, electric lighting, electrolytic processes, electric tramways and railways, home appliances, and so on. The electric motor was perhaps the key industrial innovation in the diffusion of electrical technology. Electric motors replaced the coal-using steam engine because they offered a smaller, less costly source of power that obviated the belting and shafting techniques necessary for the transmission of power in steam-powered plants. In doing so, the electric motor permitted the redesign of plant layout and mass production techniques. Although virtually absent in 1900, electric motors accounted for more than seventy-five percent of total installed horsepower in Canadian manufacturing by 1933.

In Montreal, electrical installations predated the advent of hydroelectricity. Electric street lighting, powered by steam-generated electricity, was inaugurated in 1889 and an electric tramway in 1892. But as hydroelectricity became available after 1897, the steam generation of electricity waned. In the early years of the twentieth century, the demand for electricity was restricted to electric lighting. Not until the 1920s did electrical appliances such as the refrigerator and the electric range appear on the consumer goods market. In addition to servicing the urban areas, the hydro-electric power companies also diffused power in the rural areas surrounding the main hydroelectric installations. The average cost of installing transmission lines was lowest where farms were small and grouped together. Electric lighting could more easily be applied in pen feeding than in pasture feeding or field cropping. These conditions were generally satisfied near urban areas such as Montreal, Trois-Rivières and Quebec.

The development of hydroelectric power technology completely revalued Quebec's abundant supplies of water power. To exploit the water power of a river, an entrepreneur required property rights traditionally held by the State. The history of the evolution of property rights in Quebec's rivers and streams is difficult to summarize because of the variety of rights and the frequency of changes in judicial interpretation and public policy concerning these rights. Navigation, flotation by raft, log transport, public harbors, and hydraulic power were each the object of indentifiable, sometimes conflicting property rights. At Confederation, the Quebec government obtained most of these rights in rivers that were either navigable or floatable by rafts, including the rights to hydraulic power. The provincial government withheld the property rights to hydraulic power in all non-navigable, non-floatable rivers and streams from new land concessions as of 1884. Between 1867 and 1907, however, the government separately disposed of many of its water power rights by sale. These sales involved some of the most important power sites on the Saguenay, St. Maurice, Gatineau and Lièvre Rivers. Only in 1907 did the provincial government adopt a long term leasing system that enabled it to introduce a measure of control over exports of hydroelectricity in the 1920s. (See Chapter 16)

About seventy percent of Quebec's known water power

resources lay along the St. Lawrence River and its northern tributaries. Each of the major watersheds provided a natural water power monopoly within the region. Water rights on the upper St. Lawrence, St. Maurice, Saguenay, Gatineau, Lièvre and St. François Rivers belonged to six separate firms. These companies accounted for about ninety percent of provincial hydroelectrical output. Hydro installations generally encountered high start-up costs associated with plant construction, and falling average and marginal costs up to the physical capacity of the power site. Because each firm was able to prevent the resale of its product, the power companies engaged in price discrimination based on differing marginal costs and demand elasticities among buyers.[9]

The largest industrial users of electricity in Quebec were the wood and paper and non-ferrous smelting (aluminum) industries. These two sectors accounted for almost one half of all power sales in Quebec. In the 1930s, about three-quarters of provincial power production was either sold to these industries, or exported from Canada. However, the wood and paper and non-ferrous smelting industries contributed a relatively smaller share of hydroelectric revenues than their consumption would indicate. (Dales, p. 43) Small industrial, commercial and farm users paid higher rates and contributed relatively more to hydroelectric revenues because of the hydroelectric firms' pricing policies. The retail markets for lighting and small power use occupied a much larger proportion of total power demand in Ontario as a result of lower domestic rates in that province. Public ownership of the hydroelectric industry in Ontario undoubtedly contributed to the interprovincial difference in rate structure.

* * *

Quebec's resource sector expanded after 1900 in response to technological change, shifts in demand, and new resource discoveries. Technological innovation was perhaps the most important force behind this expansion. Many technical innovations appeared first in the United States and were then adopted in Quebec and elsewhere. The transfer of technology often involved the migration of American capital and trained personnel.

According to Nathan Rosenberg, technological change in the United States reflected the relative availability of productive factors in the American economy.

> In the United States, perhaps the most enduring and pervasive influence shaping the contours of technological development has been the very high land/labour ratio, the general abundance of natural resources relative to a small population. A distinctive feature of much

American innovation, therefore, was that it was directed toward making possible the exploitation of a large quantity of such resources with relatively little labour or that it substituted units of the abundant input (natural resources) for units of the scarce input (labour, and to a lesser extent, capital).[10]

And Rosenberg goes on to say:

It was not the high level of wages as such, but rather the persistant pressures on the labour market, the numerous opportunities for labour in a resource-abundant environment, and the high degree of labour mobility that conditioned entrepreneurs to expect further future increases in the cost of labour relative to other inputs, and gave them a strong bias toward the development of labour-saving techniques.[11]

With the lower land/labor ratio prevailing in Quebec agriculture, the invention and diffusion of new processes and techniques occurred more slowly than in some other North American regions. Though relative wage rates did not differ greatly from one region to the next, Quebec farmers generally experienced less pressure to adopt labour-saving devices. Throughout most of the United States and western Canada, the cultivable land/labor ratio was relatively high; labor was the scarce factor of production. In Quebec, the farm land/labor ratio was comparatively low; cultivable land was the scarce economic factor. The incentive to adopt labor-saving techniques did not arise to the same degree as it did in many other regions.

NOTES

[1] J.P. Wampach's data shows no trend between 1926 and 1945 but the data, borrowed from an earlier study by S.H. Lok, are incomplete and unreliable.

[2] Haythorne's estimates suggest that Ontario possessed many more unpaid farm family workers than Quebec in the nineteenth century, but that this situation was reversed as of census year 1911. (Urquhart and Buckley, p. 355).

[3] The failure to produce sufficient quantities of food to feed the Quebec population, despite the relatively high proportion of the labor force in the agricultural sector, was associated with problems of product quality. Quebec cheese and butter was reputed to be of a mediocre grade. Precise information on the subject of quality is scarce, but there are indirect indicators. In 1914 the Federal Department of Agriculture published the results of a study on the bacteria count in milk supplied by the major dairy farming districts feeding Montreal. As reported by Terry Copp, fifty percent of the total sample was unfit for drinking at the point of production and this percentage increased to ninety percent by the time the sample reached Montreal. The standards adopted in the study were those of large American cities. (Copp, p. 97)

[4] The details of this allowance are not explained. Estimates of both the value of farm output per agricultural worker (including family workers and family hands) and the value of farm output per full-time agricultural worker are presented. (Haythorne and Marsh, pp. 272-274).

[5]Operators' false declarations compounded the governments' data gathering difficulties. For example, a provincial government inquiry in 1902 found operators in the St. Maurice region were declaring sprucewood as timber rather than pulpwood to avoid the high government price established in 1900 for raw pulpwood cut on provincial lands and destined for export markets. (Hardy et al, pp. 119-120).

[6]The English mining conglomerate, Turner and Newell, purchased the American owned Bell Asbestos mines at Thetford in 1934.

[7]In 1912, Quebec's northern border was again extended to include the Ungava District (Nouveau-Quebec). But the northeastern boundary with Labrador remained an issue of contention with the British colony of Newfoundland. The issue revolved around the meaning of a 'coastline' as referred to in the Royal Proclamation of 1763. In a controversial decision in 1922, the Judicial Council of the Privy Council in London decided that the coastline was defined by the headwaters of all rivers flowing into the Atlantic Ocean.

[8]The deflated price of copper in the United States diminished from 1916 until the late 1930s. American consumption per capita tripled between 1900 and 1929, but showed substantial decreases during the years 1921 and 1930-1938 (Potter and Christy, Jr., p. 38).

[9]"The fee charges for the service will depend not only on the amount of electricity purchased, but also on the ratio of peak demand to average demand ('load factor'), on the time of day when the peak demand occurs and it duration ('diversity factor'), and the type of machinery for which the power is used (for on this depends the 'power factor' of the load.)" (Dales, p. 8).

[10]*American Economic Growth: An Economist's History of the United States*, page 241, by Lance E. Davis et al. Copyright 1972 by Harper & Row, Publishers Inc. Reprinted by permission of the publisher.

[11]*American Economic Growth: An Economist's History of the United States*, page 251, by Lance E. Davis et al. Copyright 1972 by Harper & Row, Publishers Inc. Reprinted by permission of the publisher.

SELECT BIBLIOGRAPHY

Angers, François-Albert. "Documentation Statistique," in Esdras Minville, ed., *L'Agriculture*. Montreal: Editions Fides, 1943.

Angers, François-Albert. "Documentation Statistique," in Esdras Minville, ed., *La Forêt*. Montreal: Editions Fides, 1944.

Biss-Spry, Irene. "Hydro-Electric Power," in W. Stewart Wallace, ed., *The Encyclopedia of Canada*. Toronto: University Associates of Canada, 1936. Vol. III.

Biss-Spry, Irene. "Water-Powers," in W. Stewart Wallace, ed., *The Encyclopedia of Canada*. Toronto: University Associates of Canada, 1937, Vol VI.

Bouffard, Jean. *Traité du Domaine*. (Reproduction de l'édition originale de 1921). Quebec: les Presses de l'Université Laval, 1977.

Burley, Kevin H., ed. *The Development of Canada's Staples, 1867-1939: A Documentary Collection*. Toronto: McClelland and Stewart Ltd., 1970.

Copp, Terry. *The Anatomy of Poverty: The Condition of the Working Class in Montreal 1897-1929*. Toronto: McClelland and Stewart Ltd., 1974.

Dales, John H. *Hydroelectricity and Industrial Development: Quebec, 1898-1940*. Cambridge: Harvard University Press, 1957.

Davis, Lance. *et al. American Economic Growth: An Economist's History of the United States*. New York: Harper & Row, 1972.

Government of Canada, *Census of Canada, 1941*. Vol. V.

Hardy, Rene, Normand Séguin, Alain Gamelin, Andre Miville, and Guy Trepanier. *L'exploitation forestière en Mauricie. Dossier statistique: 1850-1930*. Trois-Rivières: U.Q.T.R., 1980.

Haythorne, George V. *Labour in Canadian Agriculture*. Cambridge: Harvard University Press, 1960.

Haythorne, George V. and Leonard C. Marsh. *Land and Labour: A Social Survey of Agriculture and the Farm Labour Market in Central Canada*. Toronto: Oxford University Press, 1941.

Howe, Charles W. *Natural Resource Economics: Issues, Analysis, and Policy*. New York: John Wiley & Sons, 1979.

Linteau, Paul-André, René Durocher, and Jean-Claude Robert. *Histoire du Québec contemporain: de la Confédération à la crise (1867-1929)*. Montreal: Boréal Express, 1979.

Marshall, Herbert, Frank Southard, Jr., and Kenneth W. Taylor. *Canadian-American Industry: A Study in International Investment*. Toronto: McClelland and Stewart Ltd., 1976.

McInnis, Marvin. "The Trend of Regional Income Differentials in Canada." *Canadian Journal of Economics*. May 1968.

Potter, Neal, and Francis T. Christy, Jr. *Trends in Natural Resource Commodities: Statistics of Prices, Output, Consumption, Foreign Trade, and Employment in the United States, 1870-1957*. Baltimore: Johns Hopkins Press, 1962.

Raynauld, André. *Croissance et structure économiques de la province du Québec*. Québec: Ministère de l'Industrie et du Commerce, 1961.

Schurr, Sam H. and Bruce C. Netschert. *Energy in the American Economy, 1850-1975*. Baltimore: Johns Hopkins Press, 1960.

Séguin, Normand. "L'agriculture de la Mauricie et du Québec, 1850-1950." *Revue d'histoire de l'Amérique française*. March 1982.

Séguin, Normand, ed. *Agriculture et colonisation au Québec*. Montreal: Boréal Express, 1980.

Séguin, Normand and René Hardy. "Forêt et société en Mauricie, 1850-1930." *Material History Bulletin*. Fall 1981.

Urquhart, M.C. and K.A.H. Buckley. *Historical Statistics of Canada*. Toronto: Macmillan of Canada, 1965.

Wampach, Jean-Pierre. "Les tendances de la productivité totale dans l'agriculture: Canada, Ontario, Québec, 1926-64." *Canadian Journal of Agricultural Economics*. Vol. XV, no. 1, 1967.

14
Manufacturing

A series of events coincided at the turn of the century to reshape the North American economic environment and produce changes in the size and composition of Quebec's manufacturing sector. Western Canadian settlement, economic growth in the United States, and a sharp increase in foreign investment stimulated economic activity throughout Canada. The settlement of the Canadian prairie region, for instance, created expectations of a new, tariff-protected market for eastern manufactured goods. Gross investment in Canada increased from 13.4 to 26.5 percent of GNE between 1900 and 1910 (see Chapter 16, Table 16.1) resulting in historically high rates of growth in Canadian manufacturing, construction, and transport infrastructure during the first decade of the twentieth century.[1]

The rise of the United States as a major industrial nation also created new markets for a select number of semi-manufactured goods. Despite the high level of tariff protection in the United States, American demand for paper and aluminum products stimulated Quebec manufacturing output. GNP per capita in the United States increased rapidly during the years 1899-1913 and the associated rise in American living standards created new opportunities for Quebec exporters.

The expansion of Quebec's manufacturing sector was further stimulated by an inflow of American capital and technology in the form of direct investment. In the last decade of the nineteenth century, the overall position of the United States as a net capital importer began to change. As of 1897 the United States became a net capital exporter in most years and during World War I emerged as a net creditor nation. American goods and capital embodied American technology and know-how—new products, new machinery, new organizational methods, and new resource needs. The sewing machine, the phonograph, the typewriter, the bicycle and the automobile appeared as consumer products. Technical know-how, such as that involving the harnessing of rivers to produce hydroelectricity, descended on the province like manna from heaven. The invention of new products and techniques created new opportunities for profit-seeking entrepreneurs willing to invest in resource exploitation and manufacturing production.

In this chapter, growth in Quebec manufacturing is related to conditions external to the manufacturing sector. In the discussion of industrial concentration and foreign ownership, overall Canadian trends are outlined because no provincial data is available. Following an overview of Quebec's manufacturing growth, the structure of the manufacturing sector is related to four possible sources of provincial comparative advantage: domestic demand and transport costs, the resource endowment, wage rates, and government taxes and subsidies.

Industrial Concentration in Manufacturing

Canadian manufacturing industry underwent radical structural change during the first four decades of the twentieth century. Although no empirical studies have yet focused on manufacturing industry structure in Quebec *per se*, the important contribution of Quebec firms to total Canadian manufacturing output makes it reasonable to assume the structure of the province's manufacturing sector evolved in line with Canada's. The average size of industrial firms in Canada increased substantially between 1900 and 1940, and levels of industrial concentration apparently reached all-time highs in the 1930s.[2] The "flight from competition" was closely associated with two distinct waves of corporate consolidations. Of the 374 consolidations between 1900 and 1933 recorded by the Royal Commission on Price Spreads, 58 occurred between 1909 and 1912, and 231 between 1925 and 1930. (Government of Canada, 1935, p. 28) These two merger waves laid the foundations for the structure of Canadian manufacturing industry during the rest of the twentieth century.

Industrial concentration in Canada and the United States has been attributed to diverse changes that date from the late nineteenth century: the adoption of the corporate form as the preferred legal structure of industrial companies; the growth of financial intermediaries and the development of the stock market, a shift in the international structure of interest rates that encouraged American investment in Canada, larger minimum optimum plant sizes, lower railway transport costs that increased average market area sizes, tariff barriers, and so on. All of these changes were associated with corporate mergers and the growth of concentration, but cause and effect are difficult to separate. L.G. Reynolds concluded his study of industrial concentration in Canada with the following statement:

> Most Canadian mergers seem to have been promoted by men with financial rather than industrial experience, and promoter's profits seem to have been the largest single incentive to combination. This view is supported by the fact that the two bursts of merger activity occurred during periods of relative prosperity, when fresh stock issues were quickly absorbed by optimistic investors. The hope of achieving price control has been an incentive in some cases. Economies in production, while figuring largely in company prospectuses, do not seem to have been an important incentive.[3]

Foreign Ownership

A feature closely associated with industrial concentration in Quebec's manufacturing sector was a major shift in the level, sources and composition of foreign investment. Once again, data on the precise extent of foreign investment in the province is unavailable for the period before 1940, but general trends are suggested by the data for Canada as a whole. The greatest change occurred during the years preceding World War I. In 1900, total foreign investment in Canada had attained a level of 1.2 billion dollars (current). Between 1900 and 1913, the constant dollar value of total foreign investment in Canada more than doubled.[4] During these same years, the proportion of total foreign investment originating in Great Britain declined from 85 to 75 percent. American direct investment in Canadian manufacturing already exceeded British manufacturing investment by seven fold in 1897, and the gap widened after the turn of the century. The increase in American investment, and the strong preference by American investors for direct rather than portfolio investment accelerated the growth rate of Canadian manufacturing.

Between 1913 and 1939, total constant dollar foreign investment in Canada increased again by 65 percent.[5] The proportion of this total attributable to American investors rose from 21 percent in 1913 to 50 percent in 1922, and to 60 percent by 1939. At the outbreak of World War II, one-third of total foreign investment in Canada consisted of direct investment; 38 percent of Canadian manufacturing industry was foreign owned (Marr and Paterson, p. 297). Apparently, American companies preferred to locate in southern Ontario. Of 1 030 American-owned industrial plants surveyed in Canada in 1934, Marshall, Southard and Taylor found that 66 percent lay in Ontario and only 16 percent in Quebec. However, American-owned firms were less active in the food products and textile industries than in the iron and steel, machinery, and automotive industries, so the tendency by American firms to locate in Ontario may have been related to the composition of Quebec's manufacturing sector.

An Overview of Quebec Manufacturing Growth

Owing to changes in definition and coverage, the census data on Canadian manufacturing output pose various obstacles to the construction of a consistent time series data base. An initial problem arises because the census takers excluded firms employing less than five employees for the years 1900 and 1910.[6] Fortunately, W.F. Ryan has provided estimates that allow for complete coverage of manufacturing gross output value and value added in Quebec for these years. Although Ryan's estimates make an important contribution to the construction of consistent data series, serious weaknesses remain for the years after 1910: only firms with output valued at $2 500 or more are included in the data for 1915; construction firms are excluded from the manufacturing sector as of 1917; fuel and electricity are included as raw materials in the estimation of value added beginning in 1924; employers and part-time employees appear to have been included in the census data on manufacturing employment prior to 1915; and so on. (Raynauld, pp. 596-597)

Census data on total manufacturing output growth indicate rapid growth in the first and third decades of the twentieth century. Comparable rates of growth are apparent in the data for both Quebec and Canada. (See Table 14.1) As in the 1870-1900 period, growth rates in manufacturing value added after 1900 indicate somewhat wider variations than those for total output.

Quebec's manufacturing sector entered a new phase of expansion at the turn of the century. No sharp discontinuities were involved; economic change occurred in an evolutionary way. The diffusion of applied science and engineering technology from abroad gradually transformed the production methods and final products of local manufacturing industry. The adoption of machine technology, for example, slowly altered the factor intensity of Quebec's manufacturing sector. At the same time, the

Table 14.1

GROWTH RATES OF CANADIAN AND QUEBEC MANUFACTURING, COMPOUND RATES OF GROWTH PER YEAR IN CONSTANT 1935-1939 DOLLARS, 1900-1939

Period	Gross Value of Canadian Manufacturing Output	Gross Value of Quebec Manufacturing Output	Total Value Added in Quebec Manufacturing
1900-1910	6.0*	5.7*	6.5*
1910-1919	1.9**	1.0**	1.0**
1919-1926	4.0	3.5	4.5
1926-1929	9.3	10.8	11.8
1929-1939	1.2	1.7	0.4

*The data for the years 1900 and 1910 have been adjusted to compensate for the incomplete coverage of the 1901 and 1911 censuses. The Quebec data have been calculated in 1900 dollars as per W.F. Ryan.

**The data for 1910 have been adjusted for the incomplete coverage of the 1911 census and calculated in 1935-1939 dollars.

G.W. Bertram, "Economic Growth in Canadian Industry, 1870-1915," *Approaches to Canadian Economic History*, p. 82, eds. Easterbrook and Watkins, reprinted by permission of Carleton University Press.

The Clergy and Economic Growth in Quebec, 1896-1914, p. 320, by William F. Ryan, © 1966, reprinted by permission of Les Presses de l'Universite Laval.

Marc Vallières, "Les industries manufacturières du Québec, 1900-1959. Essai de normalistation des données statistiques en dix-sept groupes industriels et étude sommaire de la croissance de ces groupes," Master's Thesis (History), Université Laval, 1973. Appendix B.

spread of hydroelectrical technology resulted in the gradual substitution of electrical current for coal and wood as the principle energy source in manufacturing production. The diffusion of hydroelectric power affected both the composition and spatial distribution of Quebec manufacturing. The pulp and paper, aluminum, petro-chemical, and electrical goods industries gradually rose to the forefront of the manufacturing sector and industry began to locate in river valleys producing hydroelectricity—the Saguenay, St. Maurice, and Gatineau regions—as well as in and around the Island of Montreal.

Quebec's manufacturing sector continued to play an important

role in supplying the aggregate Canadian demand for man\
tured products. Between 1900 and 1939, Quebec's share in C\
dian manufacturing value added per capita remained consistently
above the Canadian provincial average. (See Table 14.2) Quebec
came second only to Ontario in attracting Canadian manufacturing industries even though Quebec produced little more than half
of Ontario's value added in manufacturing. The overall composition of the manufacturing sector in Quebec and Ontario remained
quite similar up to World War I: eight of the ten leading manufacturing industries by value added were the same in the two provinces in 1915. (See Table 14.3) In Quebec the chemical and
tobacco products industries belonged to the top ten whereas in
Ontario non-ferrous metal products, together with printing and
publishing, belonged to this group. At a moderate level of aggregation, it is the similarities rather than the differences in manufacturing industry structure between the two provinces that are most
striking.

By the end of the 1920s, however, Quebec's industrial vocation
as a producer of tariff protected consumer goods, railway transport
equipment, and chemical products was becoming more apparent.
Industries requiring a more sophisticated technology in produc-

Table 14.2

INDEX OF CONCENTRATION OF
MANUFACTURING INDUSTRIES,
1870-1939*

Year	Quebec	Ontario	Rest of Canada
1870	0.97	1.11	0.92
1880	1.03	1.16	0.81
1890	0.98	1.18	0.84
1900	1.06	1.20	0.74
1910	1.03	1.45	0.52
1915	1.04	1.53	0.43
1926	1.11	1.52	0.37
1939	1.07	1.57	0.36

*The index is a location quotient, the ratio of manufacturing value added per
  capita in the region to that of Canada as a whole.

Extracted, with permission, from Tables A-1 and A-5 in Hugh McA. Pinchin, *The
Regional Impact of the Canadian Tariff*. Ottawa: Economic Council of Canada,
1979, pp. 105, 110.

Table 14.3

LEADING MANUFACTURING INDUSTRIES*
IN QUEBEC AND ONTARIO
BY VALUE ADDED, CURRENT DOLLARS, 1915

Quebec Industry (SIC)	% of Total Value Added	Ontario Industry (SIC)	% of Total Value Added
Food and beverages	13.8	Food and beverages	21.2
Iron and steel products (secondary)	11.2	Iron and steel products (secondary)	16.2
Wood products	9.7	Wood products	10.5
Clothing	9.6	Clothing	8.4
Leather products	7.7	Transportation equipment	6.6
Chemical products	7.7	Non-ferrous metal products	6.5
Transportation equipment	7.0	Printing and publishing	4.4
Paper products	6.9	Paper products	4.1
Textile products	5.9	Leather products	3.9
Tobacco and tobacco products	5.4	Textile products	3.5
All others	15.1	All others	14.7
Total	100.0	Total	100.0
Total primary	22.5	Total primary	25.4
Total secondary	77.5	Total secondary	74.6

*Firms with output valued at $2,500 and over.

Gordon W. Bertram, "Historical Statistics on Growth and Structure in Manufacturing in Canada, 1870-1957," in Canadian Political Science Association, *Conference on Statistics 1962 and 1963 Papers*. Edited by J. Henripin and A. Asimakopolous. Toronto: University of Toronto Press, 1964.

tion located in Ontario. The secondary iron and steel manufacturing industries also tended to locate in Ontario, the centre of Canadian primary iron and steel processing. (See Table 14.4) Nathan Rosenberg has suggested the machine tool industry played a particularly important role in the diffusion of mechanized technology in the United States because machine tool know-how could easily be transferred from one industry to another. (Davis *et al*, p. 257) The Canadian machinery, castings and forgings, and hardware and tools industries all located primarily in Ontario.

Table 14.4

PERCENTAGE OF TOTAL CANADIAN NET PRODUCTION IN QUEBEC AND ONTARIO FOR SELECTED MANUFACTURING INDUSTRIES, 1929

	1 Quebec	2 Ontario	Total (1+2)
Cigars and cigarettes	86	14	100
Cotton yarn and cloth	75	18	93
Rubber footwear	62	38	100
Clothing, men's	61	36	97
Boots and shoes	60	36	96
Pulp and paper	54	32	86
Railway Rolling Stock	53	23	76
Clothing, women's	40	56	96
Central electric stations	33	42	75
Hardware and tools	29	68	97
Machinery	25	72	97
Non-ferrous metal smelting	23	55	78
Hosiery and knit goods	22	72	94
Electrical apparatus and supplies	22	77	99
Castings and forgings	21	69	90
Furniture and upholstering	18	76	94
Rubber tires, etc.	4	95	99
Agricultural implements	3	95	98
Automobiles	—	96	96

The Economic Background of Dominion-Provincial Relations, p. 97, by W.A. Mackntosh, reprinted by permission of Carleton University Press.

Domestic Demand and Transport Costs

For the most part, the manufacturing industries that had located in Quebec during the second half of the nineteenth century remained in place after 1900. Both the food and textile industries increased their proportion of provincial manufacturing value added between 1900 and 1940. (See Table 14.5) The size and concentration of the provincial market as well as the variety and extent of the province's transport network offered cost advantages to manufacturers who located in the Montreal region in order to supply the Canadian market. Montreal retained its position as the pre-eminent urban conglomeration and manufacturing centre in Quebec (and Canada). Urbanization continued at a rapid rate in the province, urban dwellers rising from 36.1 percent of the provincial population in 1900 to 61.2 percent in 1940.[7] Expressed as a proportion of the total urban population in Canada, however, urban dwellers in Quebec remained at a constant level, 31.8 percent. The agricultural population in Ontario and the Canadian west continued to provide an important part of the total demand for Quebec's manufactured products.

Table 14.5

PERCENTAGE OF TOTAL VALUE ADDED IN QUEBEC MANUFACTURING PRODUCTION BY INDUSTRY GROUP, CONSTANT DOLLAR VALUE*, 1900-1939

Industry Groups (SIC)	1900	1910	1920	1929	1939
Food and beverages	12.7	9.0	9.9	13.7	15.9
Clothing	12.2	10.3	6.6	7.8	11.6
Paper products	5.0	8.4	n/a	11.1	10.5
Textile products	7.4	6.8	6.0	6.6	9.7
Iron and steel products	10.6	12.5	11.7	10.5	7.6
Non-ferrous metal products	1.3	5.7	n/a	3.5	7.4
Chemical products	3.3	2.7	4.2	4.8	5.8
Tobacco and tobacco products	7.8	6.1	6.0	6.4	4.7
Wood Products	13.6	11.2	n/a	5.5	3.7
Transport equipment	5.0	6.9	n/a	8.0	3.4
All others	21.1	20.4	—	22.1	19.7
Total	100.0	100.0	—	100.0	100.0

*The data for 1900 and 1910 are given in constant 1900 dollars as per W.F. Ryan, and the data for 1920, 1929 and 1939 in constant 1935-1939 dollars as per M. Vallières.

The Clergy and Economic Growth in Quebec, 1896-1914, pp. 316-317, by William F. Ryan, © 1966, reprinted by permission of Les Presses de l'Université Laval.

Marc Vallières, "Les industries manufacturières du Québec, 1900-1959. Essai de normalisation des données statistiques en dix-sept groupes industriels et étude sommaire de la croissance de ces groupes," Master's Thesis (History), Université Laval, 1973. Appendix B.

The Resource Endowment

The accelerated rate of development of Quebec's land, forest and mineral resources after 1900 lowered the domestic supply price of many raw materials. Manufacturing opportunities expanded in industries such as butter and cheese, pulp and paper, and non-ferrous mineral products. At the same time, the harnessing of Quebec's abundant water resources and the production of relatively cheap electrical energy, combined with the high costs of coal and iron imports, affected the aggregate size, composition, and regional distribution of Quebec's manufacturing sector.

J.H. Dales has suggested several ways in which the presence of hydroelectricity affected the province's manufacturing development up to 1940. Dales draws a distinction between the industrial uses of heat and motor power. During the period 1898-1940, electric heat was more costly than fuel-generated heat on a B.T.U. basis. As a result, electricity was seldom employed in industrial processes where large quantities of heat were required. This did not preclude small scale factories from using electricity for heating; properties such as controllability, cleanliness, and ready supply without need of storage made the adoption of electrical heating an efficient choice in many small plants. Nor did the efficiency of fuel heating preclude the use of electricity in electrolytic processes (often found in the chemical industries) or in aluminum reduction (a combination of electrolysis and heating). In some circumstances, when surplus generating capacity existed, hydroelectricity was sold below the average cost of production at a price competitive with fuel-fired steam heat. This situation arose to the advantage of some pulp and paper mills in Quebec. But given the absence of domestic iron and coal resources, abundant supplies of cheap hydroelectricity generally attracted industries requiring motor power rather than heat. Dales concludes,

> Water-power areas can support a selective industrial structure composed predominantly of "secondary" or "consumer goods" industries that require relatively small amounts of heat in their production processes...manufacturing industry in Quebec has been selectively influenced in this way.[8]

Dales identifies the aluminum reduction, carbide, pulp and paper, cement, silk, general chemicals, and textile industries as heavy consumers of electricity. Hydroelectricity was not the only factor affecting their location in Quebec; in some industries, such as pulp and paper, the manufacturing process also consumed large quantities of fuel. But manufacturing industries requiring very large quantities of heat, such as ferrous metal smelting, located outside the province.

The development of hydroelectricity as an energy source may also have influenced the size distribution of manufacturing plants in Quebec. With steam power, large steam engines were generally more physically efficient than small engines resulting in a scale economy advantage to large industrial plants. The expansion of hydroelectric plants reduced the importance of this scale advantage.

> By making small-scale production technologically feasible, and by obviating the necessity of a separate power plant for each individual factory, electric power has reduced the investment required to initiate a manufacturing enterprise and has thus made the field more accessible to small entrepreneurs.[9]

The spatial distribution of manufacturing industry appears to have been affected by hydroelectric development. The increasing costs of transmission, especially over distances exceeding one hundred miles, induced manufacturing plants into the regions endowed with water power sources. River valleys, such as the Ottawa, St. Maurice, and Saguenay, achieved more rapid rates of manufacturing growth and urbanization after 1900. Regions proximate to these valleys, the south shore communities on the St. Lawrence, for instance, also benefited. Of course low cost energy was not the sole factor affecting industrial location. The electric motor, the internal combustion engine, and the paved roadways required for overland truck transport were not really developed until the 1920s. The decentralization of manufacturing industry away from Montreal proceeded in a very gradual way.

Wage Rates

Data on wage rates in Quebec are incomplete so that the possible influence of low wage labor on the size and composition of manufacturing industry is difficult to gauge. Comparable interprovincial data for the manufacturing sector as a whole is available from 1938. Between 1938 and 1950 the average hourly wage rate differential between Quebec and Ontario is unmistakable. (See Table 14.6) Did this differential reflect low wage (cheap?) labor in Quebec manufacturing?

A variety of factors could explain the wage rate differential that appears in Table 14.6. Interprovincial differences in the industrial structure, the stock of machinery and equipment per worker, and age, education or skill levels might account for part of the wage rate differential. (See Chapter 13) These differences should then be eflected in the data on manufacturing value added for the same years. According to the estimates presented in Table 14.6, manufacturing value added in the two provinces differed by almost as much as hourly wage rates. A large part of the differential in wage rates could therefore be attributable to interprovincial differences in the productivity of labor and capital.

Two other possible explanations of the wage rate differential between Quebec and Ontario lie in the domain of unionization and the 'French fact'. Interprovincial differences in the degree of unionization or in the degree of union militancy could have affected relative wage rates. As suggested in Chapter 15, this explanation is unsatisfactory for the pre-1940 years. Since the language barrier inhibited the diffusion of information about

Table 14.6

HOURLY MANUFACTURING WAGE RATES, MANUFACTURING VALUE ADDED, AND INCOME PER CAPITA, QUEBEC AS A PERCENTAGE OF ONTARIO, 1938-1950

	Hourly Wage Rates in Manufacturing	Value Added in Manufacturing per employee-year	Personal Income per Capita
1938	79.8	82.1	71.3
1939	80.6	90.1	71.2
1940	n/a	87.5	68.2
1941	84.3	85.6	67.0
1942	84.7	83.0	67.6
1943	87.4	90.5	67.7
1944	87.5	93.1	66.9
1945	89.9	90.1	66.7
1946	89.2	94.6	70.6
1947	86.3	87.8	73.0
1948	86.4	84.3	72.9
1949	86.6	87.1	70.4
1950	84.9	85.1	70.7
1938-1950 (excl. 1940)	85.6	87.8	69.7

Croissance et structure économiques de la Province de Québec, pp. 58-60, by André Raynauld, © 1961, reprinted by permission of Ministère de l'Industrie et du Commerce du Québec.

North American labor market opportunities in Quebec, imperfect information regarding employment opportunities and wage differentials may have inhibited the efficient functioning of labor markets. This latter explanation seems more likely.

> Imperfect worker information as to alternative wages will confer on each firm a margin of monopsony power. Thus, each firm will possess a degree of dynamic monopsony power arising from the imperfect information of its employees regarding alternative wages and can therefore administer wages. Recognition that labour market decisions are taken in an environment of imperfect information underpins many of the recent developments in labour economics.[10]

Furthermore, once wage differentials were perceived, workers had to be occupationally and geographically mobile in order to eliminate them. Unskilled, unilingual francophones were relatively immobile in the North American context. Emigration outside of Quebec became a tolerable option only when occupational wage and unemployment rate differentials reached some threshold level. Higher incomes could then compensate for losses in French language and culture. To some extent, unilingual Francophone workers may have constituted a captive labor market in North America, resulting in a margin of monopsony power favorable to Quebec's employers, lower wage rates for equivalent work, and the adoption of more labor-intensive industrial processes than in Ontario. This explanation could account for the interprovincial differential between value added and wage rates indicated in Table 14.6.

Government Taxes and Subsidies

Federal government tariff and railway subsidy policies affected the size and location of manufacturing industry throughout Canada. Although little direct evidence is available, Pinchin asserts that Ontario has been the principal beneficiary of the tariff since 1867. (cf. Table 14.2) It is very difficult, however, to separate the impact of tariff policy from all other economic forces affecting the economy over this period. Manufacturing growth in Ontario was also influenced by the size of the domestic market, rapid technological change, transport innovations, western settlement, and the province's proximity to the American manufacturing belt in the Great Lakes region. Judging from information on the regional concentration of manufacturing in both the United States and Canada, manufacturing industry generally relocated in the Great Lakes region between Confederation and World War I. (Pinchin, p. 106)

New England and Middle Atlantic States then [in 1860] accounted for almost three quarters of the nation's industrial employment. A half century later, the manufacturing belt had extended itself westward to include the Great Lakes region as well; in 1910 establishments in the states east of the Mississippi and north of the Ohio employed 70 percent of U.S. industrial workers.[11]

As Faucher and Lamontagne pointed out thirty years ago, the pattern of industrial location in eastern Canada is in part attributable to resource and locational advantages. It is conceivable, therefore, that tariff policy affected the functional distribution of income within each of the provinces, the brunt of the burden being carried by landowners, without causing a significant interprovincial income transfer.[12]

The regional impact of federal government subsidies to the transcontinental railways is even more difficult to assess than the impact of tariff policy. The subsidies generally resulted in lower freight charges and passenger fares, and in the extended operation of little-used lines. Railway subsidies may also have contributed to the concentration of manufacturing industries in central Canada. The magnitude of this contribution, if any, depended upon the impact of railway subsidies on the rate of western Canadian settlement. Estimates of this impact are shaky, but government subsidized railways appear to have had some positive net influence on settlement. (See Marr and Percy) Rapid western settlement after 1900 in turn contributed to higher rates of economic growth throughout Canada. The magnitude of the prairie wheat economy's contribution to per capita Canadian economic growth has also been the subject of varying estimates, ranging from 10.5 percent (Chambers and Gordon) to 24.1 percent (Lewis) for the years 1900-1910 (ie. census years 1901-1911). To the extent that railway subsidies influenced western settlement and Canadian economic growth, the subsidies may have made some contribution to the size of the manufacturing sector in Quebec and Ontario.

Although Quebec provincial governments generally remained non-interventionist vis-à-vis the economy, resource policies provided a modest exception to this approach. At the beginning of the century, the provincial government introduced two measures to encourage the processing of domestically cut timber prior to export. In 1900 the Quebec Cabinet increased the fees for pulpwood cut from public lands to $1.90 from $0.65 per cord. If the wood was processed in the province, however, the applicable fee dropped to $0.40 per cord. In effect, this differential fee schedule resulted in an export tax on raw pulpwood. Then, in 1910, the Gouin administration placed a complete embargo on the export of raw pulpwood cut from public lands in the province. Section 13 of the Woods and Forest Regulations for that year reads:

> All timber cut on Crown Lands after the first of May, 1910, must be manufactured in Canada, that is to say, converted into pulp or paper, deals or boards, or into any other article of trade or merchandise of which such timber is only the raw material.

For the purposes of this regulation, squared timber and railway ties were considered as manufactured articles. The net effect of the embargo on the Quebec pulp and paper industry is unclear. Rapid increase in the American demand for newsprint and the removal of American tariffs on pulp and paper imports in 1913 also influenced pulp and paper production in Quebec. The net contribution of each of these contributing factors is as yet unknown.[13]

The extent of price-fixing cartelization in the private sector has been documented by L.G. Reynolds. A new development during the 1920s was the active encouragement given industrial cartels by the provincial governments in Quebec and Ontario. The Quebec government publicly supported the formation of the Asbestos Corporation, together with an asbestos price-fixing agreement, in 1925. In the forest products sector, the decline in the pulp and paper industry between 1927 and 1931 produced a reduction in the timber cut on public lands from 1.6 billion feet to 900 million feet, and a parallel decline in government revenues from the public domain. (Bates, p. 169) By participating in the creation of the unsuccessful Newsprint Institute cartel in 1928, the Quebec government indicated its willingness to promote cartelization in the private sector when government revenues were at issue.

In 1935, the Taschereau administration enacted a new Forest Resources Regulation Act that conferred on the provincial cabinet the authority to fine companies behaving in a way detrimental to the public interest (ie. refusing to adhere to a price-fixing agreement). Premiers Duplessis (Quebec) and Hepburn (Ontario) carried regulation of the provincial newsprint industry one step further:

> Hepburn and Duplessis concluded a formal Interprovincial Agreement on the newsprint question on October 17, 1937. They declared that no company in either province would be allowed to overproduce or sell below the established market price. To implement that policy the two governments in effect delegated their authority to the Newsprint Association of Canada. Its proration committee was authorized "to act as the Government's referees and arbitors." On recommendations from that committee Ontario and Quebec undertook "to penalize, without further inquiry" any newsprint manufacturer who disobeyed the instructions of the Newsprint Association officials in any manner whatsoever.[14]

When the Quebec government lobbied or legislated in the
omain of collusive or non-competitive behavior, its actions rein-
orced cartels rather than constrained them.

Despite these initiatives, it is unlikely that provincial govern-
ient activity produced significant changes in the overall structure
f Quebec's manufacturing sector. The net effects of the govern-
ient embargo on the export of timber cut from public lands and
overnment participation in the formation of price-fixing cartels
ere probably not very great. The role of the State in the growth
nd development of the Quebec economy is examined in more
etail in Chapter 16.

NOTES

[1] The timing of western settlement is commonly related to several events: an increase in wheat prices stemming from rapid economic growth in the United States and Europe; the gradual closing of the frontier in the American west; falling transport costs in the shipping of wheat; a change in expectations that affected international capital and labor inflows; and technical change in the production and processing of wheat. In a critical review of these events, K.H. Norrie has suggested that the nature of the soils and climate ultimately determined the feasible margin of western North American farming in the nineteenth century. The invention of dry-farming techniques together with an increase in wheat prices touched off the rapid increase in Canadian prairie settlement at the turn of the century. (Norrie, 1975)

[2] The asset share of the one hundred largest non-financial corporations in Canada increased to over seventy-five percent in 1933. (Government of Canada, 1978, p. 20)

[3] *The Control of Competition in Canada*, pp. 173-175, by Lloyd G. Reynolds, © 1940, reprinted by permission of Harvard University Press.

[4] Between the years 1896-1900 and 1911-1915, net foreign investment in Canada as a proportion of GNP increased from 2.5 percent to 12.4 percent. (Marr and Paterson, p. 267)

[5] Although Canada continued to receive considerable foreign investment after World War I, the economy was actually a net capital exporter during the periods 1921-1925 and 1931-1940.

[6] Even specialized studies, such as those by Bertram, Raynauld, and Vallières, have made no adjustments to the Quebec data for this imperfection.

[7] The data for 1900 refers to incorporated cities, towns and villages of one thousand and over, while the data for 1940 is an estimate based on the 1961 census definition of 'urban'. (Stone, p. 29)

[8] *Hydroelectricity and Industrial Development: Quebec 1898-1940*, p. 180, by John H. Dales, © 1957, reprinted by permission of Harvard University Press.

[9] *Hydroelectricity and Industrial Development: Quebec 1898-1940*, p. 164 by John H. Dales, © 1957, reprinted by permission of Harvard University Press.

[10]*The Market for Labour: An Analytical Treatment*, p. 169, by John T. Addison and Stanley Siebert, Copyright © 1979, reprinted by permission of Scott Foresman and Company.

[11]*The Evolution of the American Economy: Growth, Welfare and Decision*, p. 276 by Sidney Ratner, James H. Soltow and Richard Sylla © 1979, reprinted by permission of Basic Books, Inc.

[12]In his evaluation of the impact of the tariff on western Canada, Norrie present evidence to suggest that the tariff on agricultural instruments affected Prairie agricultural development by redistributing income from land to labor and capital, and by delaying the move toward larger, more mechanized operation on the part of some farmers. Norrie concludes, "the tariff on farm implement and machinery appears to have had a greater impact within the Prairie agricultural economy itself than on its relations with external industrial regions." (Norrie, 1974, p. 461)

[13]In the context of a competitive industry model, T.J.O. Dick presents evidence that the export embargo had little to do with the migration of the newsprint industry to Quebec and Ontario after World War I.

[14]*The Politics of Development: Forests, Mines and Hydro-Electric Power in Ontario 1849-1941*, pp. 456-457, by H.V. Nelles, Macmillan of Canada.

SELECT BIBLIOGRAPHY

Addison, John T. and Stanley Siebert. *The Market for Labour: An Analytical Treatment*. Santa Monica, CA: Goodyear Publishing Co., 1979.

Ankli, Robert E. "The Growth of the Canadian Economy, 1896-1920." *Explorations in Economic History*. July 1980.

Bates, Steward. *Financial History of Canadian Governments*. Appendix of the Royal Commission Report on Dominion-Provincial Relations. Ottawa: King's Printer, 1939.

Bertram, Gordon W. "Economic Growth in Canadian Industry, 1870-1915: The Staple Model," in W.T. Easterbrook and M.H. Watkins, ed., *Approaches to Canadian Economic History*. Toronto: McClelland and Stewart Limited, 1967.

Bertram, Gordon W. "Historical Statistics on Growth and Structure of Manufacturing in Canada, 1870-1957." Canadian Political Science Association, Conference on Statistics, June 1964.

Chambers, E.J. and D.F. Gordon. "Primary Products and Economic Growth: A Rejoinder." *Journal of Political Economy*. December 1967.

Dales, John H. *Hydroelectricity and Industrial Development* : *Quebec, 1898-1940*. Cambridge: Harvard University Press, 1957.

Davis, Lance E. *et al*. *American Economic Growth: An Economist's History of the United States*. New York: Harper & Row, Publishers, 1972.

Dick, Trevor J.O. "Canadian Newsprint, 1913-1930: National Policies and the North American Economy." *The Journal of Economic History*. September 1982.

Faucher, Albert and Maurice Lamontagne. "History of Industrial Development," in J-C Falardeau, ed., *Essays on Contemporary Quebec*. Quebec: les Presses de l'Université Laval, 1953.

allman, Robert E. "Gross National Product in the United States, 1834-1909," in Peter Temin, ed., *New Economic History.* Harmondsworth, England: Penguin Books Ltd., 1973.

overnment of Canada. *Report of the Royal Commission on Corporate Concentration.* Ottawa: Ministry of Supply and Services, 1978.

overnment of Canada. *Report of the Royal Commission on Price Spreads.* Ottawa: King's Printer, 1935.

reen, Alan G. "Regional Aspects of Canada's Economic Growth, 1890-1929." *Canadian Journal of Economics and Political Science.* May 1967.

ay, Keith A.J. "Early Twentieth Century Business Cycles in Canada." *Canadian Journal of Economics and Political Science.* August 1966.

ewis, Frank. "the Canadian Wheat Boom and Per Capita Income: New Estimates." *Journal of Political Economy.* December 1975.

lackintosh, W.A. *The Economic Background of Dominion-Provincial Relations.* Toronto: McClelland and Stewart Ltd., 1964.

larr, William L. and Donald G. Paterson. *Canada: An Economic History.* Toronto: Macmillan of Canada Ltd., 1980.

larr, William L. and Michael Percy. "The Government and the Rate of Settlement of the Canadian Prairies." *Canadian Journal of Economics.* August 1974.

larshall, Herbert, Frank Southard, Jr., and Kenneth W. Taylor. *Canadian-American Investment: A Study in International Investment.* New Haven: Yale University Press, 1936.

elles, H.V. *The Politics of Development: Forests, Mines and Hydro-Electric Power in Ontario, 1849-1941.* Toronto: Macmillan of Canada, 1974.

eufeld, E.P. *The Financial System of Canada: Its Growth and Development.* Toronto: Macmillan of Canada Ltd., 1972.

orrie, Kenneth H. "Agricultural Implement Tariffs, the National Policy, and Income Distribution in the Wheat Economy." *Canadian Journal of Economics.* August 1974.

orrie, Kenneth H. "The Rate of Settlement of the Canadian Prairies, 1870-1911." *Journal of Economic History.* June 1975.

aterson, Donald G. *British Direct Investment in Canada, 1890-1914.* Toronto: University of Toronto Press, 1976.

nchin, Hugh McA. *The Regional Impact of the Canadian Tariff.* Ottawa: Canadian Government Publishing Centre, 1979.

atner, Sidney, James H. Soltow and Richard Sylla. *The Evolution of the American Economy: Growth, Welfare and Decision Making.* New York: Basic Books, Inc., 1979.

aynauld, André. *Croissance et structure économiques de la Province de Québec.* Quebec: Ministère de l'Industrie et du Commerce, 1961.

eynolds, Lloyd G. *The Control of Competition in Canada.* Cambridge: Harvard University Press, 1940.

Roby, Yves. *Les québécois et les investissements américains (1918-1929)*. Quebec: les Presses de l'Université Laval, 1976.

Ryan, William F. *The Clergy and Economic Growth in Quebec, 1896-1914*. Quebec: les Presses de l'Université Laval, 1966.

Stone, Leroy O. *Urban Development in Canada: An Introduction to the Demographic Aspects*. Ottawa: Dominion Bureau of Statistics, 1967.

Urquhart, M.C., and Buckley, K.A.H. *Historical Statistics of Canada*. Toronto: Macmillan of Canada, 1965.

Vallières, Marc. "Les Industries manufacturiers du Québec, 1900-1959. Essai de normalisation des données statistiques en dix-sept groupes industriels et étude sommaire de la croissance de ces groupes." Master's Thesis (History). Université Laval, 1973.

15
The Labor Market

By the year 1900 the Quebec economy was substantially integrated into the North American market and more sensitive to the economic climate in Canada and the United States than ever before. The level of economic output and income in the province continued to depend on relative resource endowments and the state of technology. Changes in the level of economic activity resulted largely from exogenous shifts in aggregate demand. Rapid growth in the United States and western Canada, the Great War in Europe, the international recovery of the 1920s, and the Great Depression of the 1930s provided the basic economic shocks that explain fluctuations in the level of provincial economic income and output prior to World War II.

Between 1900 and 1940 several distinct trends in the industrial composition of Quebec's labor force are evident. These trends reflect developments within the province's industrial structure. The most important changes occurred in the agricultural and service sectors. For example, even though the total number of workers in agriculture continued to increase, the percentage contribution of the agricultural sector to total employment declined steadily. (See Table 15.1) The percentage contribution of the manufacturing sector to total employment also decreased over the first three decades of the twentieth century. For the most part, growth in tertiary sector employment (transport, commerce and finance, services and clerical) offset these trends.

The demand for productive resources such as labor is a derived demand that varies with the demand for final goods and services. Growth in labor demand over time is related to growth in the

Table 15.1

OCCUPATIONAL TRENDS OF THE LABOR FORCE IN QUEBEC, 1891-1941
(gainfully employed as a percentage of total employment)

Occupation	1891	1901	1911	1921	1931	1941
Agriculture	45.3*	38.2	31.3	28.1	22.5	21.5
Fishing and Trapping	0.9	0.8	0.7	0.5	0.6	0.7
Lumbering	0.9	0.7	1.7	1.4	1.5	2.6
Mining and Quarrying	0.5	0.3	0.9	0.5	0.6	0.8
Manufacturing	15.3	25.2	17.4	16.0	15.3	20.3
Construction	5.3		5.4	5.7	6.1	5.9
Transportation	3.5		5.5	5.7	6.9	7.0
Commerce and Finance	5.6	9.2	8.9	9.4	9.1	8.4
Services, prof. and personal	12.8**	13.7	12.8	14.2	17.4	18.2
Clerical	1.4	3.6	3.5	6.5	6.9	7.3
Laborers, non-specialized	8.1	8.3	11.9	11.6	13.0	6.8
Others	0.4	0.0	0.0	0.4	0.0	0.4
Total (%)	100.0	100.0	100.0	100.0	99.9	99.9
Total Labor Force	457 572	512 276	653 241	785 591	1 025 709	1 188 655

*Includes farmers' sons, 14 years and over, whether or not reported with gainful occupation.

**Clerical workers in government service included.

Government of Canada, *Occupational Trends in Canada, 1891-1931*, Table 5. *Occupational Trends in Canada, 1901-1941*, Table 5. Reproduced by permission of the Minister of Supply and Services Canada.

domestic economy's capacity to produce new and better commodities. Technological innovations, resource discoveries, and changes in the institutional environment all affect the industrial structure, and consequently the volume and composition of the demand for labor. Trends in interregional specialization and comparative advantage also help to determine the size and occupational distribution of the work force. Details of the changes in Quebec's industrial structure were outlined in Chapters 13 and 14. Of course the industrial structure of a region is not the sole determinant of labor force distribution by occupation. Labor demand and supply are mutually interdependent and difficult to separately identify in an unambiguous way.

This chapter examines the Quebec labor market over the first four decades of the twentieth century. The focus is on the supply side of the market. Regional labor supply is initially considered in the light of fertility, morality, and migration rates. Labor force participation rates are then examined to shed more light on effective labor supply. In the second part of the chapter, the influence of the trade union movement on the regional labor market is examined. Trade unions, it is suggested, played a modest role in determining aggregate labor supply and wage rates during the period prior to World War II. The third part of the chapter is devoted to a discussion of interprovincial wage rate disparities. This section offers some elements of an answer to the question as to why interprovincial wage rates differed.

Natural Population Increase

Regional labor supply depends above all on the size and composition of the region's population. Fertility, mortality, and migration contribute to regional population growth and changes in population structure over time. With zero net migration, an excess of births over deaths will increase the size of a given population. The rate at which births exceed deaths is known as the crude rate of natural population increase. Regional differences in crude natural population increase depend upon such variables as the sex and age composition of the population, levels of income, health and education, and religious attitudes. Another influence on birth rates in modern times is the opportunity cost to women of having children. The foregone income associated with child-bearing tends to be positively correlated with a women's education, labor market experience, and job opportunities. These latter variables appear to have been inversely related with birth rates in the twentieth century. Unfortunately, the variables themselves are often correlated

Table 15.2

RATES OF NATURAL POPULATION INCREASE IN QUEBEC, ONTARIO AND CANADA, SELECTED YEARS, 1921-1941
(per 1 000 population)

Year	Quebec	Ontario	Canada
1921	23.4	13.5	17.7
1926	17.3	10.1	13.3
1931	17.1	9.8	13.0
1936	14.0	6.9	10.4
1941	16.5	8.7	12.3

The Demographic Bases of Canadian Society, 2/e, p. 123. By Warren E. Kalbach and Wayne W. McVey. Reprinted by permission of McGraw-Hill Ryerson Limited.

and their precise influence on the rate of natural population increase is therefore difficult to establish.

Despite higher crude mortality rates than Ontario or any of the Western provinces, Quebec displayed the highest provincial rate of natural population increase in Canada until World War II. (See Table 15.2) This rate of natural increase was associated with a high birth rate among Francophones. Even though Quebec's birth rate declined from the middle of the nineteenth century until 1936, it remained at a high level relative to the rest of Canada. The birth rate then rose again until 1947, maintaining its position relative to that of the other Canadian provinces. The traditional explanation of Quebec's high birth rate refers to religious and family planning attitudes as the causal factor, but a re-examination of the question in the light of the economic theory of fertility is needed. Quebec's high birth rate helps to explain why the province's proportion of the total labor force in Canada expanded steadily during the years 1901-1941, while Ontario's declined.

Migration

Aggregate labor supply also depends on migration to and from the region. As explained in earlier chapters, migration, whether rural-urban or interregional, can be considered as essentially an economic decision. Population movement occurs when the net social benefits from moving exceed the associated costs. The net benefits from migration involve the consideration of earned income, job opportunities, transfer payments, and the availability of social services. Net costs include job search costs, travel expenses, and income foregone during the transition period, as well as the social costs associated with regional, cultural and linguistic changes.

The rapid rate of urbanization that characterized Quebec's population in the second half of the nineteenth century continued until the 1930s. (See Table 15.3) People moved in response to higher incomes and greater job opportunities in the non-agricul-

Table 15.3

TOTAL POPULATION, URBANIZATION AND EMIGRATION, QUEBEC CENSUS YEARS, 1900-1940

Year	Total Population	Urban Percentage*	Number of Urban Complexes**	Net Emigration of the Native-Born over the previous decade: to the Rest of Canada (Urquhart & Buckley)	to the United States (Lavoie)
1900	1 649 898	36.1	10	4 500	140 000
1910	2 005 766	44.5	13	24 000	100 000
1920	2 360 510	51.8	17	14 600	80 000
1930	2 874 662	59.5	20	24 100	130 000
1940	3 331 882	61.2	25	26 300	16 105***

*For 1900 and 1910 the urban population data refer to incorporated cities, towns and villages of 1000 and over. For 1920, 1930, and 1940 the percentages are estimates based on the 1961 census definition of urban.

**Incorporated cities of 5000 and over.

***Gross emigration of French Canadians as recorded by the United States Department of Justice.

Urban Development in Canada: An Introduction to the Demographic Aspects, pp. 29, 69, by Leroy O. Stone. Ottawa: Dominion Bureau of Statistics, 1967. Reproduced by permission of Statistics Canada.

Historical Statistics of Canada, p. 21, by M.C. Urquhart and K.A.H. Buckley, © 1965, reprinted by permission.

"Les mouvements migratoires des Canadiens entre leur pays et les Etats-Unis au XIXe et au XXe siècles: étude quantitative," by Yolande Lavoie, in Hubert Charbonneau, ed., *La Population du Québec: Etudes Retrospectives*, p. 78, reprinted by permission de Les Editions du Boréal Express.

tural sectors of the economy. Income and job opportunity differentials between Quebec and neighboring regions also induced many Quebecers to leave the province. The rate of emigration slowed after 1900, especially during the war years, but accelerated again in the 1920s. The abrupt decline in emigration to the United States during the years of the Great Depression resulted from a change in American immigration laws.

Participation Rates

Labor force participation rates indicate the proportion of a population that is actually employed. In 1911, the first year for which complete provincial labor force participation data are available, Quebec displayed participation rates comparable to those of the Maritime provinces, but lower than those in Ontario and the West. Higher participation rates in the West, however, can be accounted for by the unique age and sex distribution of the western population at the time. As this newly settled frontier region adjusted toward standardized family living patterns, average labor participation rates in Canada declined. (See Table 15.4)

The decision to participate in the labor market involves choices among labor income, housework, education, leisure, and retirement. Individual choice is influenced by wage rates, hours of work, job opportunities, alternative sources of income, and social customs, as well as personal capabilities and preferences. During the three decades prior to 1941, the participation rate of Quebec women aged 15 to 64 increased steadily. (See Table 15.4) The aforementioned decline in fertility rates is probably associated with this trend. The growth in women's labor force participation rate may also be related to changes in the quantity and quality of schooling. More education raised the opportunity cost of unpaid housework by offering potential net benefits to those who joined the labor force.

The participation of men in the age group 15 to 64 showed no particular trend in the pre-war years. But increases in wealth and earned income per capita may account for the marked tendency toward earlier retirement among men aged 65 and over. The gradual introduction of private pension schemes in the 1920s and the Quebec government's adherence to the Canada Pension Scheme in 1936 also help to account for this phenomenon.

The employment of children declined in the period leading up to World War II reflecting the gradual enforcement of child labor laws and the upgrading of the school system. The greater accessibility of education raised the opportunity cost of working at an

Table 15.4

LABOR FORCE PARTICIPATION RATES IN QUEBEC BY SEX AND AGE GROUP, CENSUS YEARS, 1911-1941 (Percentages)

Year	Males 10-14	Males 15-64	Males 65+	Females 10-14	Females 15-64	Females 65+	Total Quebec 15+	Total Ontario 15+	Total Canada 15+
1911	15.0	90.1	52.2	2.4	17.0	6.0	52.3	54.9	56.0
1921	10.4	89.4	52.1	2.4	19.5	7.8	52.8	54.3	54.6
1931	6.3	90.1	49.7	1.0	23.1	7.2	54.8	54.3	55.2
1941	3.4	84.3*	42.9	0.5	24.4*	6.1	54.2	54.8	54.2

*Excluding persons in active military service on June 2, 1941.

The Demographic Bases of Canadian Society, 2/e, p. 568. By Warren E. Kalbach and Wayne W. McVey. Reprinted by permission of McGraw-Hill Ryerson Limited.

Croissance et structure économiques de la province de Québec, p. 257, by André Raynauld, © 1961, reprinted by permission of Ministère de l'Industrie et du Commerce.

early age by offering potential net benefits to those who stayed in school. But even so, Quebec continued to have the lowest proportion of young people attending school in all of Canada. In 1931, 47.5 percent of the 5 to 24 year age group was attending school full-time in Quebec, as opposed to 51.8 percent in Canada as a whole. (Kalbach & McVey, p. 248) The Quebec government did not legislate compulsory school attendance until 1943.

Labor Organization

Quebec's trade unions appear to have exercised relatively little influence on aggregate labor supply prior to World War II. This is probably related to the variety of objectives pursued by the trade union movement and the resistance of employers and governments to trade union activities. The most important role for unions may have been one of ensuring that members were not subject to arbitrary actions by employers. Unions sought better working conditions by means of collective action and by lobbying for legal and social change through political and legislative reform. In the process of organizing labor, the trade union movement laid the foundations of the institutional arrangements for collective bargaining and employer-employee relations in the modern era.

In the early years, strikes and work stoppages often occurred outside the trade union movement. Attempts to form unions were frequently unsuccessful. Low wages, the threat of unemployment, and the absence of a legal framework for union recognition and collective bargaining made union organizing very difficult. Many of the longest and most bitter struggles involved attempts to gain simple recognition of the bargaining unit. Where successful, a process of negotiation might then lead to the achievement of a first collective agreement. In the absence of an institutional framework to ensure due process, the initial collective agreement acquired a special status. Only gradually did a system of collective bargaining evolve and expectations of wage and extra-wage gains by unionization ensue.

The apparent cyclical pattern of labor unrest has led to various attempts by social scientists to identify the economic origins of strike activity. It is often believed that the time pattern of strikes varies with the business cycle: in times of economic prosperity employers are more willing to make concessions at the bargaining table and in times of recession workers are conscious of the slack in labor markets. Although there are as yet no studies relating provincial economic activity and strikes in Quebec, J. Vanderkamp has analysed this relationship for Canada as a whole. Vanderkamp found the relationship to be weak during the period 1901-1939 and referred to the following circumstances in his explanation:

(1) the question of union recognition was still unsettled, and attempts at destroying union organizations were by no means a rare occurence; since these attempts were more concentrated during depressed economic conditions, the bargaining attitudes of the two parties would tend to diverge when the economy was depressed, leading to more strike activity;

(2) wage reductions were still socially acceptable and therefore not yet ruled out by both parties in the bargaining process;

(3) the number of firms and industries which were unionized and which experienced strike activity was relatively small, and the random element introduced by special cases was much more important than in the post World War II years.[1]

Although working men and women possessed a wide array of organizations and institutions, trade union federations constituted the backbone of the labor movement. In Quebec, the historical development of union federations reflected the special nature of Quebec society. Many French speaking workers were attracted to organizations that embodied their own linguistic and cultural traits. The rate of growth of trade unionism in the province, as indicated by membership, paralleled that in Ontario. But the way in which unions responded to the economic environment—the force and timing of their actions, the nature of their federations, and the form of political alliances they chose—differed from those in neighboring regions. As a result, the Quebec labor movement emerged with a unique experience and a different perspective than its counterparts elsewhere in Canada.

The first viable union federations emerged during the 1880s at about the same time as interindustrial unions encompassing both skilled and unskilled workers made their appearance. (See Chapter 12) In 1902 the Canadian Trades and Labour Congress (TLC) expelled from its ranks both the Knights of Labour and those unions without an American affiliation. Of the 23 union organizations affected by the TLC's decision, 17 came from Quebec. By openly disavowing any claim to represent all Canadian unions and by expelling the Quebec-based Knights of Labour, the TLC created a vacuum that Quebec labor leaders subsequently attempted to fill.

In 1903 a new federation, the National Trades and Labour Congress of Canada (NTLC), was founded to unite Canadian workers irrespective of their trade affiliation. Despite its pan-Canadian appeal, 84 percent of the NTLC's membership initially came from Quebec, almost 50 percent from Quebec City alone. (Rouillard, 1979, p. 90) Less militant than the Trades and Labour

Congress, the NTLC espoused the kind of pan-Canadian national-ism identified with Henri Bourassa. In this way, the NTLC helped to lay the groundwork for the rise of Catholic unionism during World War I. In 1908 the NTLC changed its name to the Canadian Federation of Labour (CFL). But as the CFL gained new adherents in English Canada, it lost members in Quebec. Although the CFL's activities in Quebec were marginal by 1911, the trade union movement continued to grow. Between 1901 and 1911 the total number of union members in the province increased from some 10 000 to about 25 000. Even at this latter date, however, unionists represented no more than 4 percent of the provincial labor force. Many unions were unaligned with either of the two dominant federations.

Strikes and lockouts frequently occurred outside the main-stream labor movement. Quebec was second only to British Columbia as a major centre of labor unrest before World War I. The longest struggles took place in the manufacturing sector where the division of labor was most advanced. Prolonged strikes in textiles, clothing, and the boot and shoe industries accompanied slow output growth during these years. Cultural differences between English speaking employers and French language employees often intensified the conflict over wages and working conditions. Several French language Catholic trade unions were founded before the War but they had little or no effect on the labor movement at this time.

Three events accelerated the rate of growth of the Catholic trade union movement during the war years. The French language schools question first erupted in 1912 when the Ontario Department of Education placed limitations on the use of French as a language of instruction and subject of study in Ontario's public schools (Regulation 17). This policy created an outcry in Quebec where the minority language, English, was comparatively well treated. When Ontario's legislation was upheld by the Privy Council in Britain, the Ontario government revived the controversy with more stringent legislation in 1916. At the same time, an increase in the rate of inflation beginning in 1915 and war profiteering in the private sector provoked an upswing in union organizing as profit rate increases outpaced wage rate increases. The rise in the general price level increased the year-to-year inflation rate (as measured by the CPI) to 18.4 percent between 1916 and 1917. The third and perhaps most important event that affected the development of Catholic unionism was military conscription. The passage of the War Measures Act requiring the registration of male workers in 1916, and the introduction of conscription in 1917, seriously divided the labor movement in

Canada. Under pressure from the American Federation of Labor, the TLC reversed its position on the issue and narrowly supported a resolution in favor of compulsory military service. Many Quebec unionists felt misunderstood, and even betrayed, by English Canadian trade union leaders. The door was therefore open to union organizations with a nationalist appeal, be they pan-Canadian or French Canadian.

The nationalist character of the Catholic union movement was not the sole element underlying its popularity in the province but it does help to explain the movement's initial phase of expansion. The first provincial congress of Catholic unions gathered in 1918, the year after conscription was introduced. It led to the founding of the *Confédération des travailleurs catholiques du Canada* (CTCC) in 1921. As is apparent in Table 15.5, the CTCC seems to have recruited most of its members from the CFL and unaligned unions. In this sense, the Quebec wing of the CFL served as a forerunner for the Catholic union movement.

The CTCC subsequently proved successful in organizing unions among unskilled workers often ignored by the internationals. Eighty-one percent of the CTCC'S members belonged to unions outside the Montreal area. These characteristics, together with the conservative influence of the clergy, undoubtedly contributed to the less militant stance of many Catholic unions. Rouillard has enumerated 32 strikes and lockouts involving Catholic unions during the 1920-1930 period, a figure that represented 13 percent of the provincial total. (Rouillard, 1981, p. 94) Given that the CTCC represented between 20 and 27 percent of all trade unionists during these years, it appears Catholic unions were more conciliatory than those belonging to the TLC and CFL. From the members' point of view, the clerico-nationalist ideology of the CTCC presumably compensated for the federation's comparative lack of collective bargaining and strike-support services.

As elsewhere in North America, trade union membership declined during the 1920s. The unionized proportion of Quebec's labor force fell from some 14 percent in 1921 to about 1.3 percent ten years later. A substantial part of this decline occurred before the onset of the Depression. Following rapid growth during the first two decades of the century, the trade union movement appeared to have reached its organizational limits. (See Table 15.5) In the early years of the Depression, trade union militancy almost disappeared in Quebec. From a peak of 853 773 strike days in 1919, aggregate working time lost diminished to 8 090 days in 1931. (Minville, p. 27) As a result, several pan-Canadian organizations entered the Quebec labor scene. Between 1929 and 1935, the Workers Unity League organized industrial unions, and sup-

Table 15.5

TOTAL NUMBER OF TRADE UNION BARGAINING UNITS IN QUEBEC AND PERCENTAGE DISTRIBUTION BY AFFILIATION, 1901-1931

Year	Total Number of Units	International Affiliation (%)	Canadian Affiliation or Unaffiliated (%)	Catholic Affiliation (%)
1901	136	54	46	—
1906	236	66	34	—
1911	n/a*	n/a	n/a	n/a
1916	329	72	21	7
1921	492	68	8	24
1926	450	70	7	23
1931	491	58	17	25

*190 bargaining units possessed an international affiliation in 1911.

Les sydicats nationaux au Québec de 1900 à 1930, p. 119, by Jacques Rouillard, © 1979, reprinted by permission of Les Presses de l'Université Laval.

ported strikes in the mining and dressmaking industries. But the majority of Quebec unionists continued to adhere to union federations with international affiliations.

About 1935, following the worst years of the Depression, trade union membership began to increase dramatically throughout North America. In Quebec, recruiting efforts by the CTCC were particularly fruitful. There are at least three reasons why Catholic unionism proved so successful in the mid-1930s. First, the continent-wide growth of industrial unionism, symbolized by the creation of the Committee of Industrial Organizations in the United States required new organizational forms which the TLC could not or would not accommodate. Because of its short history, the CTCC proved to be a more flexible institution than the TLC and more open to unions organized by industry rather than by skill category. Second, many of the new industrial unions were formed in small urban centres outside of Montreal where Catholic unionism had already found a home. The CTCC enjoyed lower recruitment costs than the TLC in these areas. Third, the Collective Labour Agreements Extension Act became provincial law in 1934 as a result of a promotional campaign by the CTCC. Rouillard suggests that this legislation created an impact on Catholic union organizing similar to that of the National Labour Relations or 'Wagner' Act (1935) in the United States. TLC affiliates made little recourse to the law during the first few years of its existence because of the TLC's traditional hostility to government involvement in labor relations.

The Collective Labour Agreements Extension Act constituted a second step in the elaboration of a provincial labor code. Under pressure from the CTCC, the provincial government had already introduced the Professional Syndicates Act in 1924 to permit incorporation of professional associations on an optional basis, and to provide for the legal enforcement of collective agreements negotiated by them, as was the practice in Europe. But few unions, Catholic or otherwise, incorporated under the law before 1934 because accreditation exposed them to the possibility of civil suits on the part of employers.[2] The Collective Labour Agreements Extension Act (the Arcand Act) of 1934, similarly inspired by European precedent, authorized the provincial government to extend the terms of a collective agreement acquired by one union so that it became the minimum standards for an entire industry. In a sense, the Act represented a broadening of the Women's Minimum Wage Act of 1919, the province's earliest minimum wage legislation. By March 1936, some 135 000 workers were employed in industries regulated by provincial decree. (Marsh, p. 410) According to Rouillard, the use of the decree increased the rate of unionization as non-unionized workers sought to have some input into the negotiation of their industry's minimum standards.

Between 1931 and 1940, the CTCC increased its proportion of the unionized work force from about one-fifth to about one-third. The number of bargaining units belonging to the federation increased from 121 to 239. During these same years, however, CTCC affiliated unions were involved in only 21 strikes, less than ten percent of the provincial total. The radicalization of the Catholic trade union movement, a discontinuous process that can be traced back to the 1920s, reached a pre-war peak about the time of the province-wide cotton textile industry strike in 1937. The collaboration of Premier Duplessis and Cardinal Villeneuve in ending the strike subsequently discredited the CTCC in the view of many unionists. CTCC membership declined in favor of alternative organizational forms based on regional allegiance.[3] Between 1937 and 1940, membership in the National Union of Textile Workers (CTCC) decreased from more than 13 000 to 642. (Jamieson, p. 263). Aggregate working time foregone as a result of strikes in the province fell from 358 024 days in 1937 to 10 533 days in the following year.

The measurement of the impact of trade unionization on the general wage level is a notoriously difficult problem in labor economics. Even where the union-non-union wage differential can be measured, it does not necessarily reflect the influence of the trade union movement. In estimating the true union-non-union differential, all other wage determining influences, such as skill differentials, must be controlled for. There is also a problem of causality: have unions caused higher wages or have higher wages caused unionization? Non-union employers may be paying union rates, or something close, in order to stall the collective organization of their employees, or to retain their own employees in the face of recruitment by unionized firms. Prior to World War II, the labor movement may have had its greatest impact on non-wage aspects of the work environment: hours of work, vacation pay, safety measures, grievance procedures, and of course, the institutional environment regulating collective bargaining itself. The simple existence of a collective agreement introduced a measure of due process into the vacuum of employer-employee relations. Although the trade union movement may have exercised little influence on the average level of wages in Quebec before the war, it did succeed in laying the foundations for modern collective bargaining procedures and post-war wage rates.

Interprovincial Wage Differentials

The outward migration of Quebecers was an ever present feature of the provincial economy over the first four decades of the twentieth century. (See Table 15.3) If the forces of economic competition are operating in a region, microeconomic theory leads to the belief that migration will produce a gradual narrowing of interprovincial wage rate differentials. In other words, assuming that non-wage aspects of employment are about the same, competitive forces should induce workers and firms to relocate until expected wage rates are the same in all provinces. Although comprehensive data on interprovincial wage rates are not available, differences in average wage income between Quebec and Ontario persisted through the 1920s and 1930s. (See Table 15.6) The persistence of interprovincial wage income differentials, even to the present day, requires some explanation.

A common explanation of interregional wage variations refers to the relative immobility of labor between regions. Some workers may not move to higher wage regions either because a differential is not perceived or because the differential is insufficient to cover the costs of displacement. According to this explanation, wage rate

Table 15.6

AVERAGE ANNUAL WAGES IN MANUFACTURING INDUSTRIES, QUEBEC, ONTARIO, AND CANADA, 1923-1924, 1930-1939 (Current Dollars)

Year	Quebec	Ontario	Canada
1923	870	1 044	959
1924	883	1 039	972
1930	920	1 056	1 001
1931	880	985	957
1932	777	885	852
1933	715	821	785
1934	748	891	837
1935	773	933	874
1936	798	947	896
1937	965	1 021	965
1938	853	1 008	956
1939	873	1 026	975

Government of Canada, Dominion Bureau of Statistics. *The Manufacturing Industries of Canada*, 1924, 1930-39. Reproduced by permission of Statistics Canada.

variations have never been substantial enough to eliminate the non-wage regional allegiance felt by many Quebecers. This allegiance may stem from compensating differences in conditions such as the cost of living, 'city lights' externalities, or the cultural and linguistic environment. L. Copithorne has argued that interregional migration may have little or no effect on interregional wage rate differentials even where migration does occur. Reasoning from a two sector neo-classical model of growth, with a natural resource commodity export and a tradeable manufactured good, Copithorne demonstrates how regional wage rates could be determined by productivity in the non-staple tradeable goods sector. (See Introduction) As long as interregional productivity differences remain, migration will have no impact on interregional wage rate differentials. In contrast, Albert Rees explains the persistence of regional disparities in the presence of interregional migration by reference to the dynamic nature of economic growth:

> In the case of a one-time disturbance, any positive rate of net migration in the direction of the area with higher income would eventually close the income gap. But the dynamic disturbance caused by a growth rate

of population of working age that exceeds the growth rate of employment can be alleviated only by a rate of migration larger than the difference between the two growth rates. Despite heavy out-migration, some areas can therefore have continued surpluses of unskilled labour. Like the Red Queen, they must run very fast just to stay in the same place.[4]

There are, of course, a number of further considerations that must be taken into account when examining the crude data on interprovincial wage income differentials. The average level of wage income in Quebec reflects the industrial and occupational compositon of the employed work force. The industrial structure in turn depends upon various influences, including the resource endowment, the structure of domestic demand, transport costs and, inevitably, wage rates. Are low wage rates a cause or an effect of low wage, labor intensive industries? The aggregate size, composition, age structure and degree of utilization of the capital stock further affects the average level of wage rates. Labor productivity varies with the stock of machinery and equipment available to the labor force and this may influence relative wage rates and wage incomes. The age structure of the labor force, its schooling, skills and experience also contribute to productivity differentials. As already mentioned, Quebec possessed the lowest proportion of provincial populations aged 5 to 24 attending school, and this schooling deficiency inevitably affected skills, productivity, and wages.

Given the existence of interregional wage income differentials, it is not surprising that similar differentials appear in regional comparisons of per capita income. These differentials persisted through the first four decades of the twentieth century. There is evidence the relative position of per capita income in Quebec improved between 1910-1911 and 1920-1921. (McInnis, p. 447) But this relative improvement may have resulted from the decline in labor force participation rates and per capita incomes in the Canadian West. Between 1926 and 1962, the level of variability of relative per capita income among the Canadian regions was more or less constant. (See Chart 15.1) Disparities in wages, employment, and income relative to the other provinces have characterized the Quebec economy to the present day.

The discussion in this chapter has stressed the more obvious economic determinants of regional wage income differentials. In Quebec, however, the French fact is the overwhelming cultural trait of the majority; it would be surprising if language did not have a significant role to play in economic activity. From the firm's point of view, recruiting in a second language may raise the costs of hiring new employees as well as increase the internal costs of

Chart 15.1

RELATIVE LEVELS OF PER CAPITA INCOME, CANADIAN REGIONS
(Canada = 100)

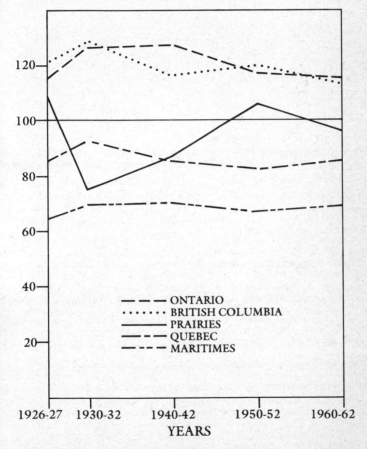

"The Trend of Regional Income Differentials in Canada," by Marvin McInnis, *Canadian Journal of Economics*, p. 442, Copyright © May 1968, reprinted by permission.

operation. Firms involved in interprovincial or international buying and selling may prefer English language recruiting. If such firms are able to pay higher wage rates because of their higher capitalization, economies of scale, and so on, then employees of these firms will be better paid than the population at large. From the employee's point of view, the existence of a dual information network complicates the job search endeavor. Wage differentials between language groups may have resulted from imperfect information flows between the two networks. Imperfect information among unilingual Francophone Quebecers regarding economic opportunities and wage differentials both inside and outside the province inhibited the efficient functioning of the provincial labor market since the eighteenth century. The growth of the trade union movement served to collect and diffuse information to Quebec labor, and eventually to improve the efficiency of the regional labor market.[5]

NOTES

[1]"Economic Activity & Strikes in Canada," by John Vanderkamp, *Industrial Relations*, p.222, February 1970. Reprinted by permission of Institute of Industrial Relations.

[2]Voluntary registrations under the provisions of Professional Syndicates Act increased in the second half of the 1930s, but many unions refused to be certified until the province's first full-fledged Labour Relations Code introduced compulsory registration in 1944.

[3]In 1937 the Quebec federations belonging to the TLC formed the Quebec Provincial Federation of Labour, the precursor of the modern-day *Fédération du Travail du Québec* (FTQ). *La Fédération catholique des institutrices rurales de la Province de Québec*, one of the early forerunners of the modern-day *Centrale de l'enseignement du Québec (CEQ)*, also made its appearance in the late 1930s.

[4]*The Economics of Work and Pay*, page 100, Second Edition by Albert Rees. Copyright © 1979 by Albert Rees. Reprinted by permission of Harper & Row, Publishers, Inc.

[5]"By far the most important function of the union is researching (gathering and processing of information on) the wage rates, working conditions, and strength of demand in closely competing types of jobs in other industries or geographical areas, and the estimation of the demand for the services of its members in the near future in the jobs within the union jurisdiction, all in order to reach an informed decision on the money wage scales that it should demand for its members. In short, the labour union acts as an economist for its members...To the degree that the informational imperfections in the labour market are lessened by the activities of labour unions, the unions tend probably to reduce the quantity of unemployment that, in equilibrium, would otherwise be experienced by their members on account of the frictions in unorganized markets." (*Inflation Policy and Unemployment Theory: The Cost-Benefit Approach to Monetary Planning*, p. 75, by Edmund S. Phelps, © 1971, reprinted by permission of W.W. Norton & Company, Inc.)

SELECT BIBLIOGRAPHY

Addison, John T. and W. Stanley Siebert. *The Market for Labour: An Analytical Treatment.* Santa Monica, CA: Goodyear Publishing Co., 1979.

Bertram, Gordon W. and Michael B. Percy. "Real Wage Trends in Canada, 1900-26: Some Provisional Estimates." *The Canadian Journal of Economics.* May 1979.

Breton, Albert. "Nationalism and Language Policies." *The Canadian Journal of Economics.* November 1978.

50 ans de lutte: histoire du mouvement ouvrier au Québec (1825-1976). Montreal: Centrale de l'enseignement du Québec, 1979.

Copithorne, Lawrence. *Natural Resources and Regional Disparities.* Ottawa: Economic Council of Canada, 1979.

Copp, Terry. *The Anatomy of Poverty: The Condition of the Working Class in Montreal, 1897-1929.* Toronto: McClelland and Stewart Ltd., 1974.

Gunderson, Morley. *Labour Market Economics: Theory, Evidence and Policy in Canada.* Toronto: McGraw-Hill Ryerson Ltd., 1980.

Henripin, Jacques and Yves Péron. "The Demographic Transition of the Province of Quebec," in D.V. Glass and Roger Revelle, ed., *Population and Social Change.* London: Edward Arnold Ltd., 1972.

Jamieson, Stuart M. *Times of Trouble: Labour Unrest and Industrial Conflict in Canada, 1900-66.* Ottawa: Task Force on Labour Relations, Study No. 22, 1968.

Kalbach, Warren E. and Wayne W. McVey. *The Demographic Basis of Canadian Society.* Toronto: McGraw-Hill Ryerson Ltd., 1979.

Lavigne, Marie and Jennifer Stoddart. "Les travailleuses montréalaises entre les deux guerres." *Labour-Le travailleur.* Vol. II. 1977.

Linteau, Paul-André, René Durocher, and Jean-Claude Robert. *Histoire du Québec contemporaine: de la Confédération à la crise (1867-1929).* Montreal: Boréal Express, 1979.

Lipton, Charles. *The Trade Union Movement of Canada, 1857-1959.* Montreal: Canadian Social Publications Ltd., 1968.

Marsh, Leonard C. "The Arcand Act: A New Form of Labour Legislation:" *The Canadian Journal of Economics and Political Science.* August 1936.

Migué, Jean-Luc. "Le Nationalisme, l'unité nationale et la théorie économique de l'information," *The Canadian Journal of Economics.* May 1970.

Minville, Esdras. *Labour Legislation and Social Services in the Province of Quebec.* A Study Prepared for the Royal Commission on Dominion-Provincial Relations. Ottawa, 1939.

McInnis, Marvin. "The Trend of Regional Income Differentials in Canada." *The Canadian Journal of Economics.* May 1968.

Ostry, Sylvia and M.A. Zaidi. *Labour Economics in Canada.* Third Edition. Toronto: Macmillan of Canada Ltd., 1979.

Pelletier, Michel and Yves Vaillancourt. *Les Politiques sociales et les travailleurs.* Cahier I: *Les années 1900 à 1929.* Cahier II: *Les années 30.* Montreal, 1974.

Phelps, Edmund S. *Inflation Policy and Unemployment Theory: The Cost-Benefit Approach to Monetary Planning.* New York: W.W. Norton & Co., 1971.

Raynauld, André. *Croissance et structure économiques de la province de Québec.* Quebec: Ministère de l'Industrie et du Commerce, Province de Québec, 1961.

Rees, Albert. *The Economics of Work and Pay.* Second Edition. New York: Harper & Row, 1979.

Rouillard, Jacques. *Histoire de la CSN (1921-1981).* Montreal: les Editions de Boréal Express, 1981.

Rouillard, Jacques. *Les syndicats nationaux au Québec de 1900 à 1930.* Quebec: les Presses de l'Université Laval, 1979.

Vanderkamp, John. "Economic Activity and Strikes in Canada." *Industrial Relations.* February 1970.

16
The Role of Government

For more than sixty years after Confederation, government activity in Quebec was essentially limited to the supply of public goods: the provision of defense, the administration of justice, and the support of civil government. With the notable exceptions of transport subsidies, tariff policy, and special war measures during World War I, systematic government 'intervention' in the Quebec economy really began in the 1930s. The role of government in stimulating and channeling economic growth and development grew to modern proportions as a result of the Great Depression, World War II, and the Quiet Revolution of the 1960s.

Between 1900 to 1939, the rate and composition of economic growth in Canada produced a gradual increase in the government sector. Government spending on goods and services increased from 7.5 percent of Gross National Expenditure (GNE) to 12.9 percent. (See Table 16.1) The prairie wheat economy expanded considerably and total exports of Canadian goods and services increased from 19.7 percent of GNE in 1900 to 26.5 percent in 1929. This growth in exports was accompanied by higher government spending on railways, shipping facilities, highways and airports. Some of the provincial governments, particularly those in the west, made large outlays in the utility field. During World War I, the demand for a basic public good, 'national' defense, also led to a substantial increase in federal government intervention in the economy. But with the return of peace in 1919, many government activities reverted to the private sector and the federal government reduced its role to pre-war levels.

Table 16.1

GROWTH OF SECTORAL EXPENDITURES IN CANADA BY DECADE, 1870-1939

(expressed as a percentage of total GNE)

	Personal expenditure on consumer goods and services	Gross investment	Government expenditure on goods and services	Exports of goods and services	Imports of goods and services	Residental error	Gross national expenditure (GNE)	Federal Government expenditures as percent of all government expenditures
1870	88.2	14.9	4.6	17.2	−24.9	—	100.0	52.4
1890	84.8	15.5	6.6	13.5	−20.4	—	100.0	37.0
1900	83.1	13.4	7.5	19.7	−23.7	—	100.0	37.7
1910	78.4	26.5	8.1	16.3	−29.3	—	100.0	34.1
1920	71.6	23.2	10.0	29.2	−34.0	—	100.0	31.8
1929	71.2	22.6	11.0	26.5	−31.5	0.2	100.0	25.4
1933	81.3	4.4	14.8	23.2	−29.3	0.3	100.0	24.7
1939	68.4	16.4	12.9	23.2	−23.3	−0.4	100.0	30.2

Reproduced with permission of Bowes & Bowes Publishers at The Bodley Head from *Canada's Economic Development*, pp. 72, 127, by O.J. Firestone.

See also "A Note on Canadian GNP Estimates, 1900-25," by R.E. Ankli, *The Canadian Historical Review*, pp. 62-63, March 1981.

The growth of government activity in Canada during the first four decades of the twentieth century also resulted from the public demand for income redistribution. A select list of essential services, such as education, was gradually taken over and expanded by the provincial governments in a move toward minimum standards and universal accessibility irrespective of family income. Education, for example, became an area of heavy provincial government spending during the 1920s, except in Quebec. Similarly health and social welfare programs became an important new area of municipal spending in most provinces after World War I. Provincial governments in the Maritimes and the West brought political pressure to bear on the federal government to reduce regional disparities by redistributing tax revenues, taxing powers, and property rights in western resources. By contrast, Quebec governments adopted a singular approach to economic growth and development that tended to leave a greater proportion of economic decision-making in the hands of the private sector. The economic depression of the 1930s exacerbated existing tensions between the federal and provincial levels of government. By undermining governments' confidence in the ability of a capitalist economy to resolve its own problems, the depression led to higher levels of government spending aimed at greater economic efficiency and equity.

In this chapter the role of the federal and provincial governments will be considered separately. Where possible, the probable impact of federal government activity upon the Quebec economy is suggested. The discussion of federal government activity is limited to the major areas of concern to Quebecers: tariffs, railway construction, income transfers, government enterprise, and taxation policy. The discussion of provincial government activity covers resource policy, road construction, income transfers, and taxation.

Tariff Policy

The Quebec economy evolved within an environment of moderately high protective tariffs during the first four decades of the twentieth century. (See Table 16.2) Between 1897 and 1907 the federal government established a reciprocal system of preferential duties applicable to trade with Great Britain. About one-third lower than the general rates, preferential duties encouraged east-west commerce and the use of the St. Lawrence transport network. As a result, the late nineteenth century trend toward substitution of American imports for British imports disappeared until World

War I. (See Chapter 9, Table 9.3) During the war a surtax of 7.5 percent was placed on the general and intermediate tariff rates, and 5 percent on the preferential rates; but the surtax disappeared in the post-war budget of 1919. Then, in the 1930s, the contraction of world trade and the atmosphere of protectionism and international tariff retaliation created by the Depression led the federal government to introduce sharp tariff increases on a number of specific items. (See Mackintosh, pp. 154-166) But no dramatic change in the overall level of protection occurred at this time. The tariff structure elaborated between 1849 and 1887 remained largely in place until World War II.

What impact did federal government tariff policy have on the growth and structure of the Quebec economy? In its broad outlines, W.A. Mackintosh's classic treatment of the regional effects of Canadian tariff policy still offers the basic answer to this question.

> The long run result of a protectionist policy (if it is effective) is a different distribution of capital and population and a different selection of industries. This is accomplished by a restriction of export industries, through raising their costs, and an expansion of industries selected for production by sheltering their selling prices from the lower cost imports...The incomes which, in the long run, will be differentially affected by a protectionist policy are those derived from the ownership of immobile and specialized resources.[1]

And Mackintosh goes on to say,

> It is not possible to give a quantitative statement of the long run effects of the protective policy on the different regions of the country. Some descriptive probabilities may be stated. Without the protective tariff, Ontario and Quebec would have had a smaller fraction of the Dominion's population than they now have. Industrialization and urbanization, particularly in the development of great metropolitan areas, would have been less.[2]

More recent studies of the tariff's regional impact prior to World War II lend support to this broad conclusion. H.M. Pinchin writes,

> While the static costs and benefits and the dynamic repercussions of one hundred years of protection cannot be measured, one can offer some reasonably well-founded generalizations. It is clear that all regions have had to pay the static costs of the Canadian tariff, and that the bulk of them have represented goods located in Ontario and Quebec.[3]

By 'static' costs, Pinchin means the price mark-up paid by consumers as a result of the tariff. These annual transfers of

Table 16.2

AVERAGE RATES OF DUTY ON CANADIAN IMPORTS,
1898-1941
(Percentages)

Year of Legislation	Years under Consideration	Ad Valorem Rate on Dutiable Imports	Ad Valorem Rate on Total Imports	Proportion of Imports Entering Free
1897	1898-1907	27.7	16.7	39.7
1907	1908-1914	26.4	16.8	36.7
1914	1914-1921*	24.1	15.7	35.0
1922	1922-1930	n/a	n/a	n/a
1930	1931-1935	28.5	17.6	38.2
1935	1936-1941	24.2	13.2	45.7

*Direct controls had more to do with the direction of trade in wartime than tariffs.

Extracted, with permission, from Table 1-2 in Hugh McA. Pinchin, *The Regional Impact of the Canadian Tariff*. Ottawa: Economic Council of Canada, 1979, p. 6.

income have also led to long term 'dynamic' advantages for the development of Central Canada.

> Even though it may be possible to show that per capita incomes would have been higher in Canada without the tariff, it would still be apparent that the tariff was associated with increased employment opportunities and levels of investment in central Canada. Protection of manufacturing raised wages and the returns to capital at the expense of returns to land resources. Job opportunities in central Canada resulting, directly and indirectly, from tariff protection attracted migrants from the rest of Canada and from Europe, but they also offset, to a large degree, the pull of industrial centres in the United States.[4]

Railway Policy

The costs to Quebecers of subsidizing transcontinental railways (through higher taxes) have been called into question by nationalist writers such as F-A. Angers. In the nineteenth century, however, no alternative seemed compatible with the political unification of the British North American colonies. The Intercolonial Railway represented a political concession necessary to the adherence of the

Maritime provinces to Confederation. Similarly, the construction of the Canadian Pacific Railway constituted a part of the Confederation package offered to British Columbia upon that province's entry in 1871. Indeed, without railway building and the settling of the Canadian West, the meaning of Canadian sovereignty in the former Hudson Bay lands would have been very unclear. However, a strong argument can be made that the subsidies accorded to the C.P.R. appear, at least in retrospect, to have been excessive.[5]

The anticipated settlement of the west, tariff barriers between the United States and Canada, and the evident profitability of the CPR attracted rival projects to build competing transcontinental rail lines at the turn of the century. Between 1900 and 1915, railway infrastructure in Canada increased from 17 657 to 45 833 miles of track. (Urquhart and Buckley, pp. 528, 532) This burst of railway building could not have been accomplished without enormous subsidies from the federal, provincial and municipal governments across Canada. The federal government alone contributed $248 million (current dollars) in direct investment, $47 million in cash subsidies, $32 million acres in land grants, $64 million in loans, and financial guarantees covering another $134 million in railway bonds between 1903 and 1916. (Mackintosh, p. 59)[6] Glazebrook has summed up the railway building of this era as follows:

> From the vantage point of later years the mistakes in policy seem clear enough. First in importance was the decision to build two additional and complete transcontinental railways, instead of adopting one of the compromises suggested. Secondly, the expensive construction of the Grand Trunk Pacific and National Transcontinental, and the route of the latter, were hostages to fortune. These were, indeed, mistakes which were to cost the country dear, and to form one of the most important contributory causes to what has come to be called "the railway problem".[7]

Subsidies to the railways by no means came to an end with the completion of the Canadian Northern Railway in 1915. Following the Report of the Royal Commission on Railway Transportation in 1916, the federal government began the process of nationalizing the Canadian Northern, the Grand Trunk, and the Grand Trunk Pacific in the following year. The new enterprise was named the Canadian National Railways in 1920. Henceforth, two major railway systems operated in Quebec and throughout Canada: the privately owned CPR and the publicly owned CNR. Through the CNR, the federal government continued to subsidize rail traffic and set rail rates across Canada. When western Canadian drought and a severe decline in wheat prices undermined the Canadian railway system in the 1930s, the federal government raised railway subsidies to yet higher levels. During the years 1932-1934, the central government subsidized nearly forty percent of the freight transport costs incurred by the CNR. (Smiley, p. 172) Together with the regulation of freight rates governing the transport of grain between the prairie provinces and ports at the Lakehead, Churchill and Vancouver (the Crow's Nest Pass rates established in 1897), federal government payments to the railways resulted in the cross-subsidization of grain merchants and farmers by all other taxpayers in Canada.

Federal Income Transfers

The severity of the economic depression of the 1930s led to a substantial increase in the role of the federal government in the Quebec economy. Government activity increased as a result of a series of *ad hoc* decisions aimed at redistributing the burden of the recession and raising the level of national income and employment. The new role of the federal government involved a new social security system, expanded regulatory policies, and more public enterprise. The rise in spending activity naturally provoked a corresponding increase in tax rates. Collectively, the new programs, responsibilities, and priorities of the federal government have been identified by V. Fowke as the beginnings of a 'new national policy' distinct from the old national policy rendered obsolete by the crisis.

The beginning of the federal government's new social welfare policy is often dated from the Old Age Pensions Act of 1927. Although the welfare of the elderly is not mentioned in the BNA Act, this responsibility was considered to be a provincial matter of a "merely local or private matter". By proposing a grants-in-aid approach to intervention, the federal government temporarily side-stepped the issue of constitutional jurisdiction. The Pensions Act offered grants-in-aid to provinces that agreed to pay one-half the cost of a non-contributory pension scheme involving a means test, to a maximum of twenty dollars a month for those over seventy years of age. The Quebec government initially declined the federal offer and the Catholic Church (together with other religious and non-profit organizations) retained responsibility for care of the aged. In 1931 the federal government's funding offer rose to 75 percent, and in 1936 the Quebec government agreed to participate in a province-wide pension scheme.

At the outset of the Depression, the Quebec government remained constitutionally responsible for unemployment assistance and social welfare ("poor relief") in the province. But given their limited powers to raise tax revenues, all of the provincial and municipal governments in Canada found themselves unable to cope with massive urban unemployment (14.5 percent in Quebec in census year 1931) and agrarian poverty. For its part, the Canadian government feared that a federally administered unemployment scheme would be unconstitutional. The central government consequently transferred revenue to the provinces in the form of additional grants-in-aid until, by constitutional amendment, it acquired the responsibility for unemployment insurance in 1940. Even though the federal government did not acquire constitutional authority to assist the unemployed until World War II, it assumed about 40 percent of total government spending on relief during the years 1930-1937. (Smiley, p. 176) Federal grants amounted to a net transfer of tax revenues from the eastern provinces to the west, the region most affected by the export-led recession.

Conscious of the regional disparities in unemployment, unemployment relief and social welfare, the federal government attempted to legislate minimum working conditions and welfare standards across the provinces. But the labor-related aspects of Prime Minister Bennett's "New Deal" legislation of 1935 were declared unconstitutional by the Judicial Committee of the Privy Council in London because they contravened the Property and Civil Rights clause of the BNA Act.[8] Similarly, an attempt to regulate the marketing of western agricultural products through the National Products Marketing Act was declared *ultra vires* the federal government. As a result, the federal government established the Royal Commission on Dominion-Provincial Relations to inquire into intergovernmental problems of jurisdiction in 1937.

Government Enterprise

The expansion of federal government activity in the 1930s extended beyond higher subsidies, more transfer payments, and greater regulation. In a number of sectors, the central government undertook to supply selected goods and services directly to consumers. Government enterprise did not represent a new concept to Quebecers. Transport and communications services had been provided by the State throughout the nineteenth century. The creation of the CNR between 1917 and 1920 extended this tradition. The failure of the private enterprise economy to maintain economic growth and full employment during the 1930s, and the 'public good' characteristics of new technologies, such as radio broadcasting, intensified the political demand for more government enterprise. Between 1932 and 1937, broadcasting, central banking, the marketing of wheat, national harbors, and air transport all came under some form of federal government ownership.[9]

Federal Taxation Policy

Until World War I, almost all federal government revenues came from tariff duties and sales taxes on liquor and tobacco. Tariff administration represented a low-cost option when compared to other instruments of revenue collection. During the first decade of the twentieth century, real national income per capita in Canada rose by almost thirty percent (Ankli, p. 63), and the value of imports increased from $190 million (current) to $420 million (Smiley, p. 221). The corresponding increase in the value of import duties allowed the federal government to realize current account surpluses in most of the years between 1900 and 1913, despite a tripling of current expenditures. This buoyant financial situation helps to explain the central government's willingness to subsidize the ill-fated transcontinental railway building projects of the period.

World War I placed a considerable strain on government revenues and expenditures.[10] At the beginning of the war, tariff duties constituted the primary source of federal government revenue (ie. 75 percent in 1913). The interruption of trans-Atlantic trade in 1914 produced a substantial decline in the value of Canadian exports, income, and import duties. The disruption of capital markets also rendered government borrowing abroad more difficult. On the expenditure side, Canada's participation in the war required a costly effort to reallocate resources from peacetime to military purposes. The resulting financial squeeze produced an embryonic system of income taxation administered by the federal government. The government first introduced a tax on business profits in 1916 (retroactive to 1915) in order to reduce war-profiteering. The war profits tax amounted to 25 percent of "the amount by which the profits exceeded, in the case of an incorporated company, the rate of 7 percent per annum, and, in the case of a business owned by any other person, the rate of 10 percent per annum upon the capital employed in such business." (6-7 George V, Chap. II, Article 3) In 1917 the federal government implemented the more general Income Tax War Act—fiscal arrangements involving additional corporate taxes and a personal income tax schedule.

With the return of peace in 1919, the central government began to disengage itself from the Canadian economy in an effort to reduce the overall role of government to pre-World War I levels. The federal government allowed the business profits war tax to expire at the end of 1921, amended the Income Tax War Act, and introduced a federal sales tax. In 1921 tariff revenues furnished only a third of federal tax revenues, but during the 1920s direct taxes on households and corporations were gradually reduced and government financing reverting to its pre-war dependence on foreign trade. By the end of the decade, customs and excise duties again produced almost two-thirds of federal government revenues. The increasingly inflexible nature of many of the central government's financial commitments (net debt charges, veterans' pensions, railway operating deficits) led to a reduction in the rate of growth of new policies and programs. Between 1921 and 1930, federal government spending increased by only 10 percent while total provincial government current spending increased by 106 percent. (Bates, p. 68)

The Great Depression of the 1930s affected the level of world trade, Canadian imports, and federal government revenues, even more dramatically than World War I. The decline in incomes, employment, and tax receipts was followed by new demands for unemployment relief and social welfare. As a result, the federal government ran enormous deficits (almost one half of total revenues in 1931) throughout the years 1930-1936. To help finance provincial and municipal transfer payments, the government raised the level of import duties, excise taxes on liquor and tobacco, the federal sales tax, and corporate income tax rates. The central government generally avoided increases in personal income tax rates, however, because most of the provinces began imposing provincial income taxes of their own (Quebec and the Maritimes being exceptions).

The Quebec Government

Throughout the first four decades of the twentieth century, the government of Quebec occupied a unique position among provincial governments in Canada. Provincial government intervention in the regional economy lagged behind all of the other provinces; the Quebec government practiced the strongest of laissez-faire strategies. This attitude was partly in reaction to the exceedingly rapid growth of provincial borrowing to finance railway building during the 1870s and 1880s. Debt charges rose from nil to 33 percent of total provincial expenditures between 1873 and 1900. (Bates, p. 148) The Quebec government was not alone in endeavoring to control spending in the 1890s, but unlike the other

Table 16.3

PER CAPITA FUNDED DEBT OF THE PROVINCIAL GOVERNMENTS IN QUEBEC, ONTARIO, AND CANADA, CENSUS YEARS, 1890-1940 (Current dollars)

	1890	1900	1910	1920	1930	1940
Quebec	14.4	21.3	12.8	17.2	26.7	119.3
Ontario	—	—	6.9	33.5	127.6	166.5
Canada	6.4	10.3	11.4	38.7	95.5	150.9

The Financial System of Canada: Its Growth and Development, p. 474, by E.P. Neufeld, reprinted by permission.

Government of Canada, *Financial Statistics of Canada*, 1930, 1940.

provincial governments, Quebec maintained this restraint during the first three decades of the twentieth century. (See Table 16.3)

Between 1900 and 1910, the Quebec government contributed less than ten percent of gross provincial government investment in capital formation across Canada. (Buckley, p. 88) Canadian provincial government spending was especially high in the western provinces; the newly settled regions required transport infrastructure, public buildings, schools and hospitals. Quebec, on the other hand, enjoyed a series of government surpluses in the pre-war years. After the war, Quebec continued to spend proportionately more of its revenues on traditional public goods such as the administration of justice and civil government, and proportionately less on economic development, education, health services and social welfare, than in the other provinces. Although Quebec contained about 28 percent of the Canadian population in 1930, Quebec's share of gross provincial investment in capital formation amounted to 13 percent. Provincial and municipal expenditure on education stood at $7.15 per capita in Quebec, as opposed to $14.03 in Ontario. (Government of Canada, Vol. I, p. 206) The Quebec government therefore possessed a comparatively small net provincial debt at the onset of the Depression. Debt charges (less interest received) amounted to only 6 percent of provincial expenditures in 1930, substantially below that of the other Canadian provinces.

The Great Depression pushed the Quebec government along the road already travelled by the others. Spending on social welfare services and road construction increased substantially, and the provincial debt rose dramatically. Of the provincial debt outstanding in June 1937, almost 60 percent had been added since 1930. The depression years marked the beginnings of a slow trend toward *rattrapage* or catching-up with the other provinces in the realm of provincial government spending and debt financing.

Resource Policy

Although Quebec governments generally adopted a laissez-faire attitude toward the provincial economy, resource policies provided a modest exception. As indicated in Chapter 14, the Gouin administration placed a total embargo on the export of raw pulpwood cut from Crown lands in the province in 1910. This timber manufacturing policy followed similar initiatives by British Columbia in 1891 and by Ontario in 1898. The provincial governments believed that a 'home manufacturing' policy constituted a legitimate exercise of powers granted them by the BNA Act, as long as the regulations applied solely to Crown (ie. provincial) lands.[11]

Despite the popular opinion that attributed growth in the paper industries to the embargo on raw timber, no effort was made to extend this policy to the mineral industries. In the case of asbestos, the Quebec government could not intervene to encourage the domestic transformation of asbestos fibre because preceding governments had relinquished control of mineral rights in the nineteenth century. The province no longer possessed the same property rights in asbestos as it had regarding timber. Although the Taschereau government toyed with the possibility of imposing an embargo on the export of raw asbestos fibre in the 1920s, it abandoned the idea. By this time an export embargo or tax on government-owned asbestos deposits would have been meaningless. Because it had alienated most of its property rights in asbestos during the nineteenth century, the Quebec government was deprived of this particular instrument for increasing the size of the domestic asbestos manufacturing industry.

The Taschereau government did extend the embargo policy to hydroelectricity in 1926 so as to prevent the export of electricity from government-owned waterfalls. By this time, however, property rights in a large number of the province's waterfalls had already been sold to private entrepreneurs. Until 1907, when the Gouin administration adopted a leasing system, the Quebec government alienated property rights in waterfalls by outright sale. In this way many of Quebec's greatest falls—Shipshaw, Grand Décharge, Shawinigan Falls—as well as the falls at La Tuque, Grans'Mère and on the Ottawa, Gatineau, and Lièvre Rivers, were acquired by private enterprise. (Dales, pp. 30-31) The embargo legislation of 1926 applied only to the export of hydroelectricity from government-owned waterfalls. The provincial government possessed no jurisdiction over international trade in hydroelectricity generated from privately owned waterfalls.[12] Although various provincial electricity commissions and boards nominally supervised hydroelectric producers in the years that followed, the Quebec government took no further steps to regulate the industry until the Quebec Hydro-Electric Commission purchased the Montreal Light, Heat and Power Consolidated in 1944.

A more traditional form of resource development, colonization in unsettled regions continued until World War II. Areas of new settlement in the twentieth century included the Abitibi, Temiscamingue, upper St. Maurice and Saguenay regions. Government spending took the form of colonization roads, administered land prices, seed distribution, school grants and the diffusion of technical information. Some colonization programs were viable in the first two decades of the century as long as high agricultural prices prevailed. But the recession of 1921 and the net benefits from farm mechanization in established regions worked against colonization in marginal agricultural areas during the 1920s. In 1924 the Quebec government introduced subsidies for clearing new land and for its first ploughing. Following the worst years of the Depression, the government stepped up its expenditures on rural colonization in a renewed effort to retain French speaking people in the province. In this context the Quebec Farm Credit Bureau was established as a government agency to provide subsidized credit to the farm population.

Road Construction

For the first three decades of the twentieth century, most of the growth in provincial investment programs in Quebec can be attributed to two items: roadways and building construction. Twentieth century automobile travel constituted a major innovation in transportation that required a complementary commodity, smooth roadways. Owing to the assignment of powers at Confederation, roads and highways fell under the province's constitutional jurisdiction. In the early years, public road building devolved to Quebec's municipalities: the provincial legislation of 1907 permitted annual subsidies to municipalities equal to one-half the costs of road construction and improvement. The Good Roads Act finally authorized provincial government road construction in 1912. Between 1915 and 1926 the network of provincial highways increased from 1 600 miles to 7 500 miles (Buckley, p. 89) and road building became the most important provincial government investment expenditure.

The Quebec government took over responsibility for the maintenance of all roads from the municipalities in 1927. By the end of the decade, highway spending had grown to 24 percent of current expenditures. Although the revenue requirements occasioned by the Depression created a slowdown in road building programs, investment in highways accounted for about one-third of the total new debt accumulated during the years 1928-1936. By 1937 the province possessed over 17 000 miles of improved roadway. (Bates, pp. 155-156)

Provincial Income Transfers

Throughout the first four decades of the twentieth century, the Quebec government left the provision of basic social welfare, health and educational services to religious and other private sector organizations. The provincial government made annual grants to mental institutions, as well as to certain health and welfare organizations, but did not attempt to direct policy in these areas. The Public Assistance Act of 1921 provided for one-third of the health care costs of the chronically ill hospitalized in public charitable institutions. But the strenuous denunciation of government health care funding by the Catholic press of the time (*Le Devoir*, l'*Action Catholique*, etc.) obliged the Taschereau administration to condede several amendments to the Act in 1924 and 1925. When the federal government offered grants-in-aid to the provinces through the Old Age Pensions Act of 1927, the Taschereau government declined on the grounds that the requisite tax increase would be too great, that pensions should be left to "individual responsibility", and that the central government's proposed scheme derogated the province's constitutional powers.

The onset of the Depression resulted in substantially greater income transfers by the provincial government. The total costs of unemployment relief through provincial and municipal agencies increased by more than fifteen times between 1930 and 1934. Montreal, the largest urban conglomeration in Canada, was especially hard-hit by the economic slowdown. Provincial welfare expenditures (leaving aside unemployment and 'poor' relief) increased from 10 to 16 percent of total provincial spending between 1929 and 1936. Even though health, welfare, and educational institutions generally remained exempt from government regulation, adherence to the federal government's Old Age Pension scheme in 1936 signalled a wider recognition of social welfare as a legitimate concern of the state. The election of Maurice Duplessis's Union Nationale government in August 1936, however, put a damper on depression-era initiatives in this domain.

Provincial Taxation Policy

All of the provincial governments in Canada found themselves financially dependent upon federal government subsidies, resource sales, and licence fees in the post-Confederation years. In Quebec, the recession (1873-96) together with large scale subsidies to railway building during the 1870s and 1880s induced the government to introduce new forms of provincial taxation. In 1882, Quebec became the first province to introduce a 'direct tax'

Table 16.4

PROVINCIAL GOVERNMENT REVENUES IN QUEBEC, YEAR ENDED JUNE 30, SELECTED YEAR, 1869-1937 (Percentages)

	1869	1900	1914	1921	1929	1937
Total Taxes	n/a	n/a	n/a	n/a	n/a	47.5
Direct Taxes	—	10.6	29.7	24.7	21.0	n/a
Gasoline Taxes	—	—	—	—	8.1	n/a
Federal Transfers	60.4	25.1	22.5	12.7	5.8	5.7
Natural Resource Revenues	24.1	30.2	21.3	23.1	14.3	13.4
Licenses, Fees, Fines, etc.	9.6	8.9	12.7	8.1	4.0	19.1
Motor Vehicles	—	—	n/a	8.7	11.9	n/a
Liquor Control	4.3	12.4	9.1	2.7	21.3	9.6
Interest, etc.	0.7	11.9	1.7	3.3	3.0	3.0
Miscellaneous	0.9	0.1	3.1	10.3	10.6	1.7
Total	100.0	99.2	100.1	100.0	100.0	100.0

Financial History of Canadian Governments, pp. 149, 151, by Stewart Bates. Ottawa: King's Printer, 1939. Reproduced by permission of the Minister of Supply and Services Canada.

Financial Statistics of Provincial Government in Canada, pp. 4-7. Government of Canada, 1929, 1947. Reproduced by permission of the Minister of Supply and Services Canada.

on corporations. The tax was a nominal charge based on the value of "paid-up capital", and on the number and location of establishments. The legislation constituted an innovation in the field of provincial taxation and was vigorously contested until the Privy Council upheld its validity in 1887. In 1892 the Quebec government also introduced succession duties. Both of the foregoing concepts were borrowed from examples set by American state governments. (Perry, pp. 110-112) By 1900, direct taxation from these two sources had grown to 10.6 percent of Quebec provincial government revenues. (See Table 16.4) In 1914 succession taxes accounted for 18.3 percent of total provincial revenues and corporation taxes for 10.8 percent.

Direct taxes diminished in relative importance as a source of Quebec government revenues during the war years. As authorized under the Quebec Mining Act of 1892, the provincial government imposed mineral royalties for the first time. In 1917 the Cabinet imposed a royalty of 5 percent on the net benefits from asbestos production. Under pressure from asbestos producers, the royalty was changed to a 2 percent levy on the gross value of mineral extracted, a calculation more easily verifiable and therefore considered more equitable than producers' estimates of profits. Of all the provincial governments, only Quebec failed to introduce a wartime land tax. The Quebec government did introduce a sales tax on entertainment and substantial fees for racetrack operations in 1916. The revenue from motor vehicle licensing also increased considerably during the war years in step with the diffusion of this new means of transport.

Most of the Canadian provinces widened their tax base during the 1920s in order to finance heavy spending in the areas of social welfare, education and highways. The Quebec government imitated this widening of the tax base even though its role in the regional economy did not substantially change during these years. The greatest increases in Quebec government revenues came from liquor control subsequent to the creation of a government retail sales monopoly in 1921, motor vehicle licences, and gasoline taxes (introduced in 1924). In 1926 the provincial government introduced a new sales tax on hotel and restaurant meals. Given the government's conservative spending outlook, the wider tax base in the latter half of the 1920s resulted in a stationary provincial debt, recurrent surpluses on current account, and a reduction in federal government revenue transfers. (See Table 16.4)

With the Depression of the 1930s, Quebec government revenues decreased along with the decline in the level of provincial economic activity. As elsewhere, the demand for social welfare and unemployment relief intensified. To meet the demand for greater income transfers, most of the provincial governments attempted to widen their tax base. But the Quebec government maintained its conservative attitude toward new forms of taxation at this time. The corporate profits tax introduced in 1933, for example, amounted to 1.5 percent. Not until the election of the Godbout government in 1940, did Quebec introduce a provincial income tax (20 percent of the federal tax) and a general provincial sales tax (2 percent) in line with the majority of the other provinces.

* * *

Throughout Canada, provincial government activities expanded at a faster rate than federal government activity after Confederation. Between 1870 and 1900 federal government expenditures on goods and services declined from 52.4 percent of total government expenditures in Canada to 37.7 percent. (See Table 16.1) However, action by the federal government to restrain or disallow provincial programs and initiatives often succeeded because of the broad interpretation of federal powers accorded by the supreme court of the day (ie. the Judicial Committee of the Privy Council in London).[13] Beginning with the 'Local Prohibition Case' in 1896, the centralizing trend in judicial decisions was reversed. By 1929, federal government expenditures on goods and services had diminished to 25.4 percent of total government expenditures in Canada. During these years, greater scope for the decentralization of political power in Canada led to more provincial government intervention in almost every province except Quebec. But major problems concerning divided dominion-provincial jurisdiction and provincial government financing remained. Until World War I, federal transfers remained the largest source of total provincial revenues in Canada.

The Depression of the 1930s induced the federal and provincial governments into a wider range of public sector activity. Increasingly, the federal government assumed a responsibility for attaining a high rate of economic growth by promoting greater economic efficiency. The federal government also assumed the responsibility of reducing inter-provincial disparities by assuring minimum standards with respect to certain economic and social services. At the provincial level, Quebec governments acknowledged a wider role for the public sector. But this did not result in any fundamental shift in overall economic development strategy at this time. A change in outlook concerning the appropriate role of the Quebec government in the regional economy awaited the Quiet Revolution of the 1960s.

NOTES

[1]*The Economic Background of Dominion-Provincial Relations*, p. 144, by W.A. Mackintosh, reprinted by permission of Carleton University Press.

[2]*The Economic Background of Dominion-Provincial Relations*, p. 150, by W.A. Mackintosh, reprinted by permission of Carleton University Press.

[3]*The Regional Impact of the Canadian Tariff*, by Hugh McA Pinchin *Census of Canada, 1851-1901*, p. 8, reproduced by permission of the Minister of Supply and Services Canada.

[4]*The Regional Impact of the Canadian Tariff*, by Hugh McA Pinchin *Census of Canada, 1851-1901*, p. 11, reproduced by permission of the Minister of Supply and Services Canada.

[5]P. George has estimated that the private rate of return to the C.P.R. (net of subsidies) averaged 3.2 percent over the decade 1886-95. Given going rates of return of 6 to 10 percent, George's figures suggest that subsidies were justified, but not to the amount actually granted.

[6]The Quebec government also contributed both cash subsidies and land grants to the new transcontinental rail links.

[7]*A History of Transportation in Canada*, Vol. II, p. 146, by G.P. de T. Glazebrook, reprinted by permission of Carleton University Press.

[8]viz. The Employment and Social Insurance Act, the Weekly Rest in Industrial Undertakings Act, the Minimum Wages Act, and the Limitation of Hours of Work Act.

[9]viz. The Canadian Radio Broadcasting Commission (1932), the Bank of Canada (1934), the Canadian Wheat Board (1935), the National harbours Board (1936), and Trans-Canada Air Lines (1937).

[10]Many Quebecers opposed Canada's participation in the Great War and this was reflected in the weak provincial response to voluntary recruiting and majority opposition to conscription. However, the 'public good' characteristics of many wartime government activities resulted in the coercion of the anti-war minority, and social conflict. (See Chapter 15).

[11]In a 1900 decision of the Ontario Court of Appeal, Smylie v. The Queen, the Court decided that section 92(5) of the BNA Act, concerning "the Management and Sale of the Public Lands belonging to the Province and of the Timber and Wood thereon", overrode any federal powers contained in Section 91. In the recent opinion of one jurist, "the principle articulated in Smylie that the legislature can legislate under Section 92(5) as it pleases, flies in the face of every decision ever rendered on the question of provincial legislative power under Section 92. The decision appears to be wrong. [Mr. Justice] Osler's view that the legislation was not a regulation of trade and commerce is clearly not tenable today. The conclusion is that no valid rule of law can be gleaned from the case." (An article by S. Ian Bushnell which appeared in *Canadian Public Policy—Analyse de Politiques*, Vol. VI:2, pp. 321-322, Spring 1982. Reprinted by permission.

[12]The federal government had imposed an export tax on all hydroelectricity leaving Canada in 1925.

[13]The federal government's constitutional power to reserve (hold in abeyance)

or disallow provincial legislation carried with it a quasi-judicial function with considerable economic ramifications. Using this power, the federal government reserved 51 provincial bills and disallowed 65 during the first three decades after Confederation.

SELECT BIBLIOGRAPHY

Angers, François-Albert. "L'évolution économique du Canada et du Québec en cent ans de Confédération." *Revue d'histoire de l'Amérique française*. Vol. XXI (1967).

Ankli, Robert E. "A note on Canadian GNP Estimates, 1900-25." *Canadian Historical Review*. March 1981.

Bates, Stewart. *Financial History of Canadian Governments*. Appendix of the Royal Commission Report on Dominion-Provincial Relations. Ottawa: King's Printer, 1939.

Bird, Richard M. *The Growth of Government Spending in Canada*. Toronto: Canadian Tax Foundation, 1970.

Bouffard, Jean. *Traité du Domaine*. (Reproduction de l'édition originale de 1921). Quebec: les Presses de l'Université Laval, 1977.

Buckley, Kenneth. *Capital Formation in Canada, 1896-1930*. Toronto: McClelland and Stewart Limited, 1974.

Bushnell, S.I. "The Control of Natural Resources through the Trade and Commerce Power and Proprietary Rights." *Canadian Public Policy*. Spring 1980.

Dales, John H. *Hydroelectricity and Industrial Development: Quebec, 1898-1940*. Cambridge: Harvard University Press, 1957.

Faucher, Albert and Maurice Lamontagne. "History of Industrial Development," in J-C Falardeau, ed., *Essays on Contemporary Quebec*. Quebec: les Presses de l'Université Laval, 1953.

Firestone, O.J. *Canada's Economic Development, 1867-1953, With Special reference to Changes in the Country's National Product and National Wealth*. London: Bowes and Bowes Publishers Ltd., 1958.

Fowke, Vernon C. "The National Policy - Old and New," in W.T. Easterbrook and M.H. Watkins, ed., *Approaches to Canadian Economic History*. Toronto: McClelland and Stewart Ltd., 1967.

George, Peter J. "Rates of Return in Railway Investment and Implications for Government Subsidization of the Canadian Pacific Railway: Some Preliminary Results." *The Canadian Journal of Economics*. November 1968.

Glazebrook, G.P. de T. *A History of Transportation in Canada*. Vol. II. Toronto: McClelland and Stewart Ltd., 1964.

Government of Canada. *Report of the Royal Commission on Dominion-Provincial Relations*. 3 Vol. Ottawa: King's Printer, 1940.

Green, Christopher. *Canadian Industrial Organization and Policy*. Toronto: McGraw-Hill Ryerson Ltd., 1980.

Hodgetts, J.E. "The Public Corporation in Canada," in W. Friedmann and J.F.

Garner, eds., *Government Enterprise: A Comparative Study*. London: Stevens and Sons, 1970.

Linteau, Paul-André, René Durocher, and Jean-Claude Robert. *Histoire du Québec contemporain: de la Confédération à la crise (1867-1929)*. Montreal: les Editions de Boréal Express, 1979.

Mackintosh, W.A. *The Economic Background of Dominion-Provincial Relations*. Toronto: McClelland and Stewart Ltd., 1964.

Marr, William L. and Michael Percy. "The Government and the Rate of Settlement of the Canadian Prairies." *Canadian Journal of Economics*. November 1978.

Minville, Esdras. *Labour Legislation and Social Services in the Province of Quebec*. A Study Prepared for the Royal Commission on Dominion-Provincial Relations in Canada, 1939.

McDiarmid, O.J. *Commercial Policy in the Canadian Economy*. Cambridge: Harvard University Press, 1946.

Nelles, H.V. *The Politics of Development: Forest, Mines and Hydro-Electric Power in Ontario, 1849-1941*. Toronto: Macmillan of Canada, 1974.

Norrie, Kenneth H. "Agricultural Implement Tariffs, the National Policy, and Income Distribution in the Wheat Economy." *The Canadian Journal of Economics*. August 1974.

Perry, J.H. *Taxes, Tariffs; and Subsidies: A History of Canadian Fiscal Development*. Vol. 2, Toronto: University of Toronto Press, 1955.

Pinchin, Huch McA. *The Regional Inpact of the Canadian Tariff*. Ottawa: Canadian Government Publishing Centre, 1979.

Ratner, Sidney, James H. Soltow and Richard Sylla. *The Evolution of the American Economy: Growth, Welfare and Decision Making*. New York: Basic Books, Inc., 1979.

Roby, Yves. *Les québécois et les investissements américains (1918-1929)*. Quebec: les Presses de l'Université Laval, 1976.

Smiley, Donald V. ed. *The Rowell-Sirois Report*. An Abridgement of the Royal Commission Report on Dominion-Provincial Relations. Toronto: McClelland and Stewart Ltd., 1963.

Urquhart, M.C. and K.A.H. Buckley, ed. *Historical Statistics of Canada*. Toronto: Macmillan of Canada, 1965.

Epilogue

The flow of European labor and capital to North America began in the sixteenth century. Mobile factors moved toward the *in situ* resources of the St. Lawrence Valley in search of profitable opportunities. The early history of the region was associated with the discovery and exploitation of fish stocks, fur-bearing animals, cultivable land and the labor services of the Amerindian people. The rate of European migration to North America was greatest in the direction of those regions where expected profits and rents were highest. Consequently, migration to Quebec proceeded slowly. The volume and spatial distribution of arable land in the St. Lawrence Valley as well as the climate and location of the region were comparatively disadvantageous. From the beginnings of the colony, the size of Quebec's population depended heavily on natural population increase.

The discovery and exploitation of economic opportunities is influenced by the prevailing institutional environment. In the seventeenth century, the French State transferred the seigneurial system of property rights to the St. Lawrence Valley. Even after the British Conquest of New France, the seigneurial system continued intact for more than half a century. From the beginning, however, the rights and customs associated with the system were adapted to the higher land/population ratio and alternative labor market opportunities available on the frontier. There is little evidence that the structure of incentives embedded in the seigneurial system constrained economic growth in the seventeenth and eighteenth centuries. But a change may have occurred during the nineteenth century. Though it is unlikely that the seigneurial system contributed to the agricultural 'crisis' of the 1830s and 1840s in a fundamental way, its abolition in 1854 may have hastened economic recovery in the second half of the nineteenth century.

Until the final decades of the eighteenth century, income and productivity levels were low and roughly equal throughout the world. Economies experienced alternating periods of feast and famine, but there was little trend change in average income levels. Beginning in the late eighteenth century, a small number of the world's nations embarked one after another on a process of modern economic growth. The prime mover in this process appears to have been the rate of technological change. By and large, the fund of technological knowledge was pooled among nations; regional differences in the actual rate of change seem to have been linked to the technology diffusion process. From this perspective, the substantial differences in the rate of spread of modern economic growth are attributable to constraints on the dissemination of new information.

Language plays an essential role in the diffusion of information pertaining to production and exchange. The British Conquest resulted in the delimitation of a French speaking region in the St. Lawrence Valley. Canada's ties to Britain permitted the English speaking minority to acquire a prominent political and economic position in Quebec society. This position was reinforced by the gradual removal of impediments to interregional trade with the rest of English speaking North America in the nineteenth century. As interregional transport costs diminished, the language barrier came to play a more prominent role in economic activity. The difference in average literacy rates between Francophones and Anglophones contributed an additional burden on economic exchange. The transaction costs associated with language differences and illiteracy slowed the rate of diffusion of market information and cost-saving innovations. These costs also hampered the diffusion of information about alternative employment opportunities outside of Quebec and raised the population/arable land ratio above the North American average. The modernization of Quebec agriculture was delayed and the net per capita income differential between Quebec's producers and those of the continental interior increased. The per capita income disparity between Quebec and Ontario that has persisted to the present day was established by the middle of the nineteenth century.

Given the excess of population relative to the *in situ* resource endowment of the region, French speaking Quebecers faced a dilemma. Life in the northeastern United States or Ontario offered a higher average expected income than life in Quebec. But immigration to either of these regions required giving up one's language and culture. Faced with his dilemma, some native-born Quebecers moved while others accepted a lower income as the price of living in a French speaking environment.

In a region where returns to agricultural activity diminish unexpectedly, the development of a manufacturing sector may be assisted by rigidities in the labor market. Uncertainty, the costs of information, and capital market inperfections, all compounded by language and schooling differences, reinforced the immobility of Quebec labor. Though high by some standards, the rate of emigration was not sufficient to eliminate interregional income differences. The volume of regional labor supply was one factor contributing to the growth of a sizeable manufacturing sector centred in

Montreal.

French language and culture are the defining characteristics of Quebec society, but they have not exempted the history of the St. Lawrence Valley from modern economic trends. The progress of the years 1500-1940 resulted from the adaptation of modern technology to the region's endowment of resources. The broad features of Quebec's economic history are similar to those of Ontario and the northeastern United States. Any secular disparities in per capita output and income cannot be attributed to differences in *mentalité*. The attitudes of Quebecers toward net income maximization and risk-bearing have not been measurably different. Quebecers have pursued economic and political objectives similar to other North Americans even though their preferences and institutional arrangements are distinct.

Index